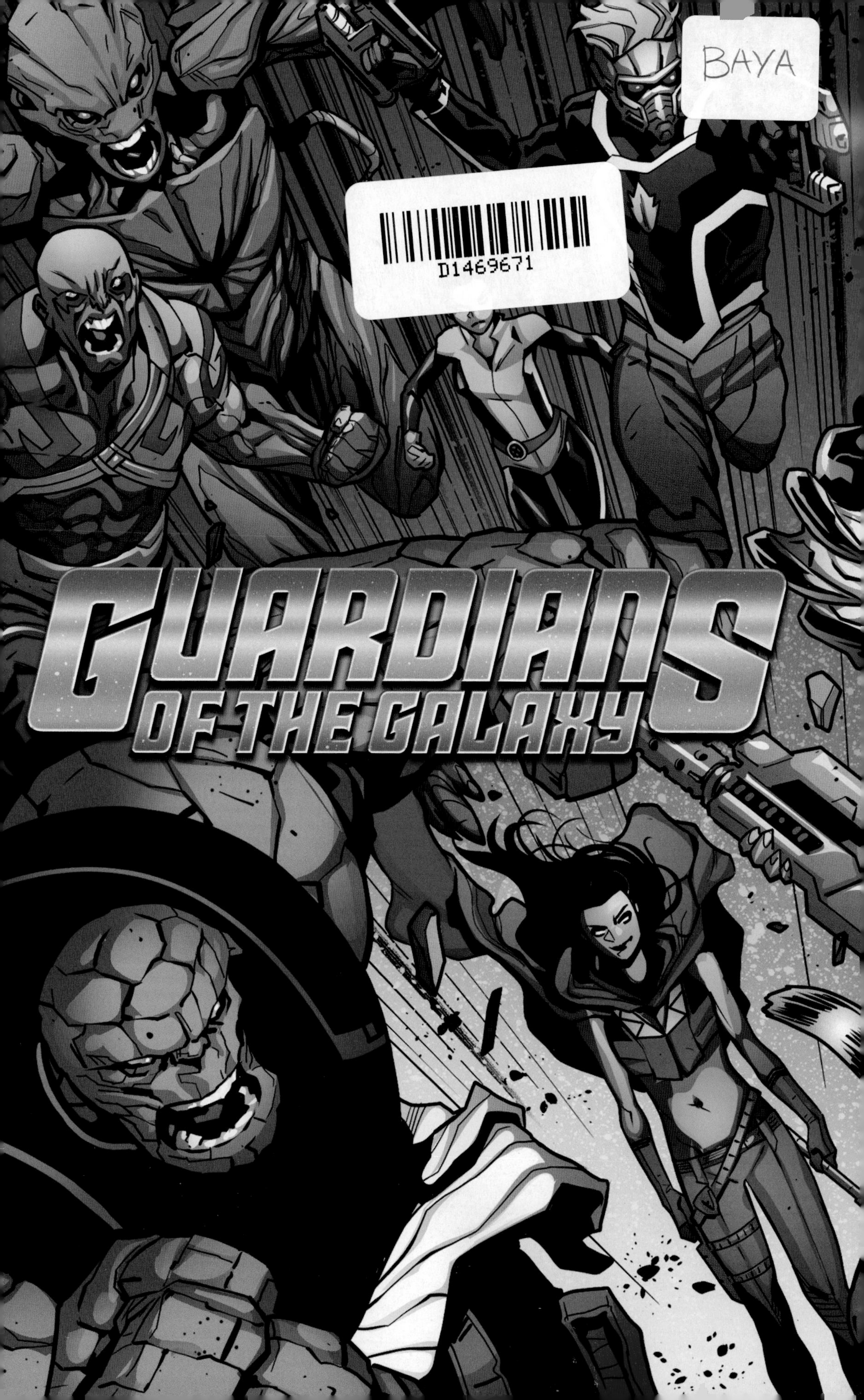
GUARDIANS
OF THE GALAXY

The entire galaxy is a mess. Warring empires and cosmic terrorists plague every corner. Someone has to rise above it all and fight for those who have no one to fight for the
A group of misfits – Drax the Destroyer, Gamora, Rocket Raccoon, Groot and Flash Thompson (A.K.A. Venom) – joined together under the leadership of Peter Quill (A.K.A. Star-Lord) to fight for those who have no one to fight for them. They serve a higher cause as the...

# GUARDIANS OF THE GALAXY

In the midst of an all-out super hero battle, the Guardians lost their ship and were stranded on Earth. In the aftermath, Gamora discovered Peter had withheld the location of her enemy and estranged foster father, Thanos, who is imprisoned in the Triskelion. Enraged, the rest of the Guardians abandoned Peter...

## GROUNDED


BRIAN MICHAEL BENDIS
WRITER

VALERIO SCHITI
ARTIST

RICHARD ISANOVE
COLOR ARTIST

ISSUE NO. 19 GUEST ARTISTS

PHIL NOTO
PP. 9-10

ANDREA SORRENTINO
PP. 11-12

ED McGUINNESS & MARK MORALES
PP. 17-18

ARTHUR ADAMS
PP. 23-24

KEVIN MAGUIRE
PP. 25-26

MARK BAGLEY & ANDREW HENNESSY
PP. 27-28

SARA PICHELLI
PP. 29-30

FILIPE ANDRADE
PP. 31-32

VC's CORY PETIT
LETTERER

ARTHUR ADAMS & JASON KEITH
COVER ART

KATHLEEN WISNESKI
ASSISTANT EDITOR

DARREN SHAN
ASSOCIATE EDITOR

JORDAN D. WHITE
EDITOR



COLLECTION EDITOR: JENNIFER GRÜNWALD
ASSISTANT EDITOR: CAITLIN O'CONNELL
ASSOCIATE MANAGING EDITOR: KATERI WOODY
EDITOR, SPECIAL PROJECTS: MARK D. BEAZLEY

VP PRODUCTION & SPECIAL PROJECTS: JEFF YOUNGQUIST
SVP PRINT, SALES & MARKETING: DAVID GABRIEL
BOOK DESIGNER: ADAM DEL RE WITH JAY BOWEN

EDITOR IN CHIEF: AXEL ALONSO
CHIEF CREATIVE OFFICER: JOE QUESADA
PRESIDENT: DAN BUCKLEY
EXECUTIVE PRODUCER: ALAN FINE



**GUARDIANS OF THE GALAXY: NEW GUARD VOL. 4 — GROUNDED.** Contains material originally published in magazine form as GUARDIANS OF THE GALAXY #15-19. First printing 2017. ISBN# 978-1-302-90670-2. Published by M WORLDWIDE, INC., a subsidiary of MARVEL ENTERTAINMENT, LLC. OFFICE OF PUBLICATION: 135 West 50th Street, New York, NY 10020.



**Printed in the U.S.A.** DAN BUCKLEY, President, Marvel Entertainment; JOE QU Chief Creative Officer; TOM BREVOORT, SVP of Publishing; DAVID BOGART, SVP of Business Affairs & Operations, Publishing & Partnership; C.B. CEBULSKI, VP of Brand Management & Development, Asia; DAVID GABRIEL, SVP of S Marketing, Publishing; JEFF YOUNGQUIST, VP of Production & Special Projects; DAN CARR, Executive Director of Publishing Technology; ALEX MORALES, Director of Publishing Operations; SUSAN CRESPI, Production Manager; STA Chairman Emeritus. For information regarding advertising in Marvel Comics or on Marvel.com, please contact Vit DeBellis, Integrated Sales Manager, at vdebellis@marvel.com. For Marvel subscription inquiries, please call 888-511 **Manufactured between 8/25/2017 and 9/26/2017 by LSC COMMUNICATIONS INC., KENDALLVILLE, IN, USA.**

10 9 8 7 6 5 4 3 2 1

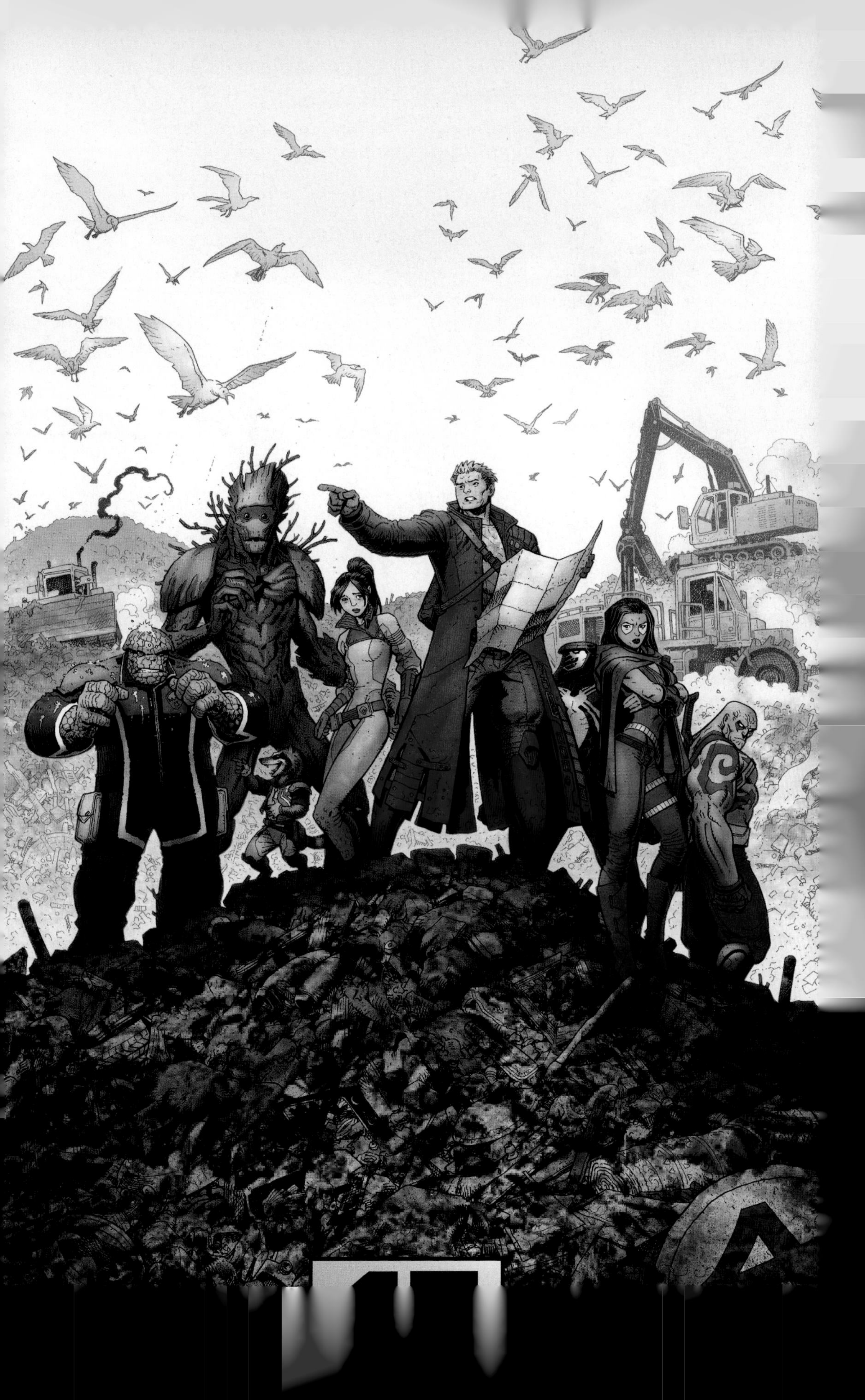

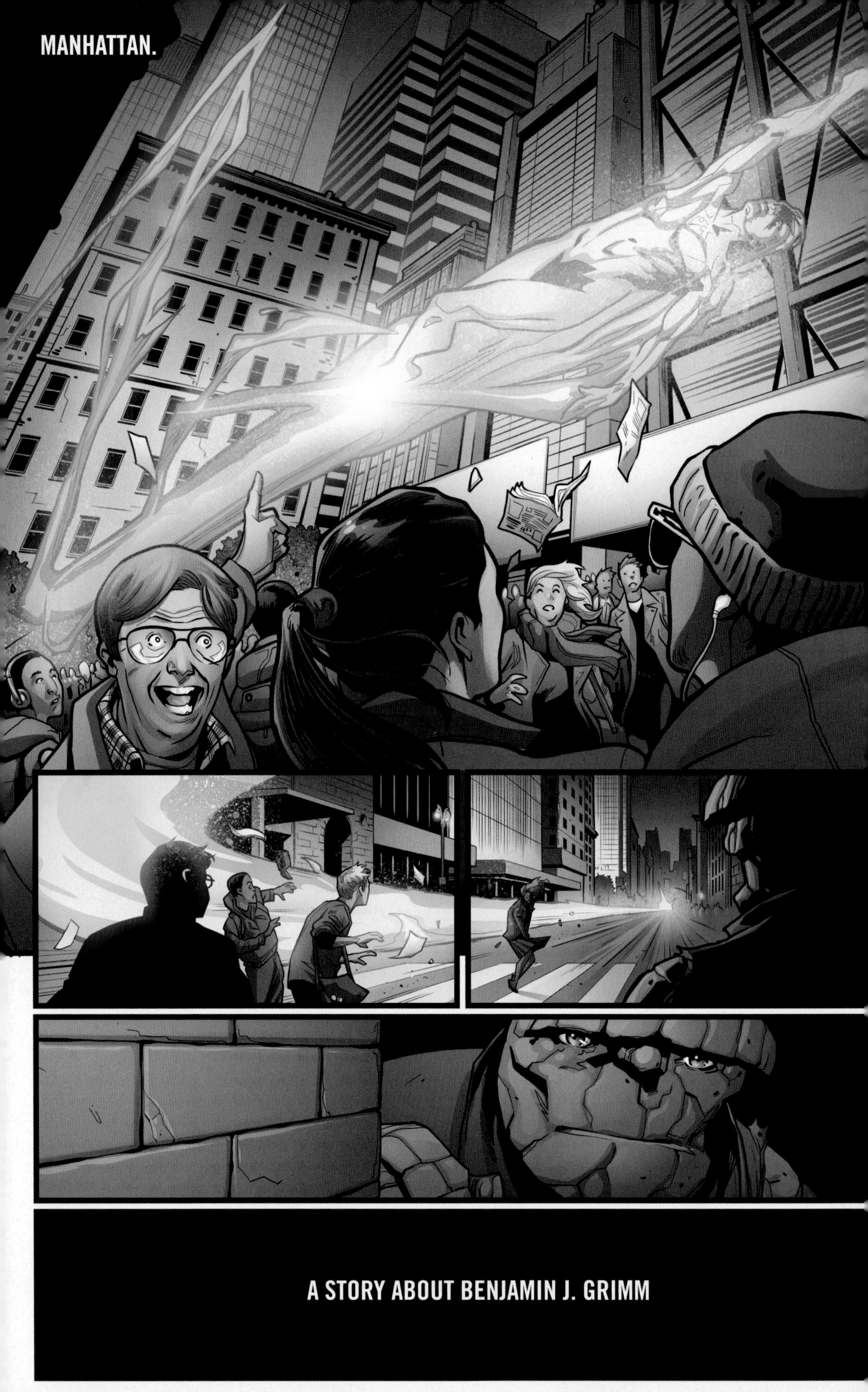
MANHATTAN.
A STORY ABOUT BENJAMIN J. GRIMM

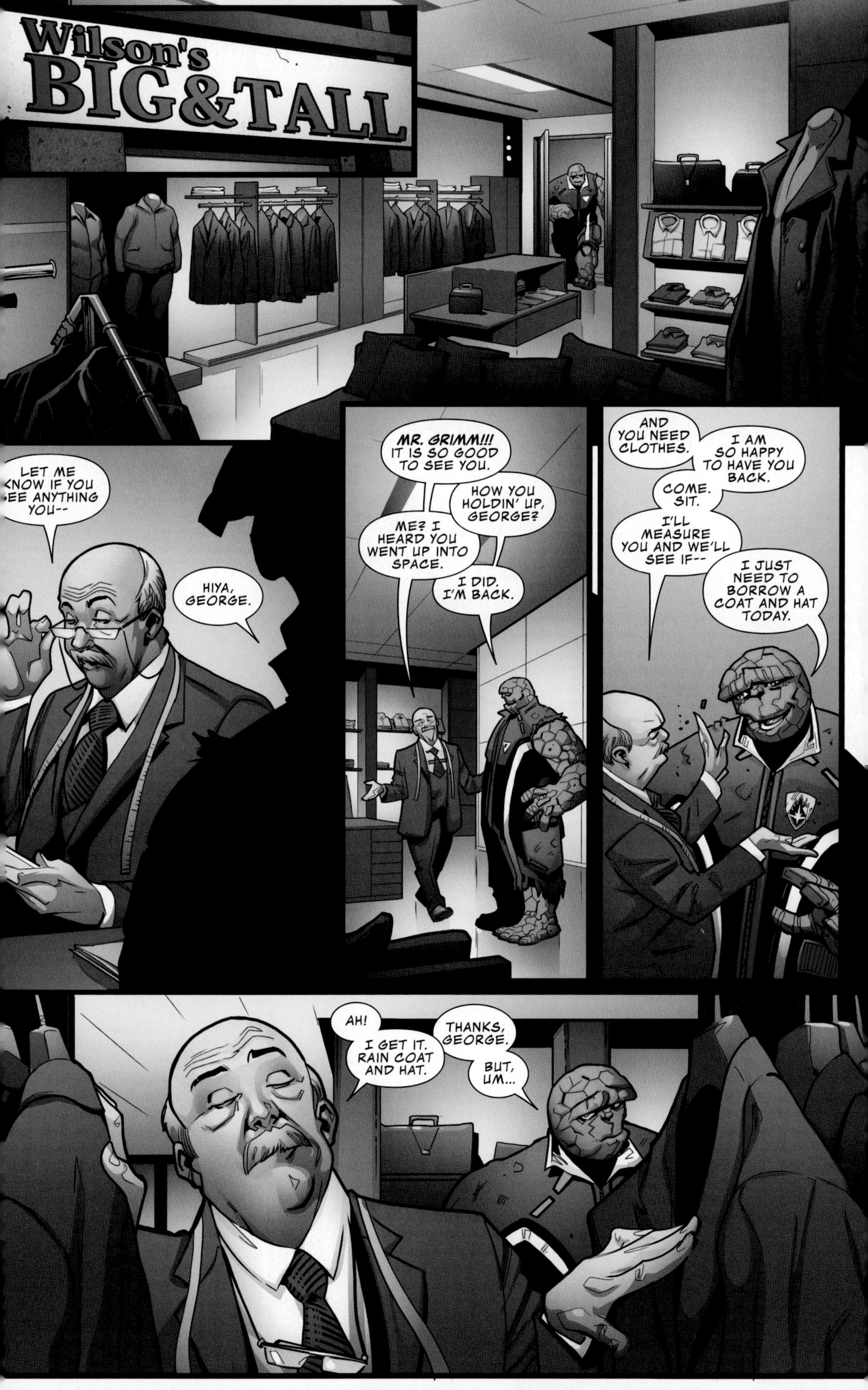
Wilson's BIG&TALL
LET ME KNOW IF YOU SEE ANYTHING YOU--
HIYA, GEORGE.
MR. GRIMM!!! IT IS SO GOOD TO SEE YOU.
HOW YOU HOLDIN' UP, GEORGE?
ME? I HEARD YOU WENT UP INTO SPACE.
I DID. I'M BACK.
AND YOU NEED CLOTHES.
I AM SO HAPPY TO HAVE YOU BACK.
COME. SIT.
I'LL MEASURE YOU AND WE'LL SEE IF--
I JUST NEED TO BORROW A COAT AND HAT TODAY.
AH!
I GET IT. RAIN COAT AND HAT.
THANKS, GEORGE.
BUT, UM...

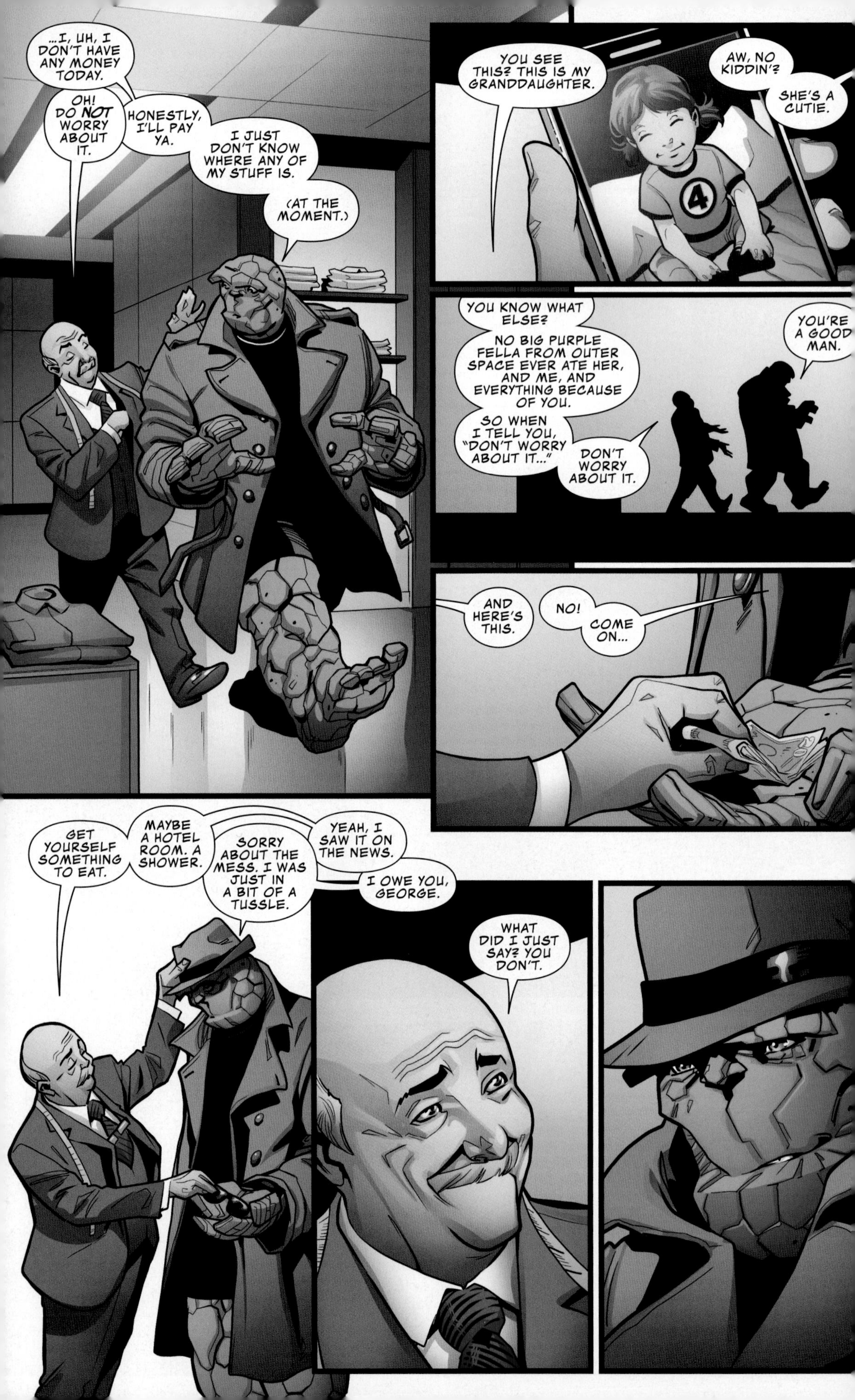

...I, UH, I DON'T HAVE ANY MONEY TODAY.
OH! DO NOT WORRY ABOUT IT.
HONESTLY, I'LL PAY YA.
I JUST DON'T KNOW WHERE ANY OF MY STUFF IS.
(AT THE MOMENT.)
YOU SEE THIS? THIS IS MY GRANDDAUGHTER.
AW, NO KIDDIN'?
SHE'S A CUTIE.
YOU KNOW WHAT ELSE?
NO BIG PURPLE FELLA FROM OUTER SPACE EVER ATE HER, AND ME, AND EVERYTHING BECAUSE OF YOU.
SO WHEN I TELL YOU, "DON'T WORRY ABOUT IT..."
DON'T WORRY ABOUT IT.
YOU'RE A GOOD MAN.
AND HERE'S THIS.
NO!
COME ON...
GET YOURSELF SOMETHING TO EAT.
MAYBE A HOTEL ROOM. A SHOWER.
SORRY ABOUT THE MESS. I WAS JUST IN A BIT OF A TUSSLE.
YEAH, I SAW IT ON THE NEWS.
I OWE YOU, GEORGE.
WHAT DID I JUST SAY? YOU DON'T.

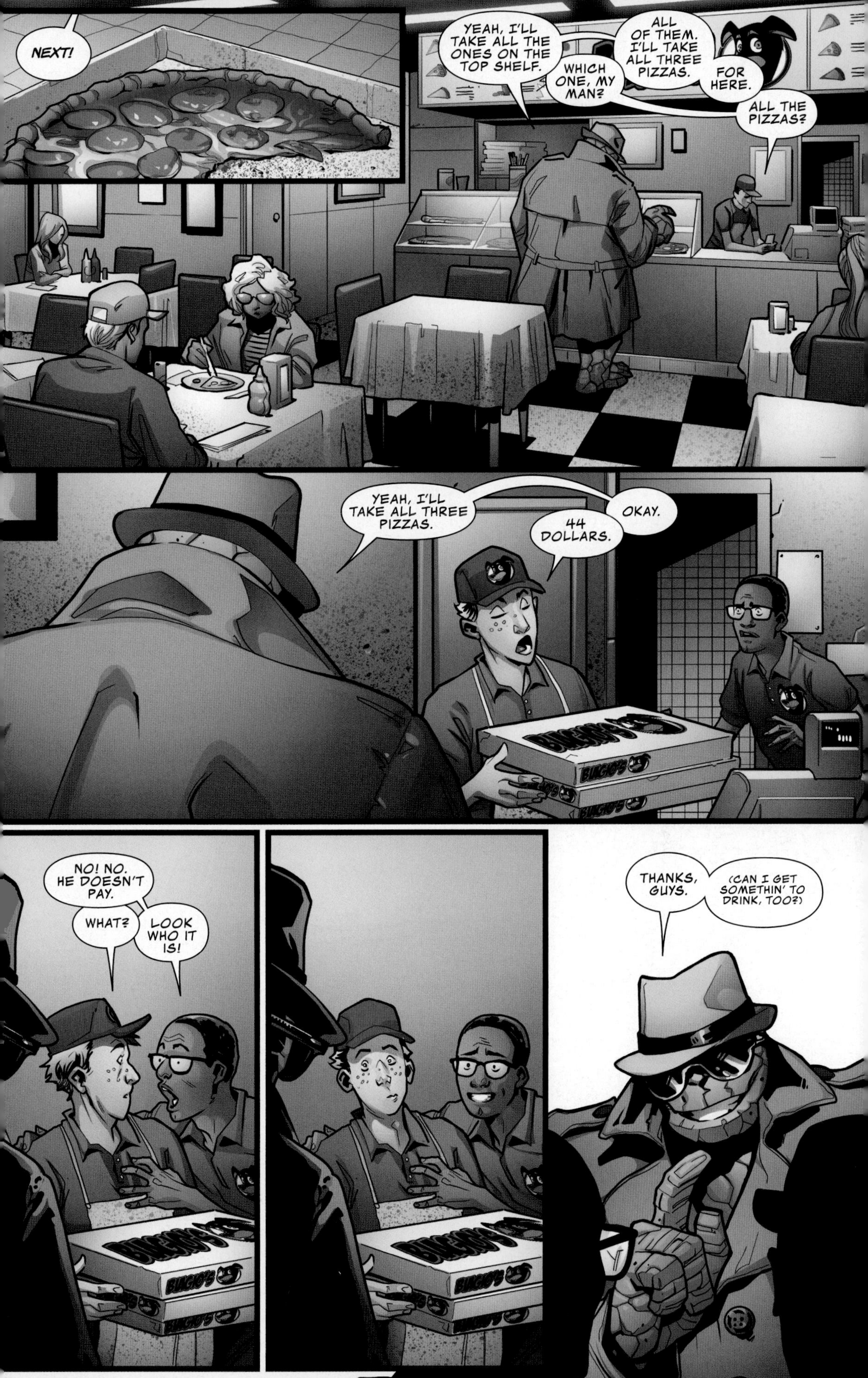
NEXT!
YEAH, I'LL TAKE ALL THE ONES ON THE TOP SHELF.
WHICH ONE, MY MAN?
ALL OF THEM. I'LL TAKE ALL THREE PIZZAS.
FOR HERE.
ALL THE PIZZAS?
YEAH, I'LL TAKE ALL THREE PIZZAS.
OKAY.
44 DOLLARS.
BIAGIO'S
NO! NO. HE DOESN'T PAY.
WHAT?
LOOK WHO IT IS!
THANKS, GUYS.
(CAN I GET SOMETHIN' TO DRINK, TOO?)

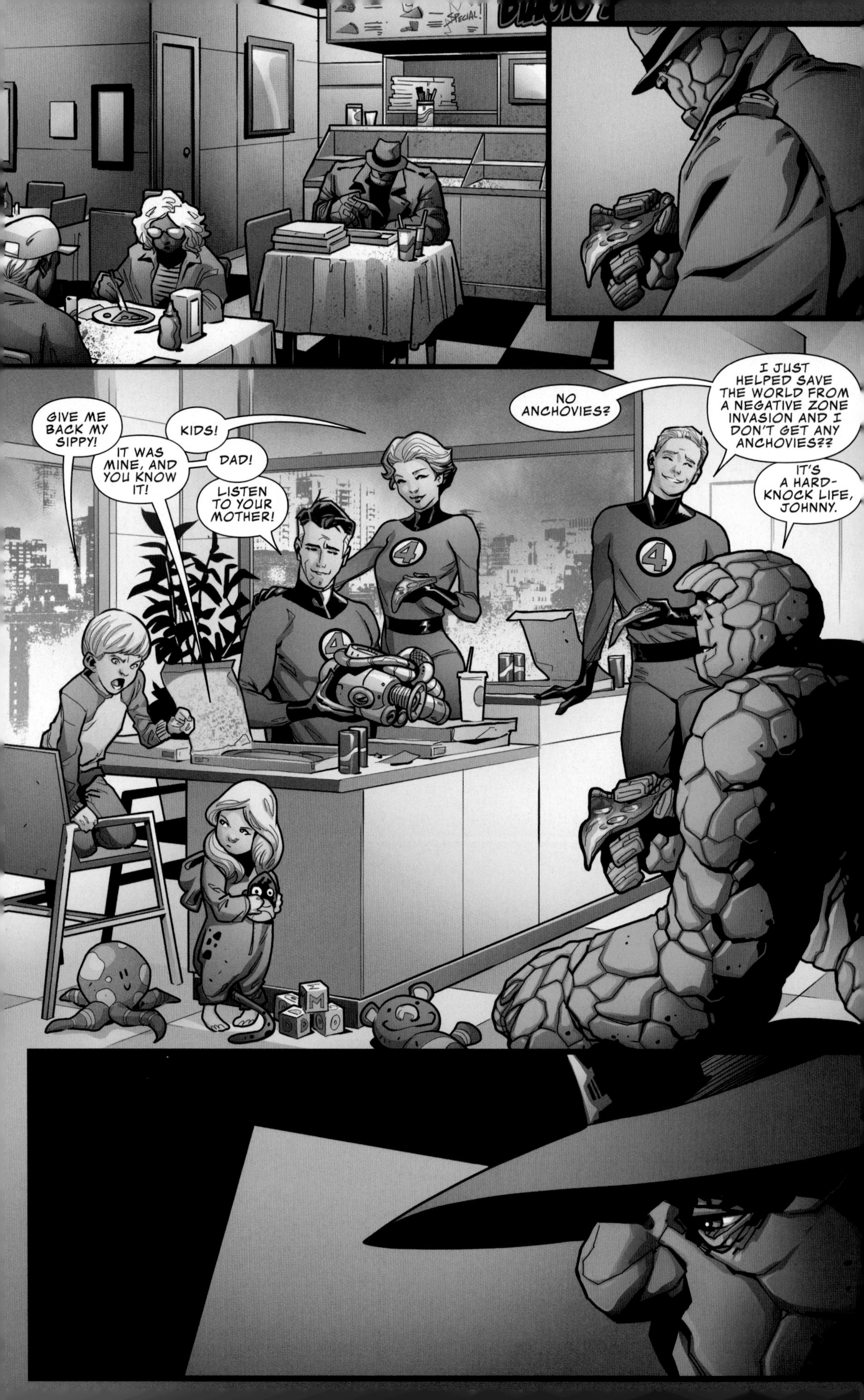
SPECIAL!
GIVE ME BACK MY SIPPY!
IT WAS MINE, AND YOU KNOW IT!
KIDS!
DAD!
LISTEN TO YOUR MOTHER!
NO ANCHOVIES?
I JUST HELPED SAVE THE WORLD FROM A NEGATIVE ZONE INVASION AND I DON'T GET ANY ANCHOVIES??
IT'S A HARD-KNOCK LIFE, JOHNNY.

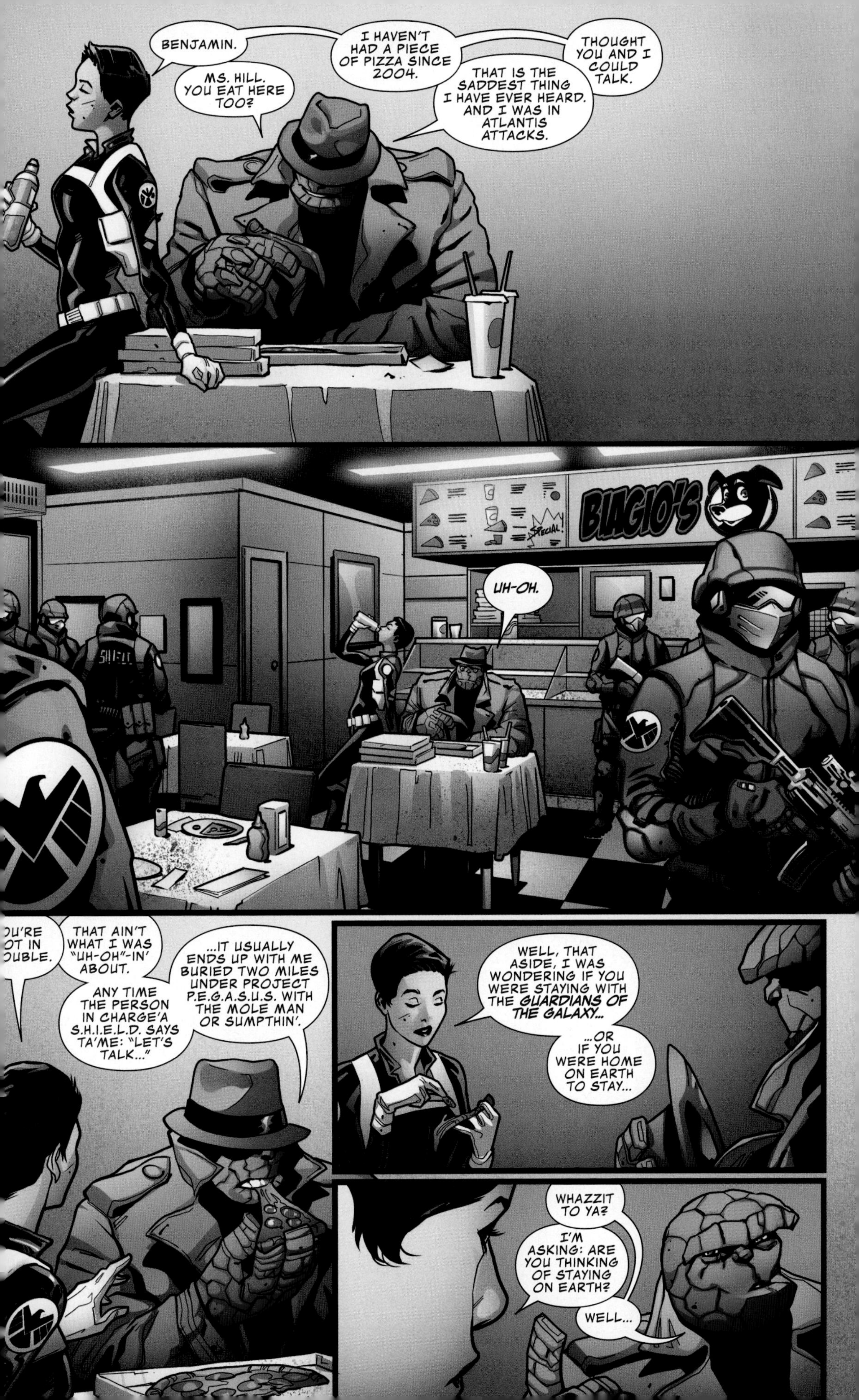
BENJAMIN.
MS. HILL. YOU EAT HERE TOO?
I HAVEN'T HAD A PIECE OF PIZZA SINCE 2004.
THAT IS THE SADDEST THING I HAVE EVER HEARD. AND I WAS IN ATLANTIS ATTACKS.
THOUGHT YOU AND I COULD TALK.
BIAGIO'S
SPECIAL!
UH-OH.
THAT AIN'T WHAT I WAS "UH-OH"-IN' ABOUT.
ANY TIME THE PERSON IN CHARGE'A S.H.I.E.L.D. SAYS TA'ME: "LET'S TALK..."
...IT USUALLY ENDS UP WITH ME BURIED TWO MILES UNDER PROJECT P.E.G.A.S.U.S. WITH THE MOLE MAN OR SUMPTHIN'.
WELL, THAT ASIDE, I WAS WONDERING IF YOU WERE STAYING WITH THE *GUARDIANS OF THE GALAXY...*
...OR IF YOU WERE HOME ON EARTH TO STAY...
WHAZZIT TO YA?
I'M ASKING: ARE YOU THINKING OF STAYING ON EARTH?
WELL...

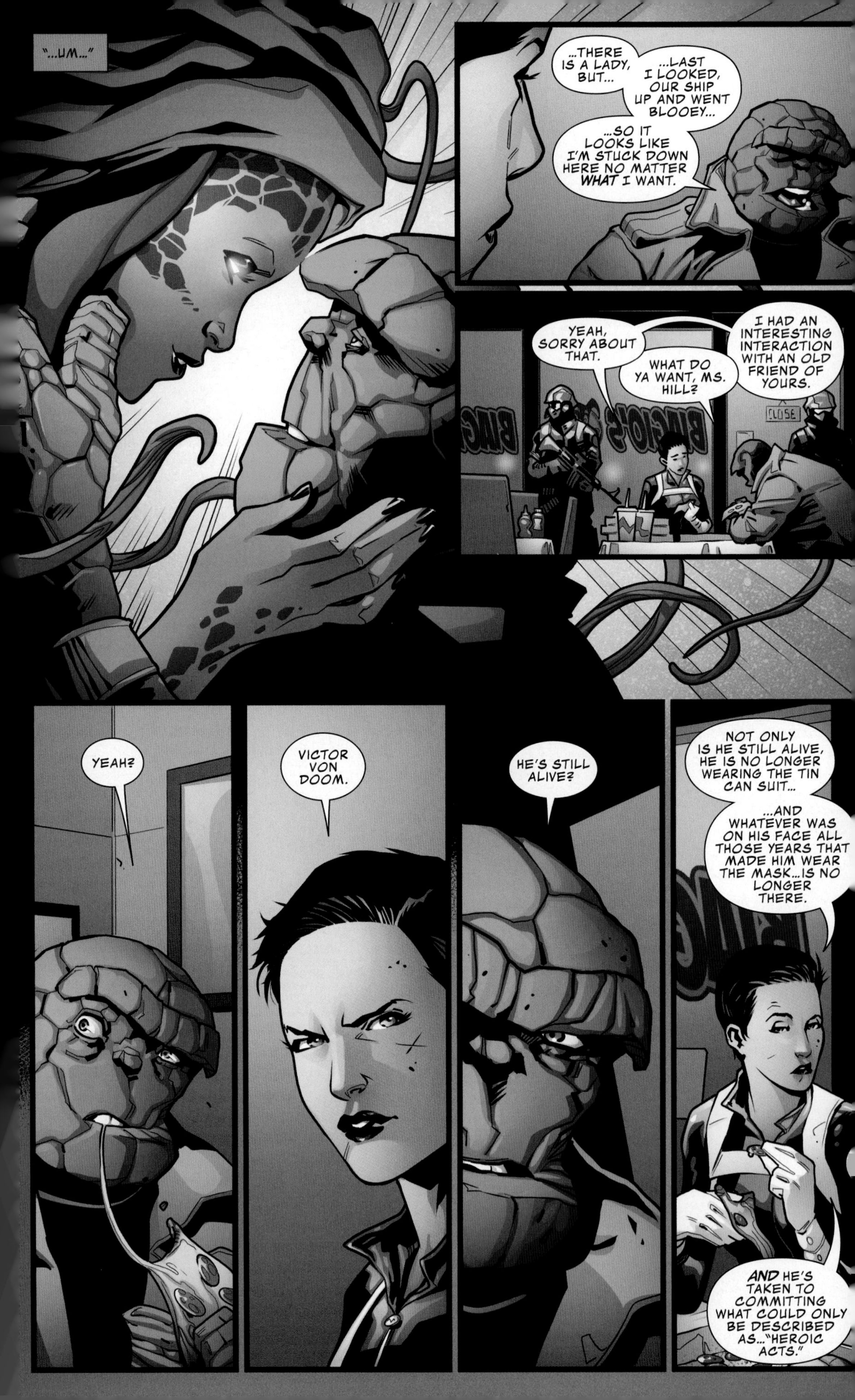
"...UM..."
...THERE IS A LADY, BUT...
...LAST I LOOKED, OUR SHIP UP AND WENT BLOOEY...
...SO IT LOOKS LIKE I'M STUCK DOWN HERE NO MATTER *WHAT* I WANT.
YEAH, SORRY ABOUT THAT.
WHAT DO YA WANT, MS. HILL?
I HAD AN INTERESTING INTERACTION WITH AN OLD FRIEND OF YOURS.
CLOSE
YEAH?
VICTOR VON DOOM.
HE'S STILL ALIVE?
NOT ONLY IS HE STILL ALIVE, HE IS NO LONGER WEARING THE TIN CAN SUIT...
...AND WHATEVER WAS ON HIS FACE ALL THOSE YEARS THAT MADE HIM WEAR THE MASK...IS NO LONGER THERE.
*AND* HE'S TAKEN TO COMMITTING WHAT COULD ONLY BE DESCRIBED AS..."HEROIC ACTS."

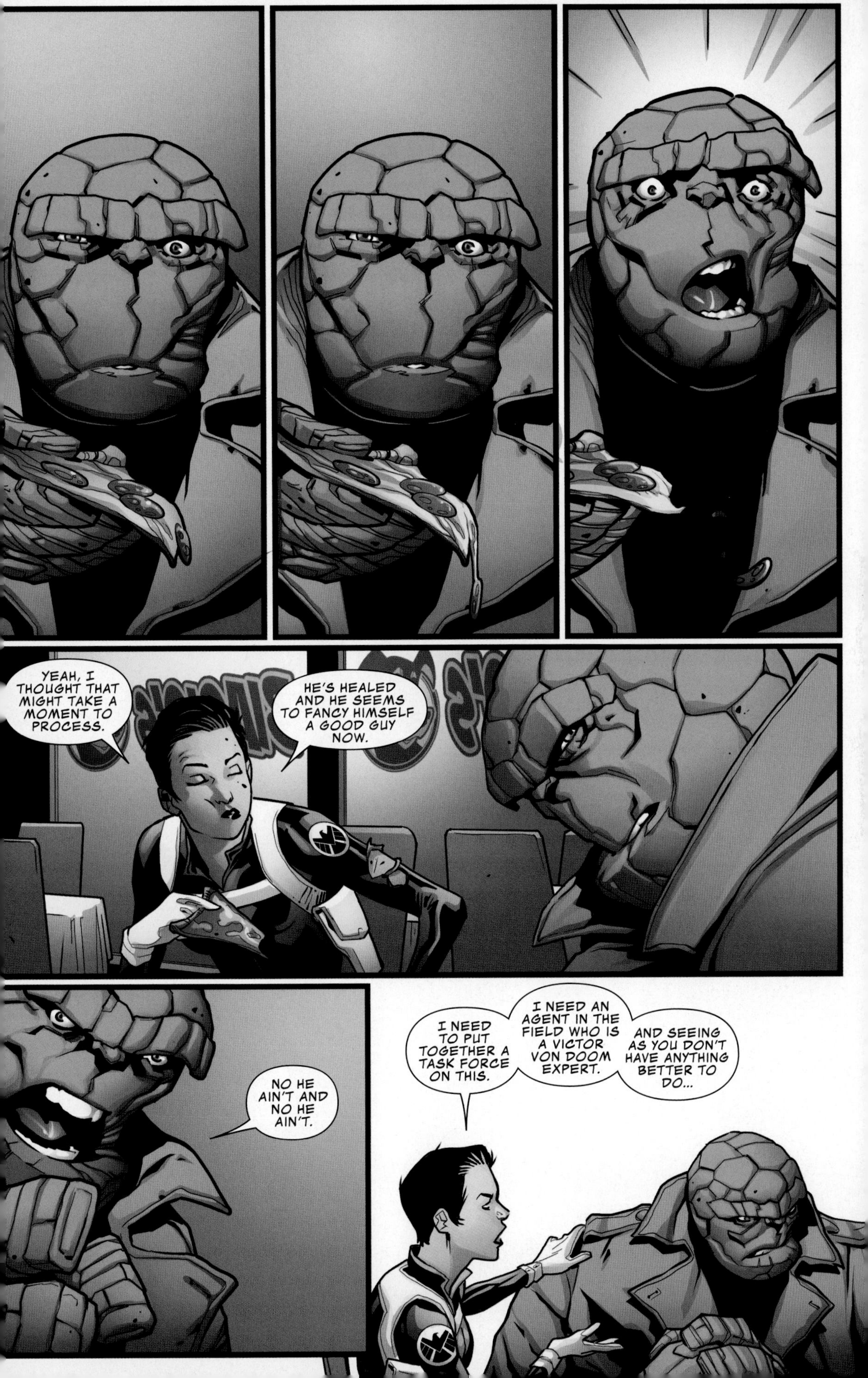
YEAH, I THOUGHT THAT MIGHT TAKE A MOMENT TO PROCESS.
HE'S HEALED AND HE SEEMS TO FANCY HIMSELF A GOOD GUY NOW.
NO HE AIN'T AND NO HE AIN'T.
I NEED TO PUT TOGETHER A TASK FORCE ON THIS.
I NEED AN AGENT IN THE FIELD WHO IS A VICTOR VON DOOM EXPERT.
AND SEEING AS YOU DON'T HAVE ANYTHING BETTER TO DO...

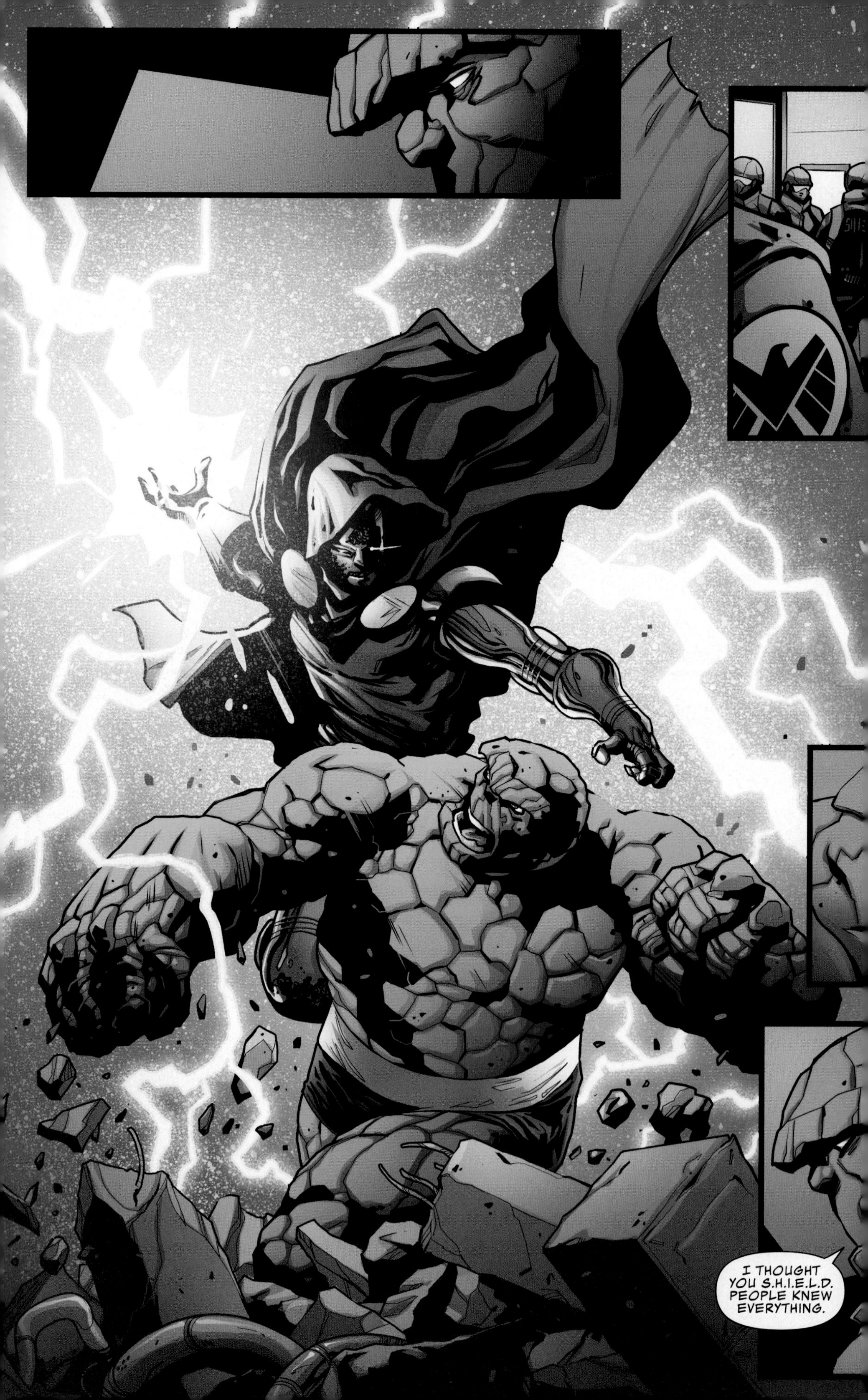
I THOUGHT YOU S.H.I.E.L.D. PEOPLE KNEW EVERYTHING.

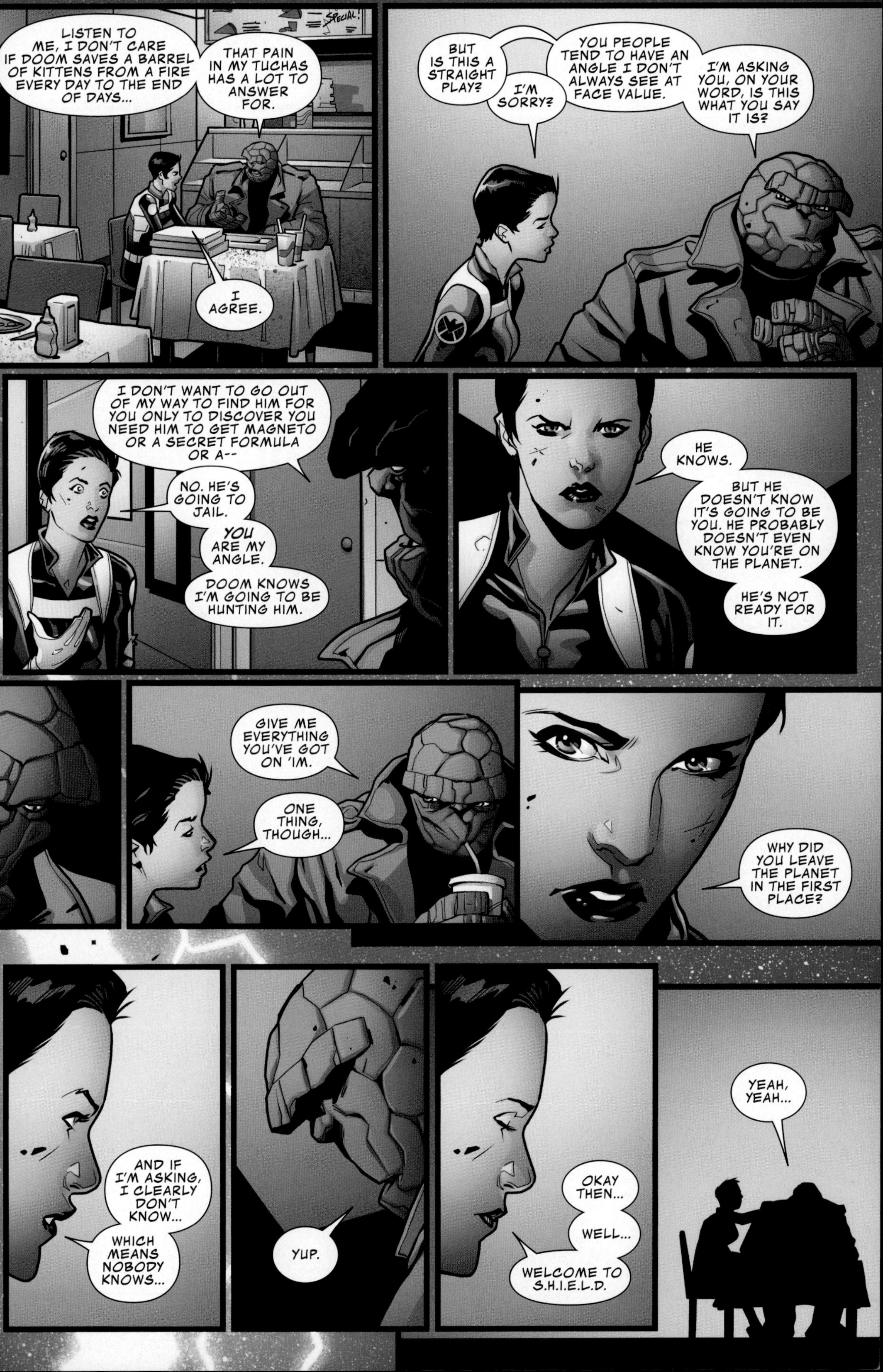
LISTEN TO ME, I DON'T CARE IF DOOM SAVES A BARREL OF KITTENS FROM A FIRE EVERY DAY TO THE END OF DAYS...
THAT PAIN IN MY TUCHAS HAS A LOT TO ANSWER FOR.
I AGREE.
BUT IS THIS A STRAIGHT PLAY?
I'M SORRY?
YOU PEOPLE TEND TO HAVE AN ANGLE I DON'T ALWAYS SEE AT FACE VALUE.
I'M ASKING YOU, ON YOUR WORD, IS THIS WHAT YOU SAY IT IS?
I DON'T WANT TO GO OUT OF MY WAY TO FIND HIM FOR YOU ONLY TO DISCOVER YOU NEED HIM TO GET MAGNETO OR A SECRET FORMULA OR A--
NO. HE'S GOING TO JAIL.
YOU ARE MY ANGLE.
DOOM KNOWS I'M GOING TO BE HUNTING HIM.
HE KNOWS.
BUT HE DOESN'T KNOW IT'S GOING TO BE YOU. HE PROBABLY DOESN'T EVEN KNOW YOU'RE ON THE PLANET.
HE'S NOT READY FOR IT.
GIVE ME EVERYTHING YOU'VE GOT ON 'IM.
ONE THING, THOUGH...
WHY DID YOU LEAVE THE PLANET IN THE FIRST PLACE?
AND IF I'M ASKING, I CLEARLY DON'T KNOW...
WHICH MEANS NOBODY KNOWS...
YUP.
OKAY THEN...
WELL...
WELCOME TO S.H.I.E.L.D.
YEAH, YEAH...

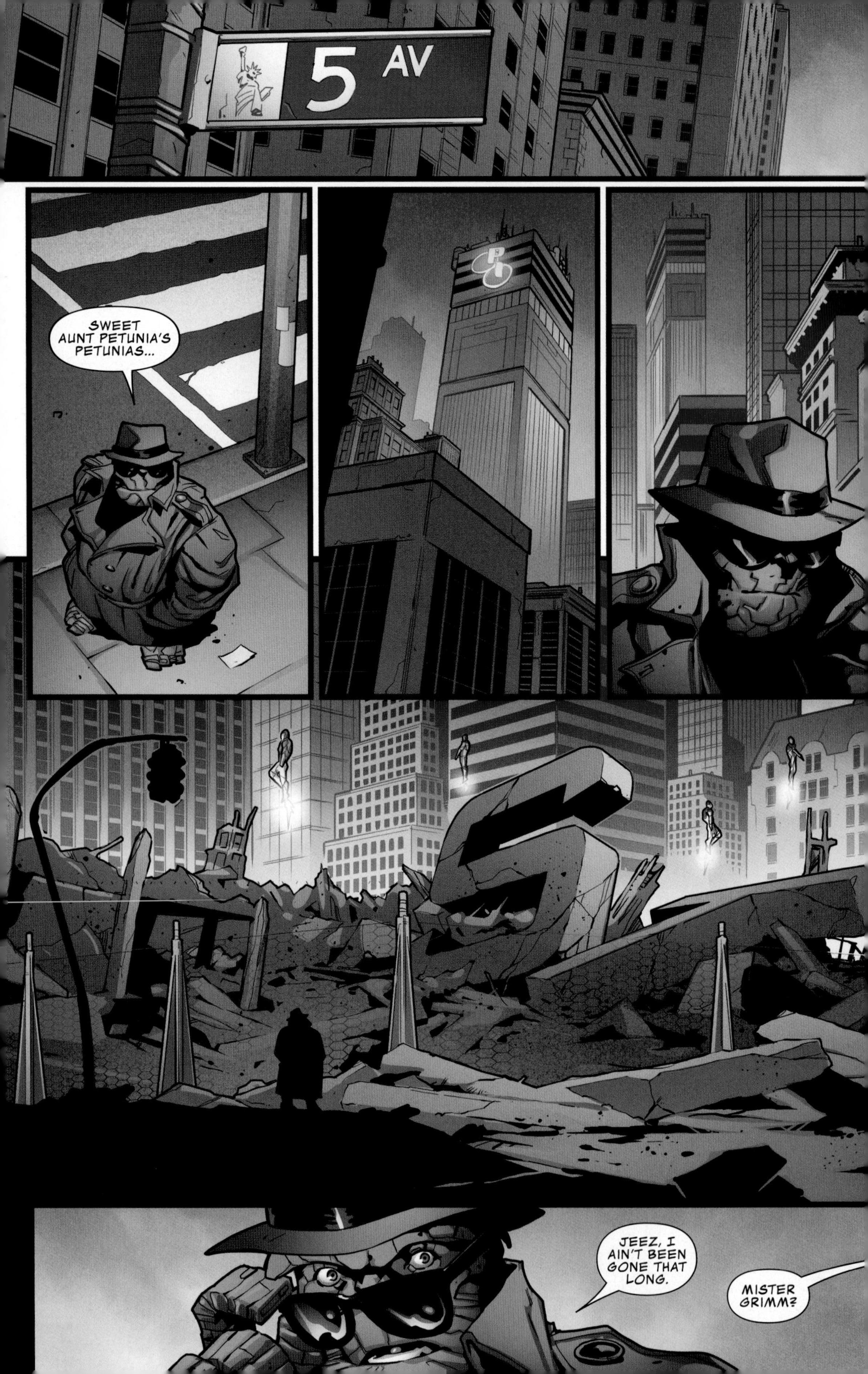
5 AV
SWEET AUNT PETUNIA'S PETUNIAS...
JEEZ, I AIN'T BEEN GONE THAT LONG.
MISTER GRIMM?

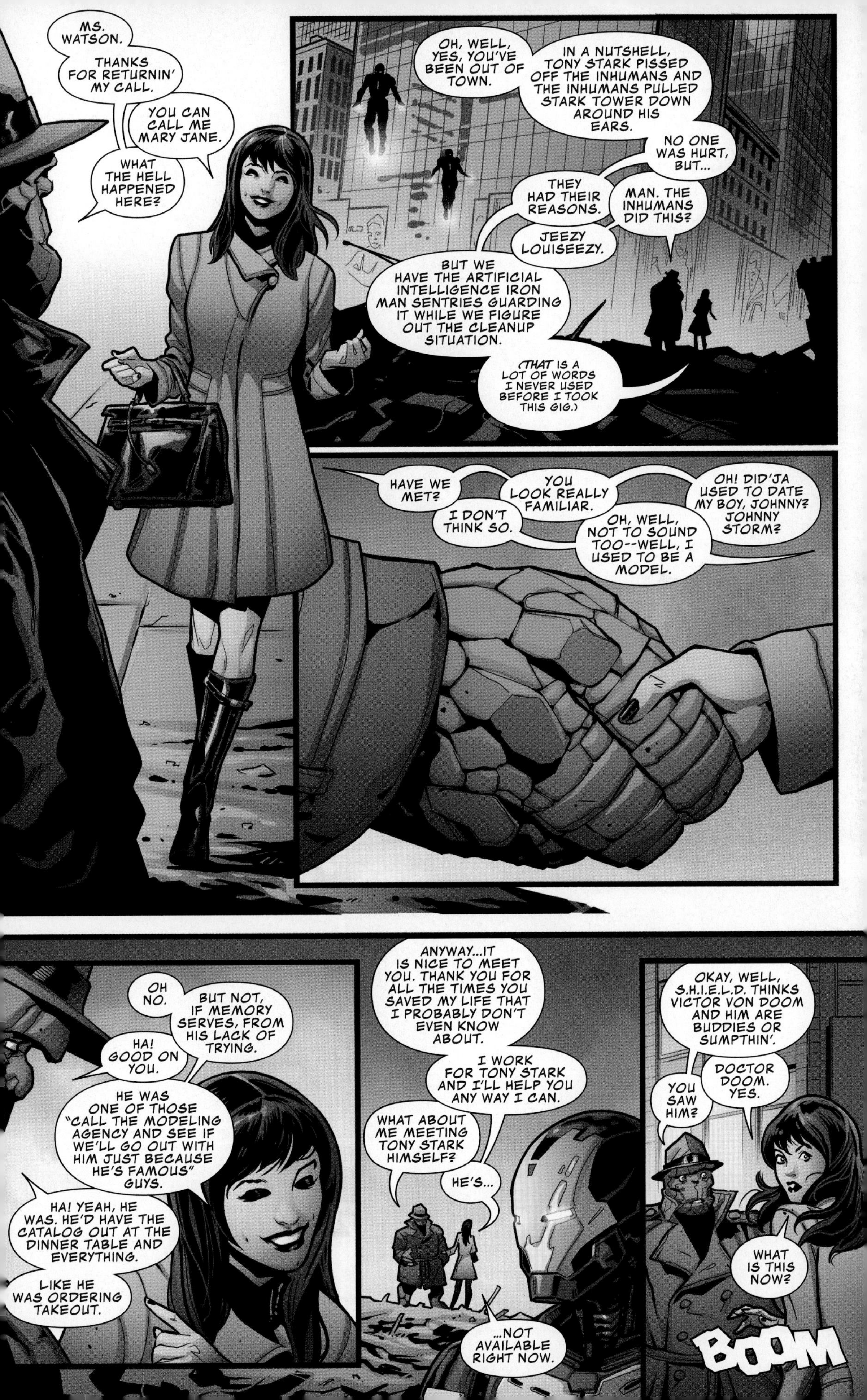
MS. WATSON.
THANKS FOR RETURNIN' MY CALL.
YOU CAN CALL ME MARY JANE.
WHAT THE HELL HAPPENED HERE?
OH, WELL, YES, YOU'VE BEEN OUT OF TOWN.
IN A NUTSHELL, TONY STARK PISSED OFF THE INHUMANS AND THE INHUMANS PULLED STARK TOWER DOWN AROUND HIS EARS.
NO ONE WAS HURT, BUT...
MAN. THE INHUMANS DID THIS?
THEY HAD THEIR REASONS.
JEEZY LOUISEEZY.
BUT WE HAVE THE ARTIFICIAL INTELLIGENCE IRON MAN SENTRIES GUARDING IT WHILE WE FIGURE OUT THE CLEANUP SITUATION.
(THAT IS A LOT OF WORDS I NEVER USED BEFORE I TOOK THIS GIG.)
HAVE WE MET?
YOU LOOK REALLY FAMILIAR.
I DON'T THINK SO.
OH! DID'JA USED TO DATE MY BOY, JOHNNY? JOHNNY STORM?
OH, WELL, NOT TO SOUND TOO--WELL, I USED TO BE A MODEL.
OH NO.
BUT NOT, IF MEMORY SERVES, FROM HIS LACK OF TRYING.
HA! GOOD ON YOU.
HE WAS ONE OF THOSE "CALL THE MODELING AGENCY AND SEE IF WE'LL GO OUT WITH HIM JUST BECAUSE HE'S FAMOUS" GUYS.
HA! YEAH, HE WAS. HE'D HAVE THE CATALOG OUT AT THE DINNER TABLE AND EVERYTHING.
LIKE HE WAS ORDERING TAKEOUT.
ANYWAY...IT IS NICE TO MEET YOU. THANK YOU FOR ALL THE TIMES YOU SAVED MY LIFE THAT I PROBABLY DON'T EVEN KNOW ABOUT.
I WORK FOR TONY STARK AND I'LL HELP YOU ANY WAY I CAN.
WHAT ABOUT ME MEETING TONY STARK HIMSELF?
HE'S...
...NOT AVAILABLE RIGHT NOW.
OKAY, WELL, S.H.I.E.L.D. THINKS VICTOR VON DOOM AND HIM ARE BUDDIES OR SUMPTHIN'.
DOCTOR DOOM. YES.
YOU SAW HIM?
WHAT IS THIS NOW?
BOOM

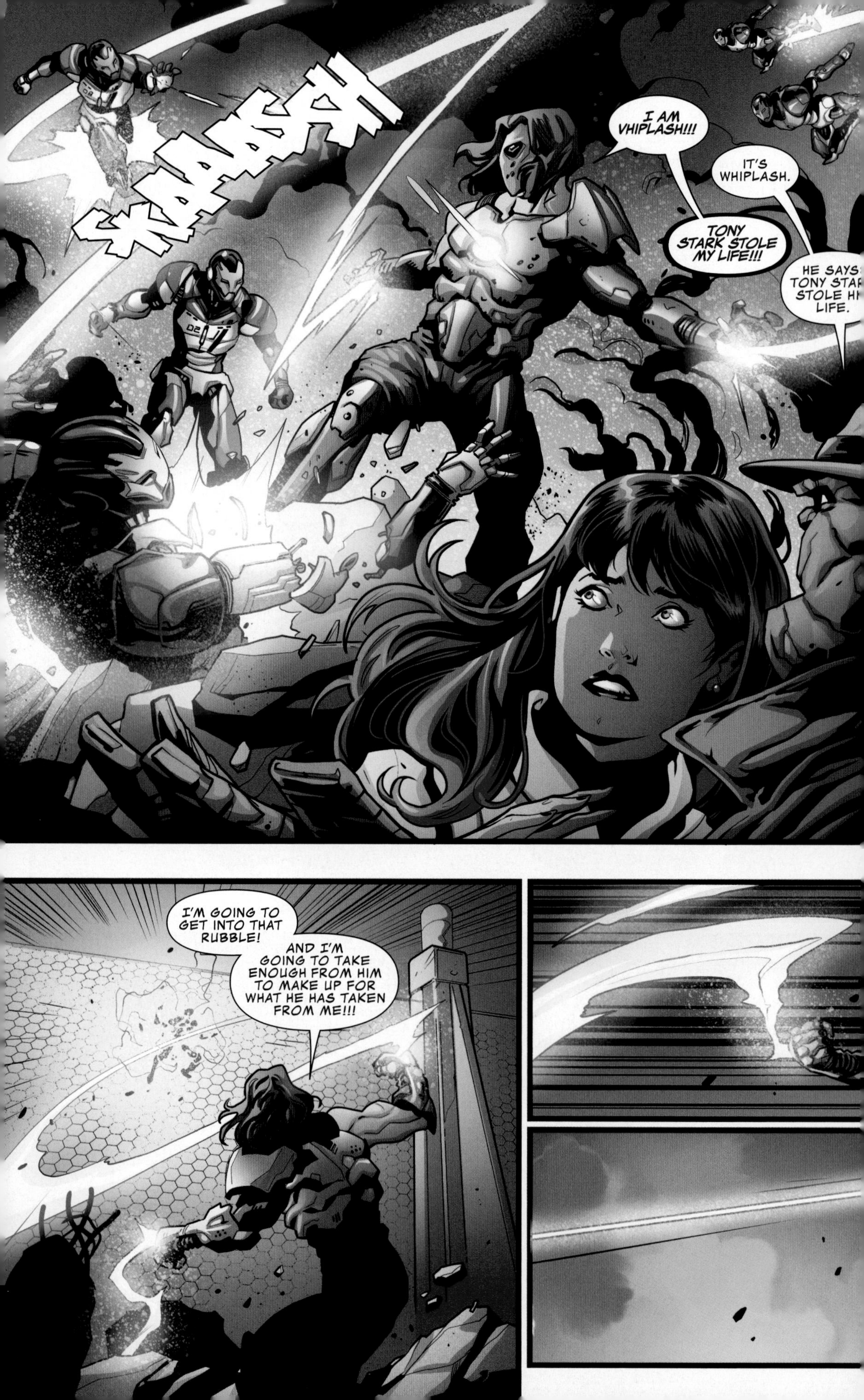
I AM VHIPLASH!!!
IT'S WHIPLASH.
TONY STARK STOLE MY LIFE!!!
HE SAYS TONY STAR STOLE HI LIFE.
I'M GOING TO GET INTO THAT RUBBLE!
AND I'M GOING TO TAKE ENOUGH FROM HIM TO MAKE UP FOR WHAT HE HAS TAKEN FROM ME!!!

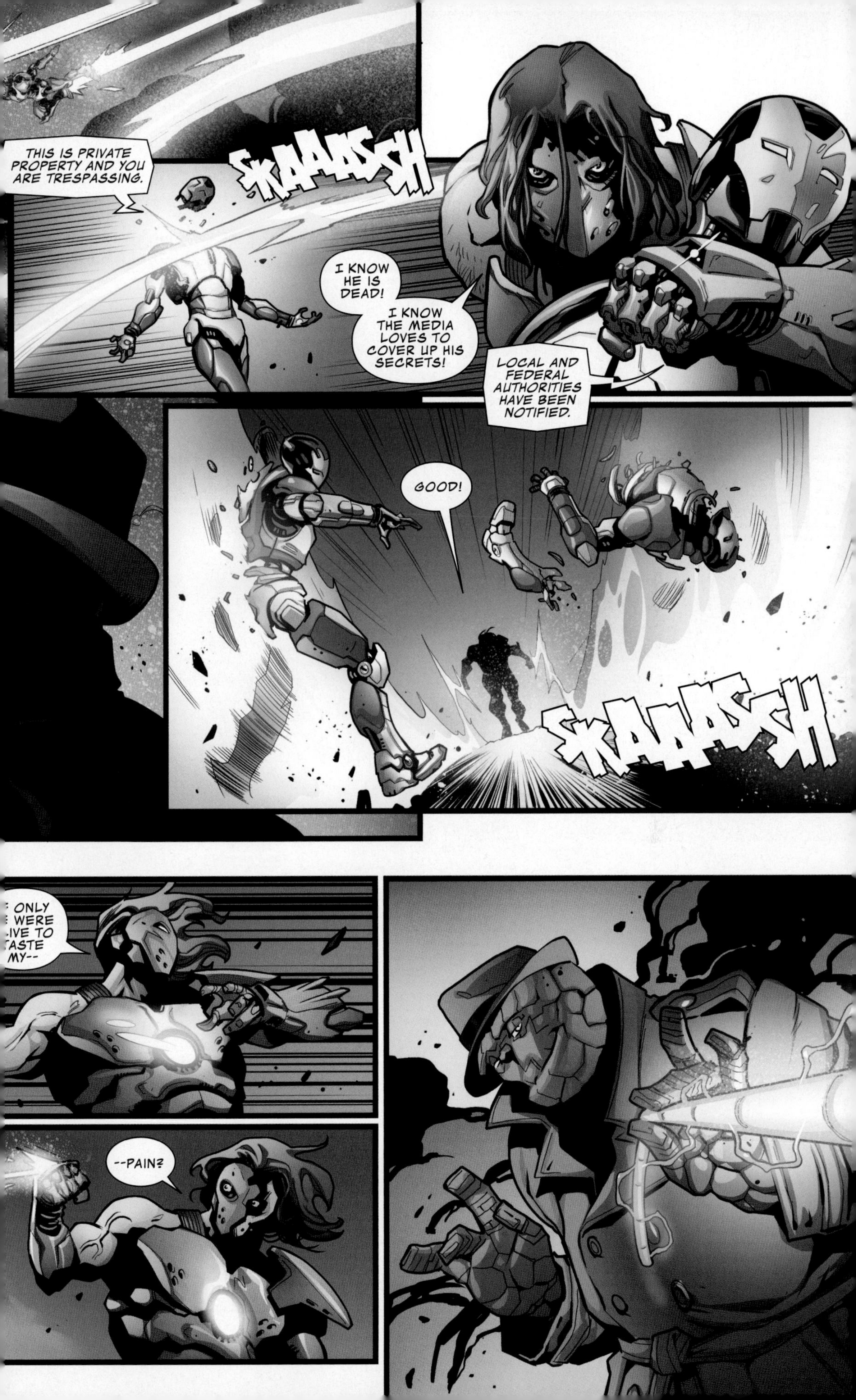
THIS IS PRIVATE PROPERTY AND YOU ARE TRESPASSING.
SKAAASSH
I KNOW HE IS DEAD!
I KNOW THE MEDIA LOVES TO COVER UP HIS SECRETS!
LOCAL AND FEDERAL AUTHORITIES HAVE BEEN NOTIFIED.
GOOD!
SKAAASSH
ONLY WERE IVE TO TASTE MY--
--PAIN?

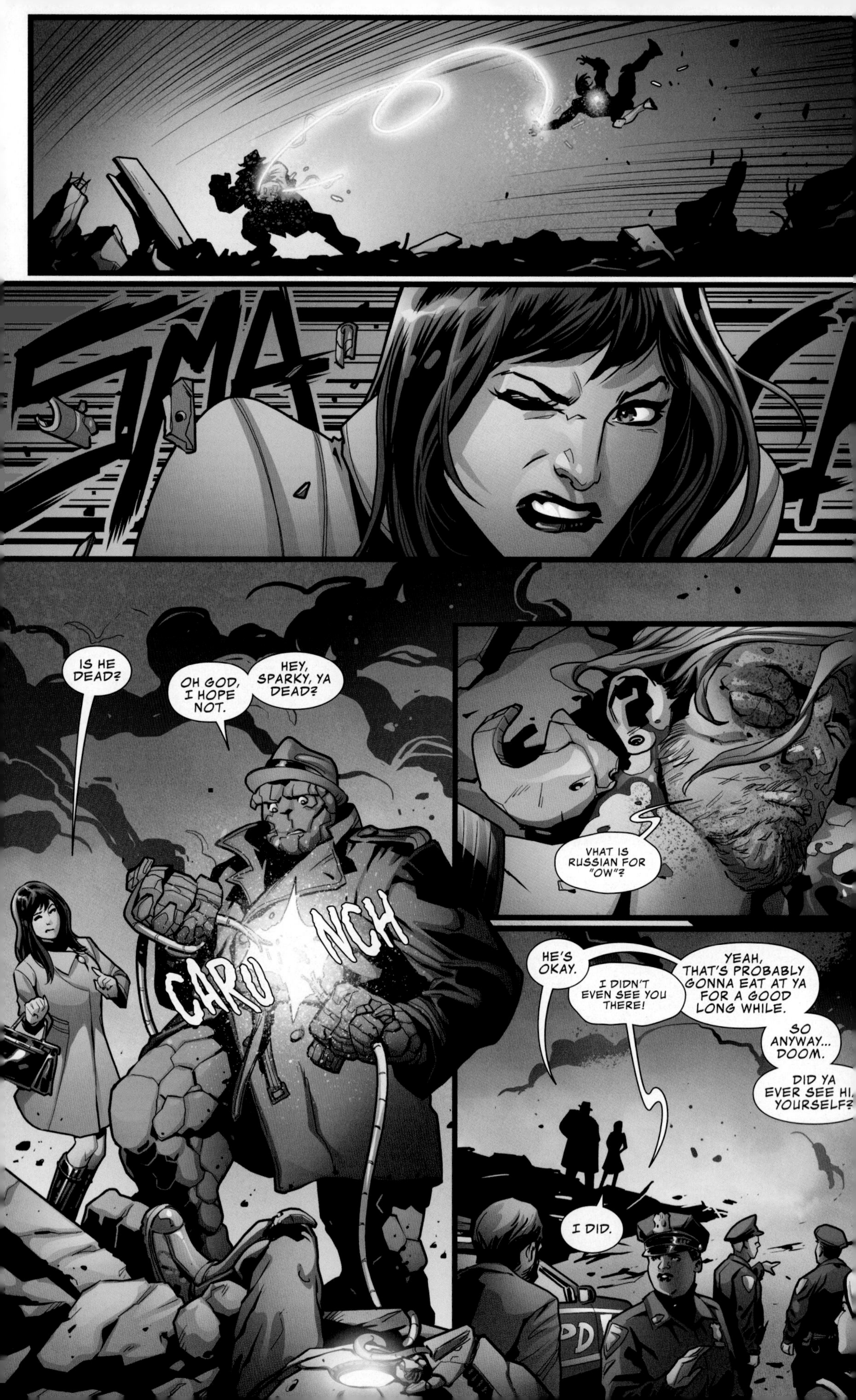
SMA
IS HE DEAD?
OH GOD, I HOPE NOT.
HEY, SPARKY, YA DEAD?
CARU NCH
VHAT IS RUSSIAN FOR "OW"?
HE'S OKAY.
I DIDN'T EVEN SEE YOU THERE!
YEAH, THAT'S PROBABLY GONNA EAT AT YA FOR A GOOD LONG WHILE.
SO ANYWAY... DOOM.
DID YA EVER SEE HI YOURSELF?
I DID.

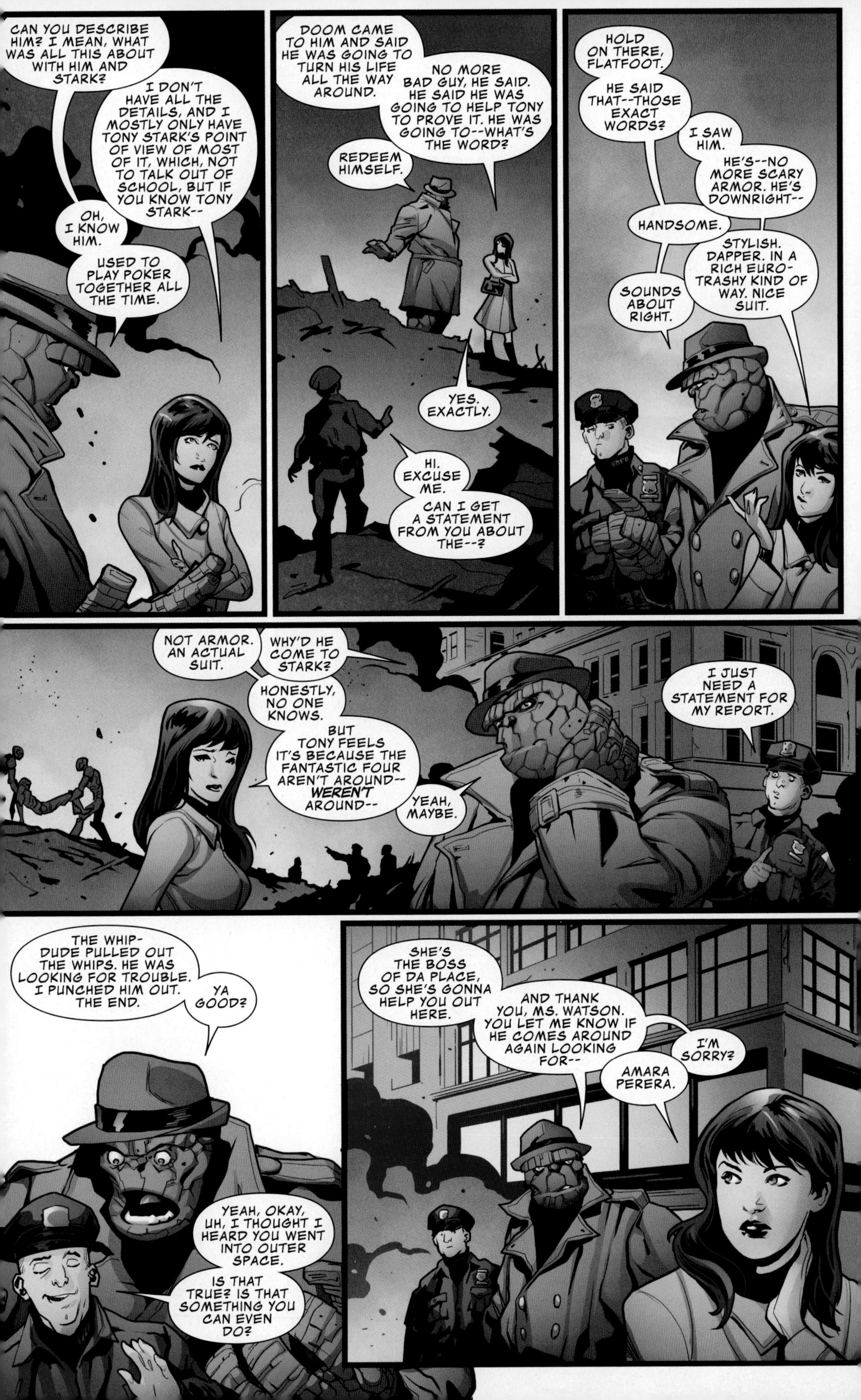

CAN YOU DESCRIBE HIM? I MEAN, WHAT WAS ALL THIS ABOUT WITH HIM AND STARK?
I DON'T HAVE ALL THE DETAILS, AND I MOSTLY ONLY HAVE TONY STARK'S POINT OF VIEW OF MOST OF IT, WHICH, NOT TO TALK OUT OF SCHOOL, BUT IF YOU KNOW TONY STARK--
OH, I KNOW HIM.
USED TO PLAY POKER TOGETHER ALL THE TIME.
DOOM CAME TO HIM AND SAID HE WAS GOING TO TURN HIS LIFE ALL THE WAY AROUND.
NO MORE BAD GUY, HE SAID. HE SAID HE WAS GOING TO HELP TONY TO PROVE IT. HE WAS GOING TO--WHAT'S THE WORD?
REDEEM HIMSELF.
YES. EXACTLY.
HI. EXCUSE ME.
CAN I GET A STATEMENT FROM YOU ABOUT THE--?
HOLD ON THERE, FLATFOOT.
HE SAID THAT--THOSE EXACT WORDS?
I SAW HIM.
HE'S--NO MORE SCARY ARMOR. HE'S DOWNRIGHT--
HANDSOME.
STYLISH. DAPPER. IN A RICH EURO-TRASHY KIND OF WAY. NICE SUIT.
SOUNDS ABOUT RIGHT.
NOT ARMOR. AN ACTUAL SUIT.
WHY'D HE COME TO STARK?
HONESTLY, NO ONE KNOWS.
BUT TONY FEELS IT'S BECAUSE THE FANTASTIC FOUR AREN'T AROUND-- *WEREN'T* AROUND--
YEAH, MAYBE.
I JUST NEED A STATEMENT FOR MY REPORT.
THE WHIP-DUDE PULLED OUT THE WHIPS. HE WAS LOOKING FOR TROUBLE. I PUNCHED HIM OUT. THE END.
YA GOOD?
YEAH, OKAY, UH, I THOUGHT I HEARD YOU WENT INTO OUTER SPACE.
IS THAT TRUE? IS THAT SOMETHING YOU CAN EVEN DO?
SHE'S THE BOSS OF DA PLACE, SO SHE'S GONNA HELP YOU OUT HERE.
AND THANK YOU, MS. WATSON. YOU LET ME KNOW IF HE COMES AROUND AGAIN LOOKING FOR--
I'M SORRY?
AMARA PERERA.

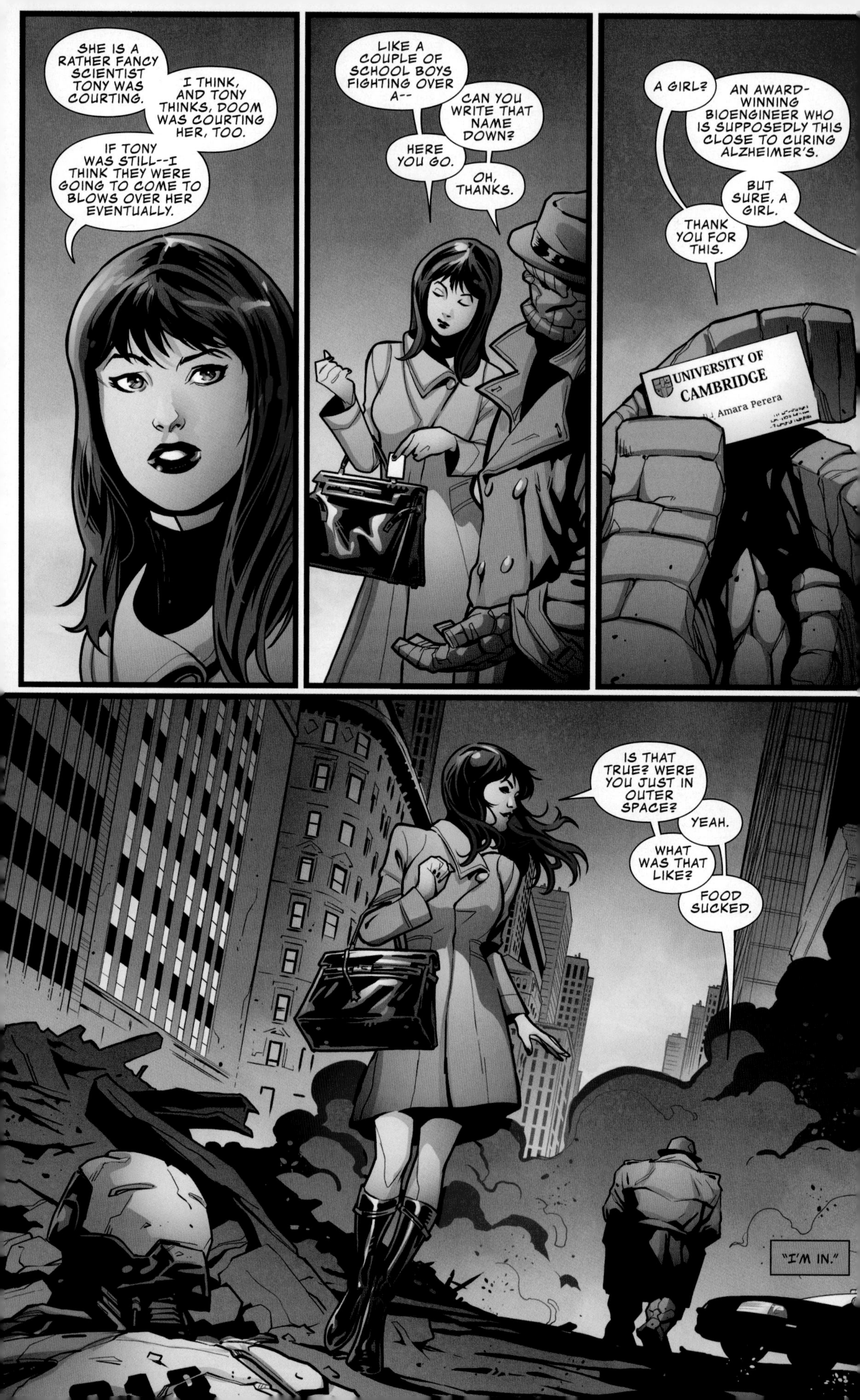

SHE IS A RATHER FANCY SCIENTIST TONY WAS COURTING.
I THINK, AND TONY THINKS, DOOM WAS COURTING HER, TOO.
IF TONY WAS STILL--I THINK THEY WERE GOING TO COME TO BLOWS OVER HER EVENTUALLY.
LIKE A COUPLE OF SCHOOL BOYS FIGHTING OVER A--
CAN YOU WRITE THAT NAME DOWN?
HERE YOU GO.
OH, THANKS.
A GIRL?
AN AWARD-WINNING BIOENGINEER WHO IS SUPPOSEDLY THIS CLOSE TO CURING ALZHEIMER'S.
BUT SURE, A GIRL.
THANK YOU FOR THIS.
UNIVERSITY OF CAMBRIDGE
Amara Perera
IS THAT TRUE? WERE YOU JUST IN OUTER SPACE?
YEAH.
WHAT WAS THAT LIKE?
FOOD SUCKED.
"I'M IN."

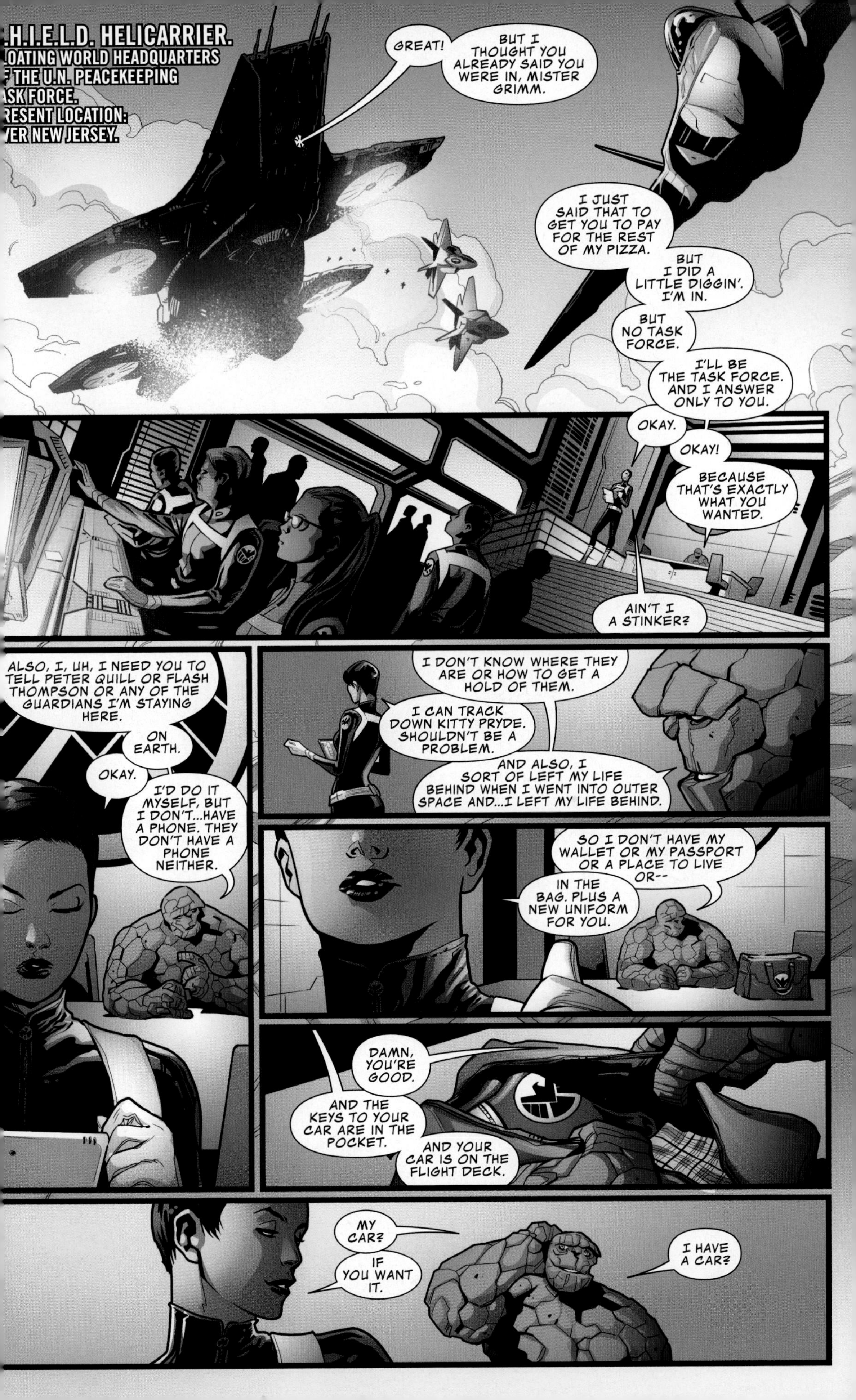

.H.I.E.L.D. HELICARRIER.
LOATING WORLD HEADQUARTERS
F THE U.N. PEACEKEEPING
ASK FORCE.
RESENT LOCATION:
VER NEW JERSEY.
GREAT!
BUT I THOUGHT YOU ALREADY SAID YOU WERE IN, MISTER GRIMM.
I JUST SAID THAT TO GET YOU TO PAY FOR THE REST OF MY PIZZA.
BUT I DID A LITTLE DIGGIN'. I'M IN.
BUT NO TASK FORCE.
I'LL BE THE TASK FORCE. AND I ANSWER ONLY TO YOU.
OKAY.
OKAY!
BECAUSE THAT'S EXACTLY WHAT YOU WANTED.
AIN'T I A STINKER?
ALSO, I, UH, I NEED YOU TO TELL PETER QUILL OR FLASH THOMPSON OR ANY OF THE GUARDIANS I'M STAYING HERE.
ON EARTH.
OKAY.
I'D DO IT MYSELF, BUT I DON'T...HAVE A PHONE. THEY DON'T HAVE A PHONE NEITHER.
I DON'T KNOW WHERE THEY ARE OR HOW TO GET A HOLD OF THEM.
I CAN TRACK DOWN KITTY PRYDE. SHOULDN'T BE A PROBLEM.
AND ALSO, I SORT OF LEFT MY LIFE BEHIND WHEN I WENT INTO OUTER SPACE AND...I LEFT MY LIFE BEHIND.
SO I DON'T HAVE MY WALLET OR MY PASSPORT OR A PLACE TO LIVE OR--
IN THE BAG. PLUS A NEW UNIFORM FOR YOU.
DAMN, YOU'RE GOOD.
AND THE KEYS TO YOUR CAR ARE IN THE POCKET.
AND YOUR CAR IS ON THE FLIGHT DECK.
MY CAR?
IF YOU WANT IT.
I HAVE A CAR?

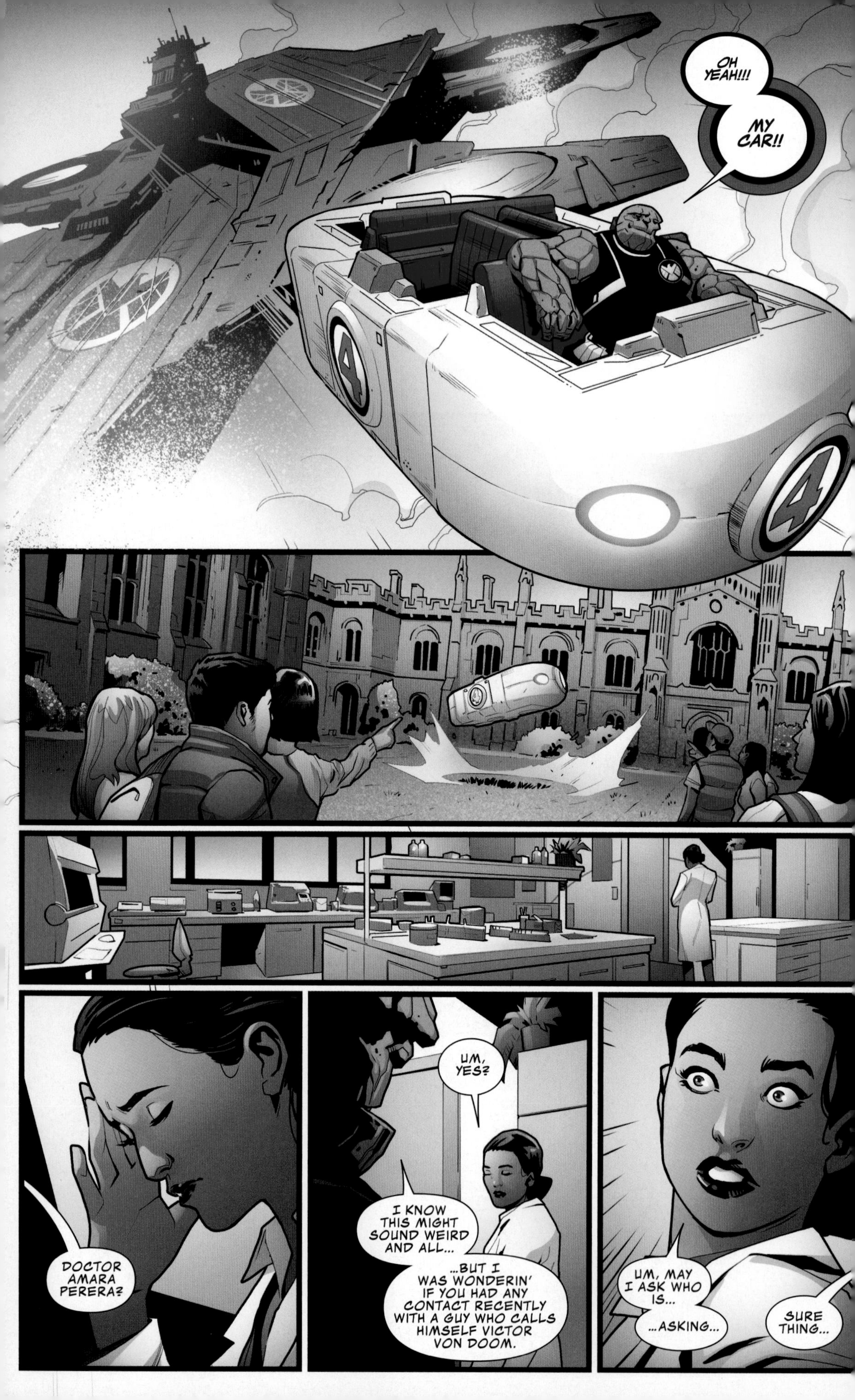
OH YEAH!!!
MY CAR!!
UM, YES?
DOCTOR AMARA PERERA?
I KNOW THIS MIGHT SOUND WEIRD AND ALL...
...BUT I WAS WONDERIN' IF YOU HAD ANY CONTACT RECENTLY WITH A GUY WHO CALLS HIMSELF VICTOR VON DOOM.
UM, MAY I ASK WHO IS...
...ASKING...
SURE THING...

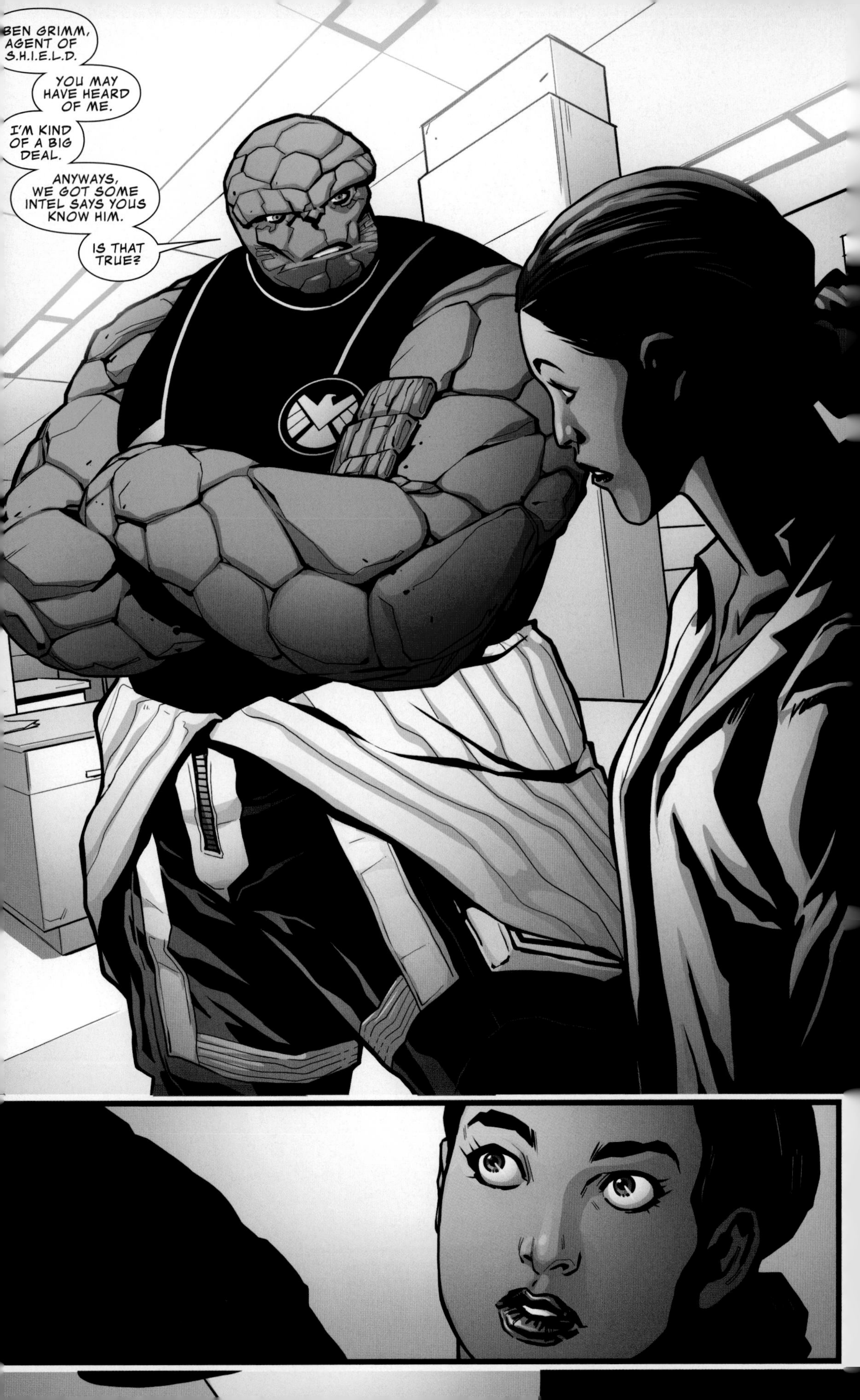
BEN GRIMM, AGENT OF S.H.I.E.L.D.
YOU MAY HAVE HEARD OF ME.
I'M KIND OF A BIG DEAL.
ANYWAYS, WE GOT SOME INTEL SAYS YOUS KNOW HIM.
IS THAT TRUE?

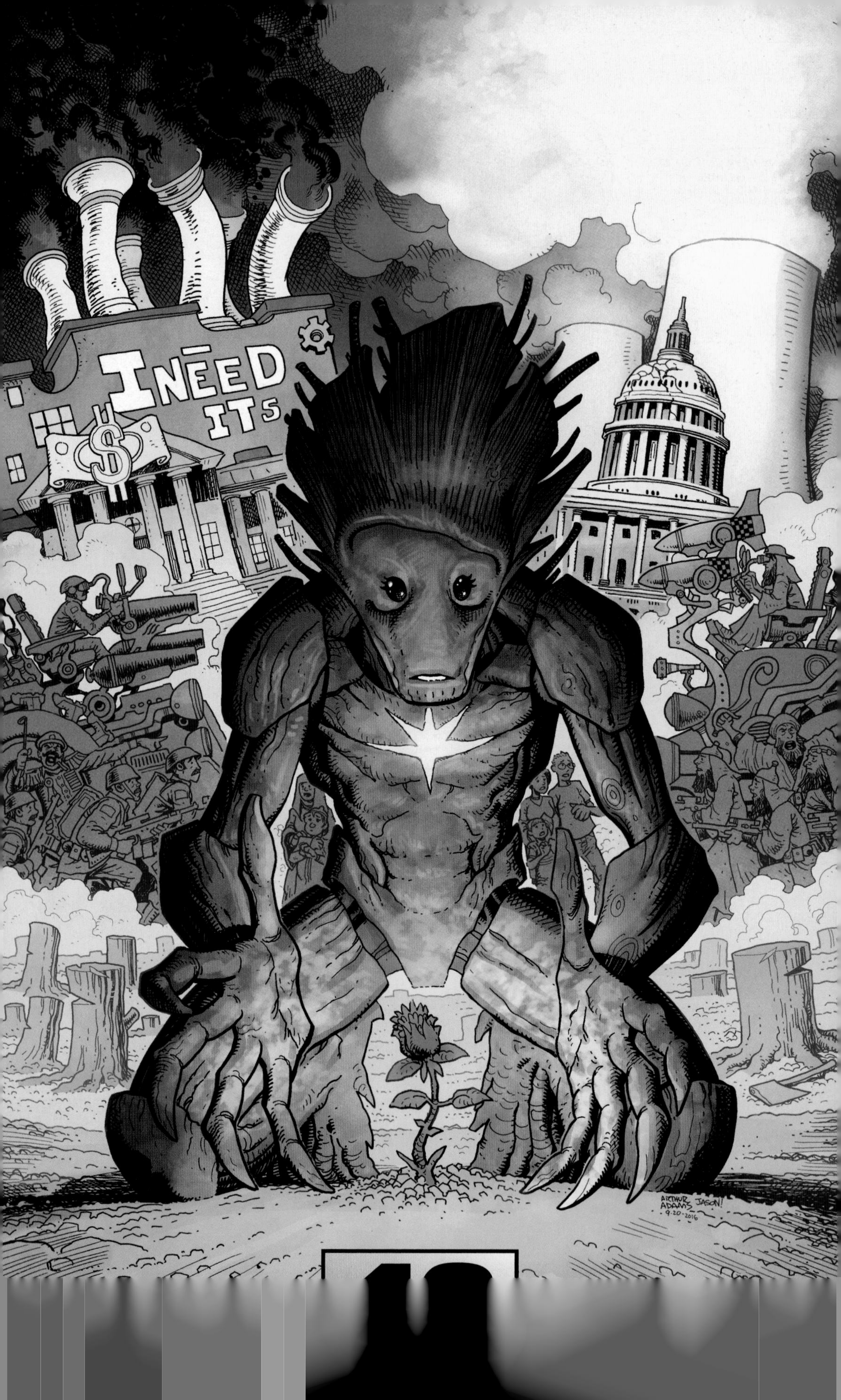
INEED
ITS
ARTHUR ADAMS JASON!
9-20-2016

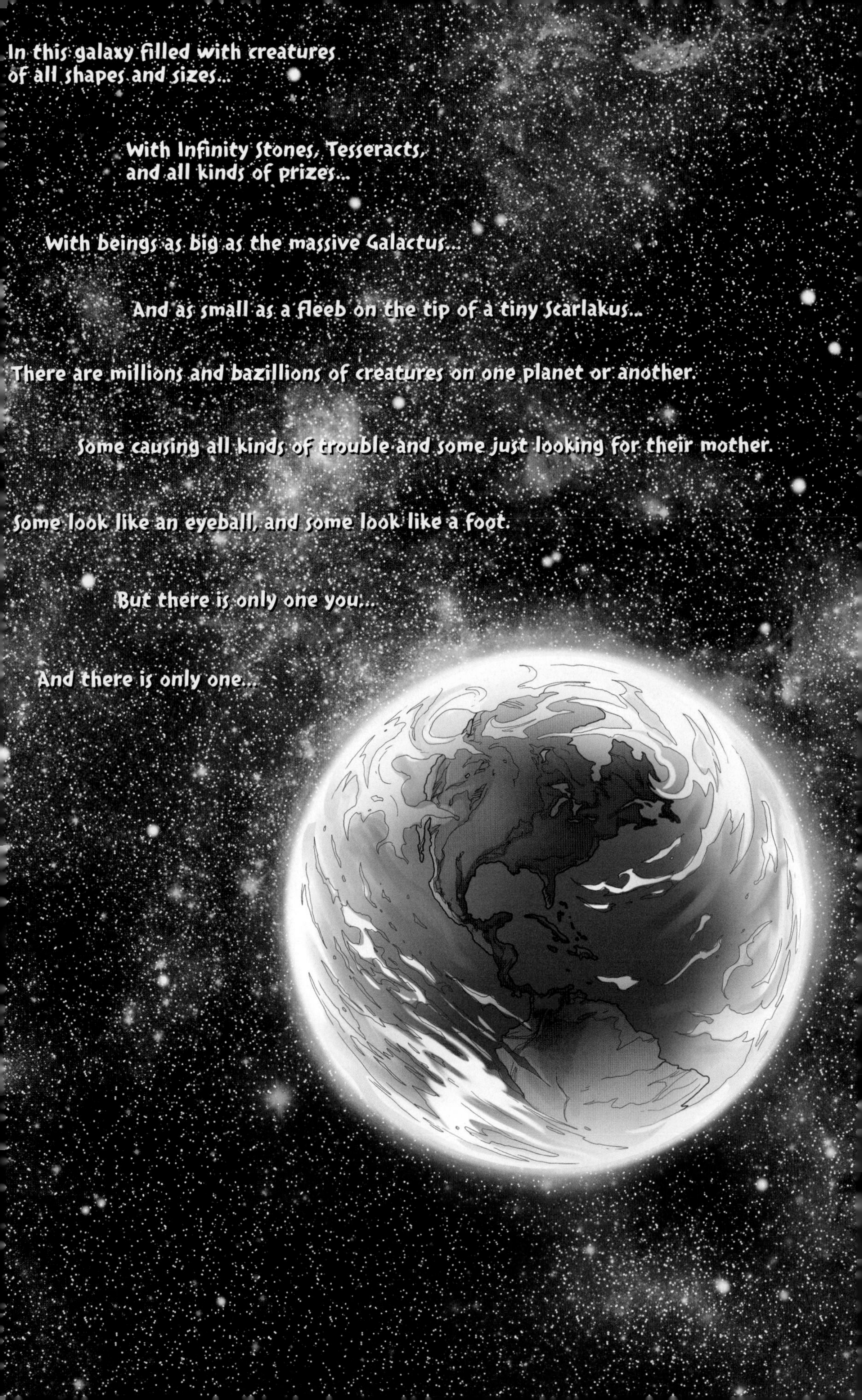
In this galaxy filled with creatures of all shapes and sizes...
With Infinity Stones, Tesseracts, and all kinds of prizes...
With beings as big as the massive Galactus...
And as small as a fleeb on the tip of a tiny Scarlakus...
There are millions and bazillions of creatures on one planet or another.
Some causing all kinds of trouble and some just looking for their mother.
Some look like an eyeball, and some look like a foot.
But there is only one you...
And there is only one...

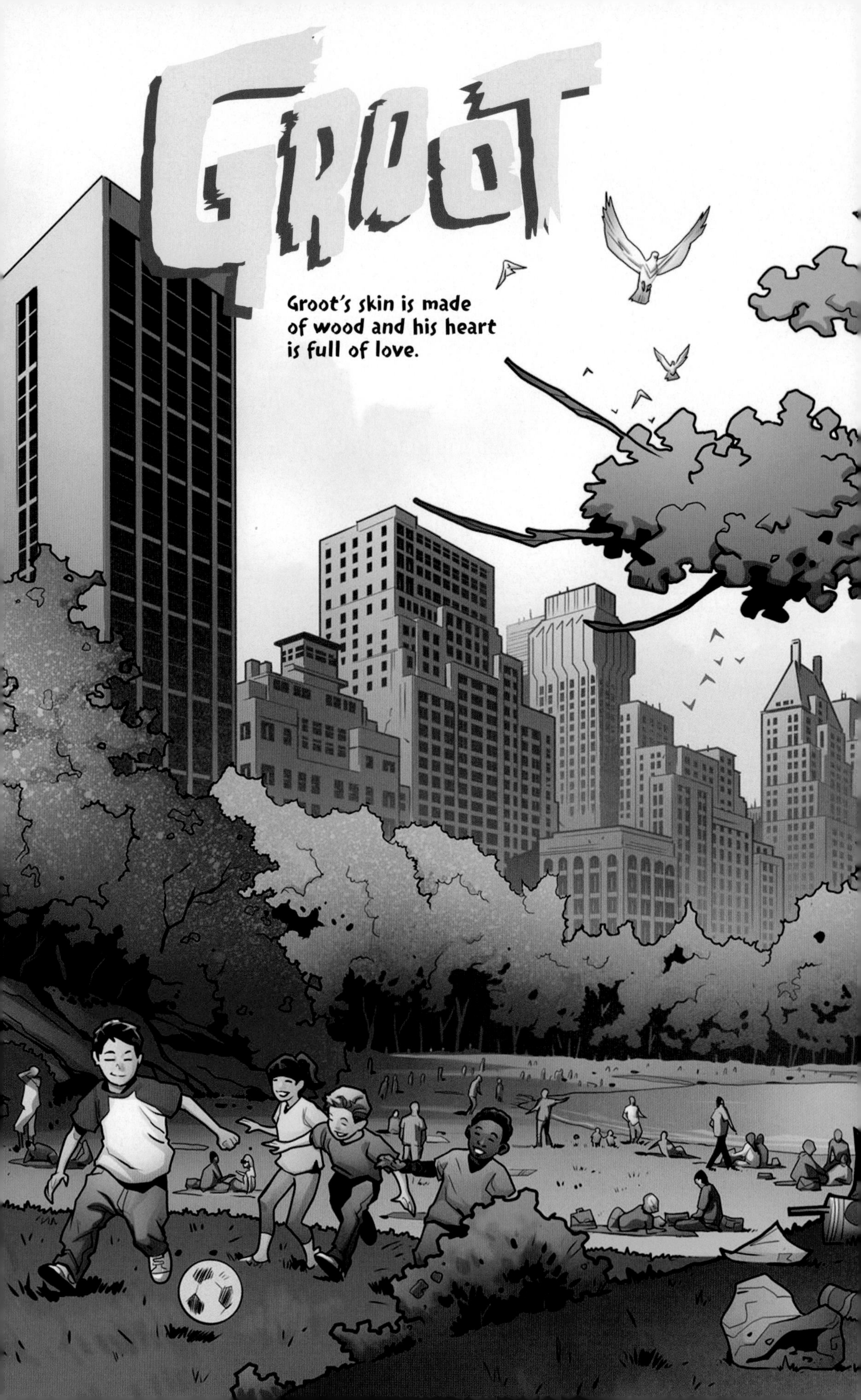
GROOT
Groot's skin is made
of wood and his heart
is full of love.

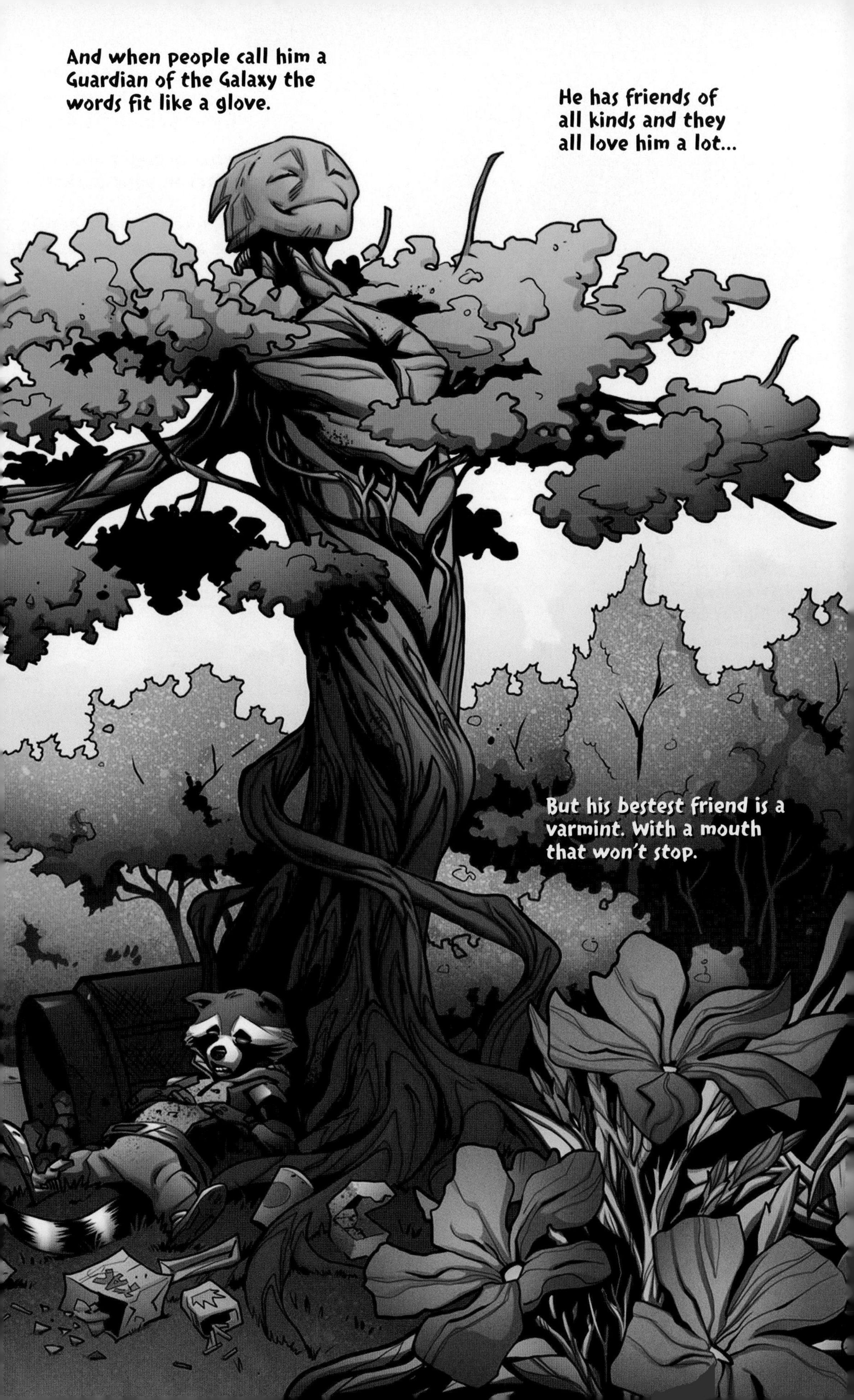
And when people call him a Guardian of the Galaxy the words fit like a glove.
He has friends of all kinds and they all love him a lot...
But his bestest friend is a varmint. With a mouth that won't stop.

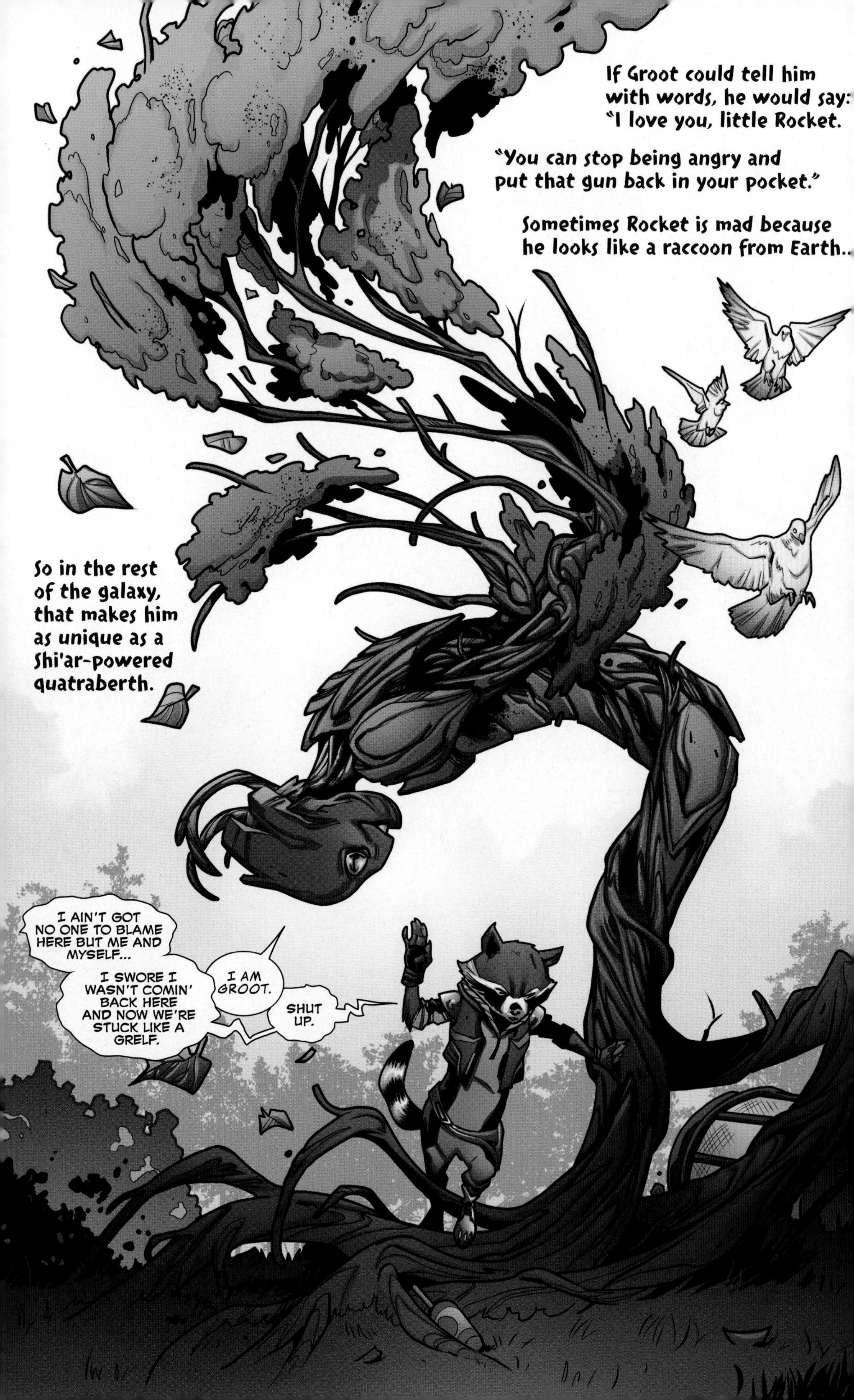
If Groot could tell him with words, he would say: "I love you, little Rocket.
"You can stop being angry and put that gun back in your pocket."
Sometimes Rocket is mad because he looks like a raccoon from Earth..
So in the rest of the galaxy, that makes him as unique as a Shi'ar-powered quatraberth.
I AIN'T GOT NO ONE TO BLAME HERE BUT ME AND MYSELF...
I SWORE I WASN'T COMIN' BACK HERE AND NOW WE'RE STUCK LIKE A GRELF.
I AM GROOT.
SHUT UP.

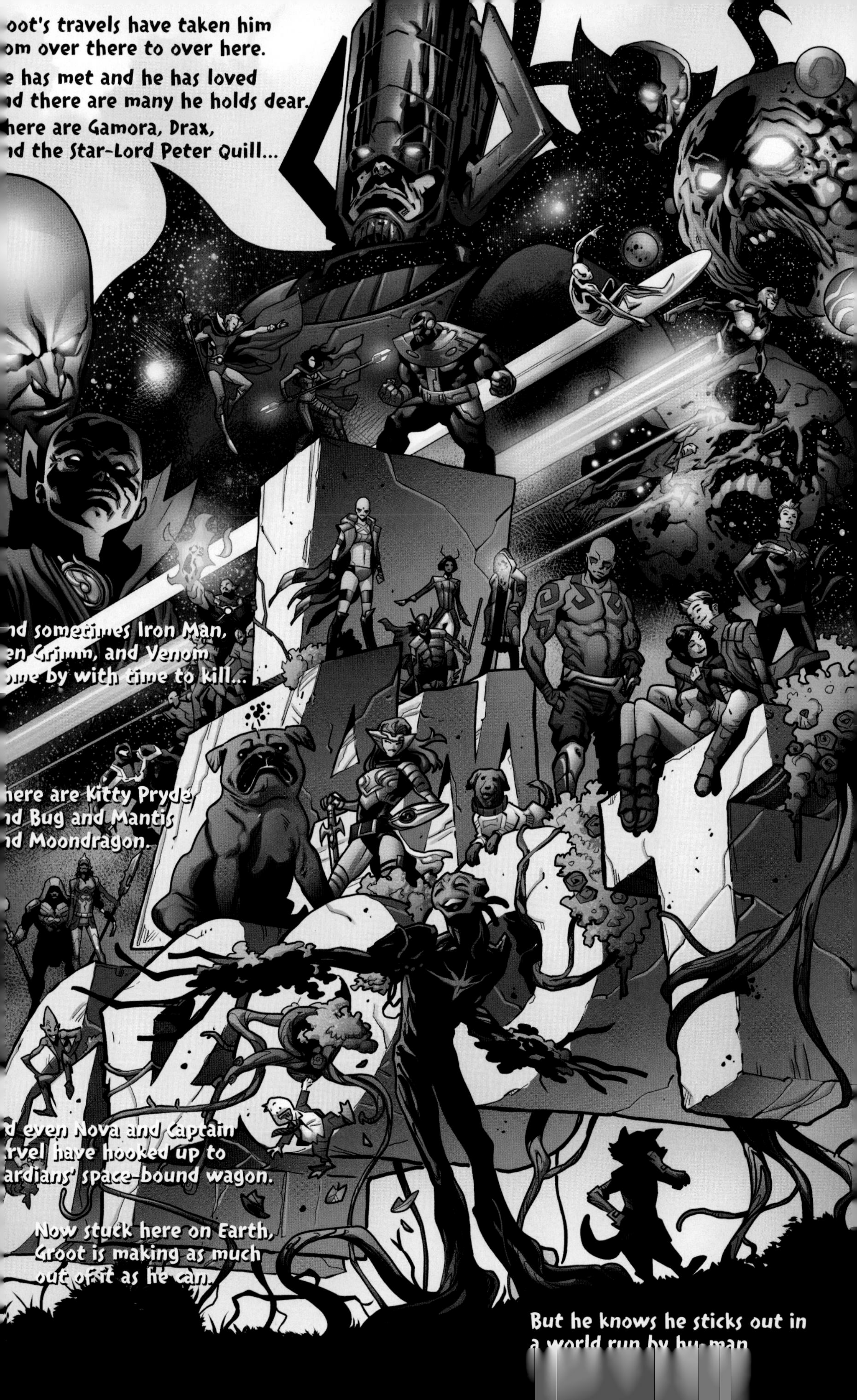

oot's travels have taken him
om over there to over here.
e has met and he has loved
nd there are many he holds dear.
here are Gamora, Drax,
nd the Star-Lord Peter Quill...
nd sometimes Iron Man,
en Grimm, and Venom
ome by with time to kill...
here are Kitty Pryde
nd Bug and Mantis
nd Moondragon.
d even Nova and Captain
rvel have hooked up to
ardians' space-bound wagon.
Now stuck here on Earth,
Groot is making as much
out of it as he can.
But he knows he sticks out in
a world run by hu-man

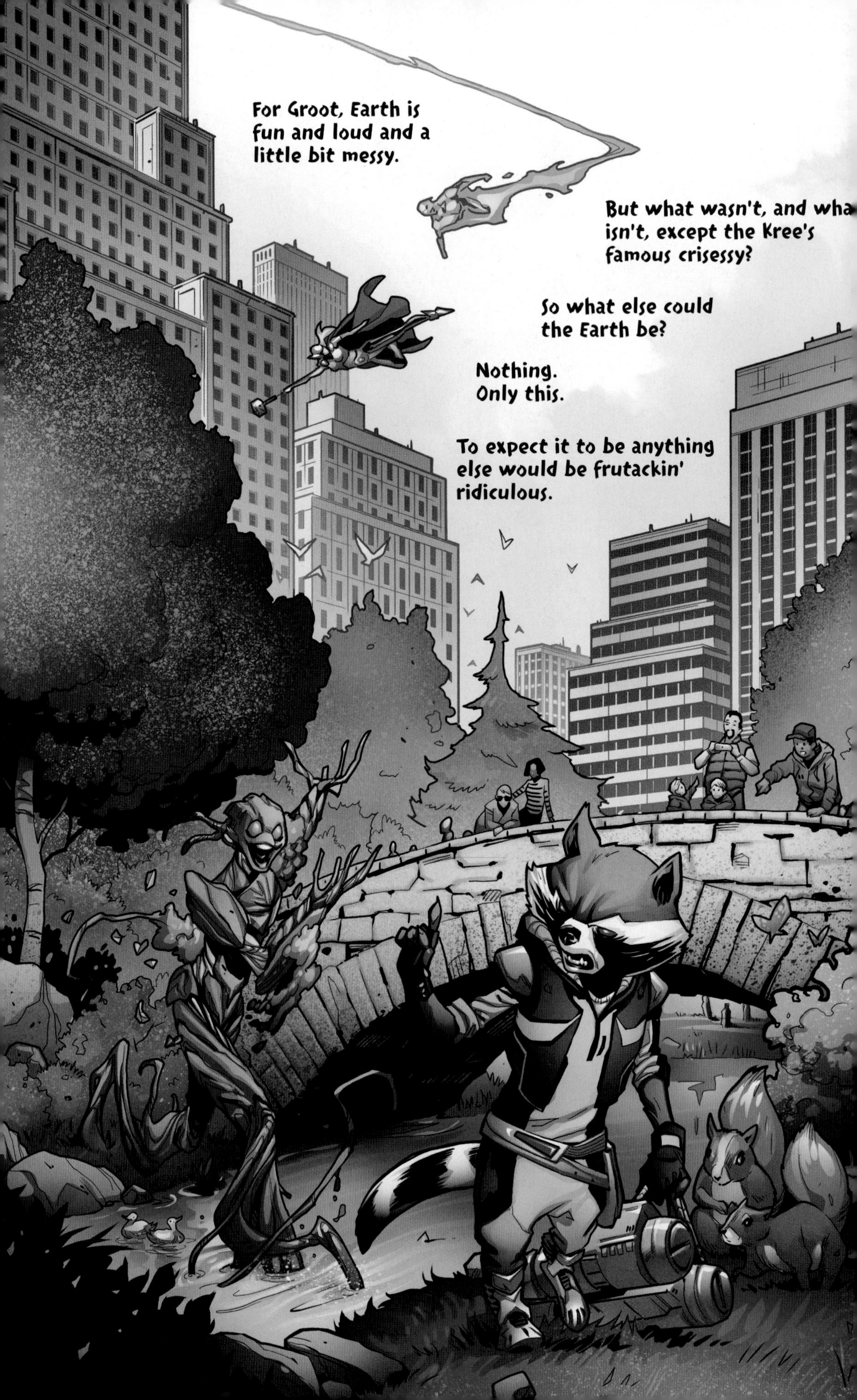
For Groot, Earth is fun and loud and a little bit messy.
But what wasn't, and wha isn't, except the Kree's famous crisessy?
So what else could the Earth be?
Nothing. Only this.
To expect it to be anything else would be frutackin' ridiculous.

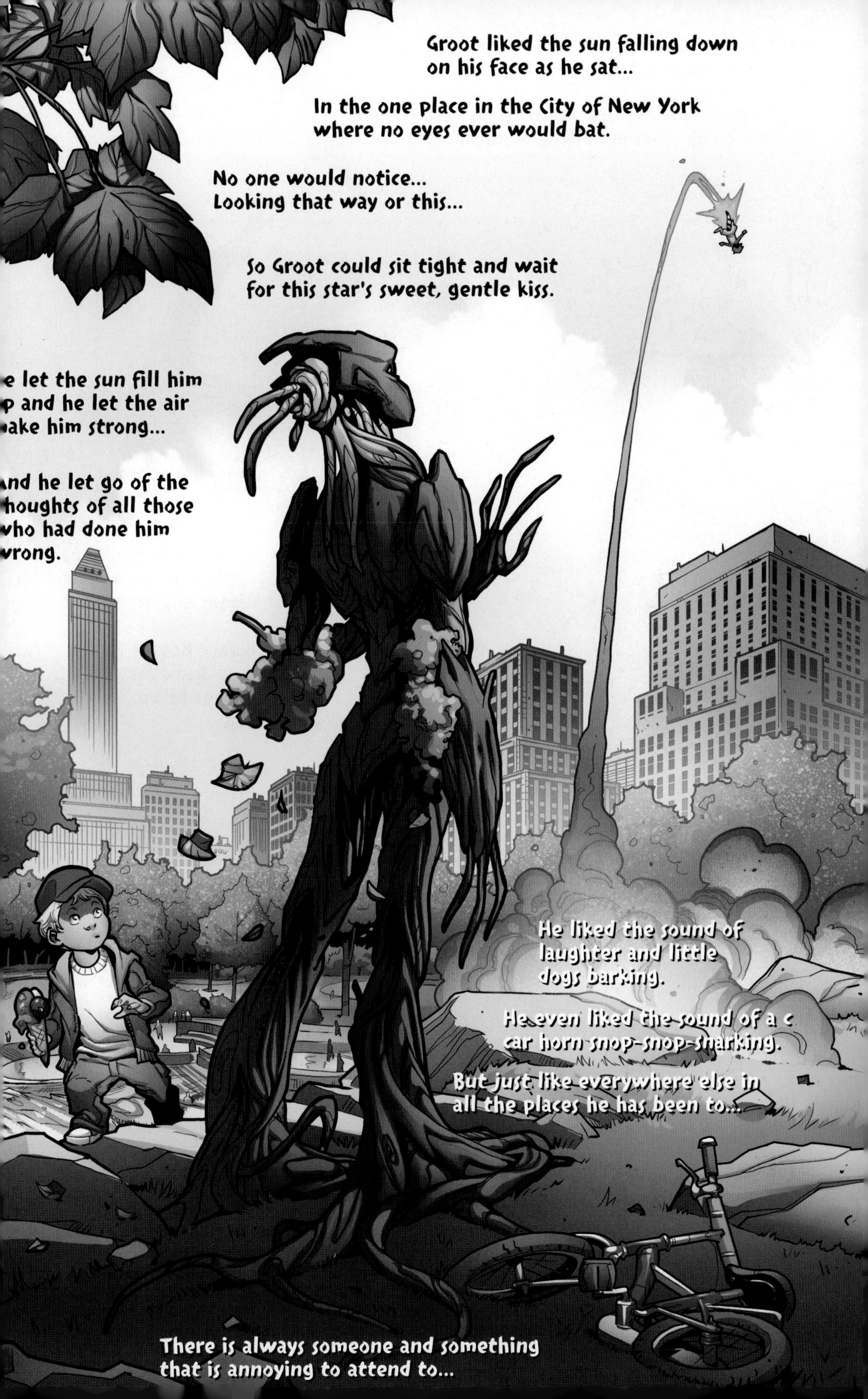
Groot liked the sun falling down
on his face as he sat...
In the one place in the City of New York
where no eyes ever would bat.
No one would notice...
Looking that way or this...
So Groot could sit tight and wait
for this star's sweet, gentle kiss.
e let the sun fill him
p and he let the air
ake him strong...
nd he let go of the
houghts of all those
who had done him
vrong.
He liked the sound of
laughter and little
dogs barking.
He even liked the sound of a c
car horn snop-snop-snarking.
But just like everywhere else in
all the places he has been to...
There is always someone and something
that is annoying to attend to...

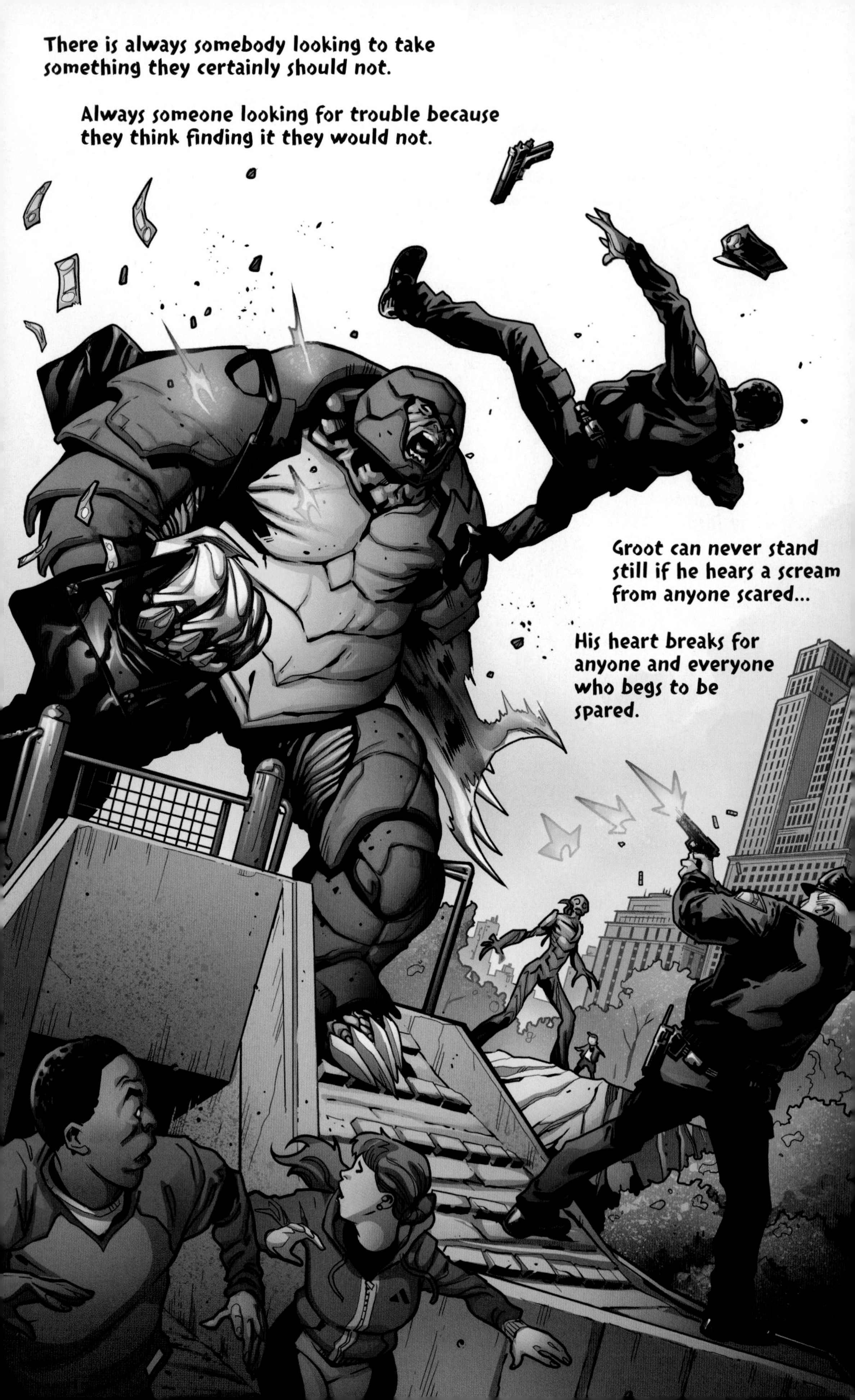
There is always somebody looking to take something they certainly should not.
Always someone looking for trouble because they think finding it they would not.
Groot can never stand still if he hears a scream from anyone scared...
His heart breaks for anyone and everyone who begs to be spared.

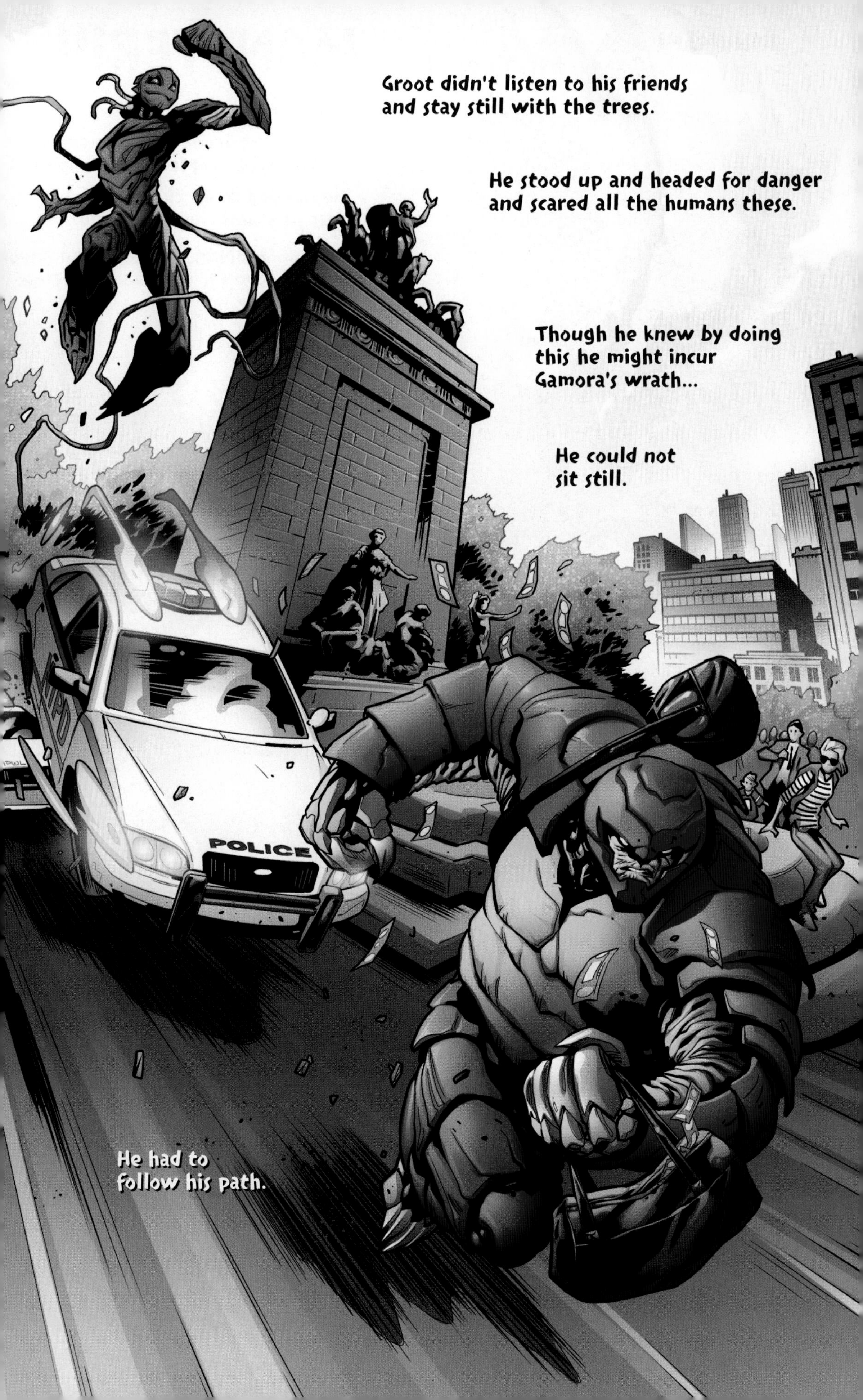
Groot didn't listen to his friends
and stay still with the trees.
He stood up and headed for danger
and scared all the humans these.
Though he knew by doing
this he might incur
Gamora's wrath...
He could not
sit still.
POLICE
He had to
follow his path.

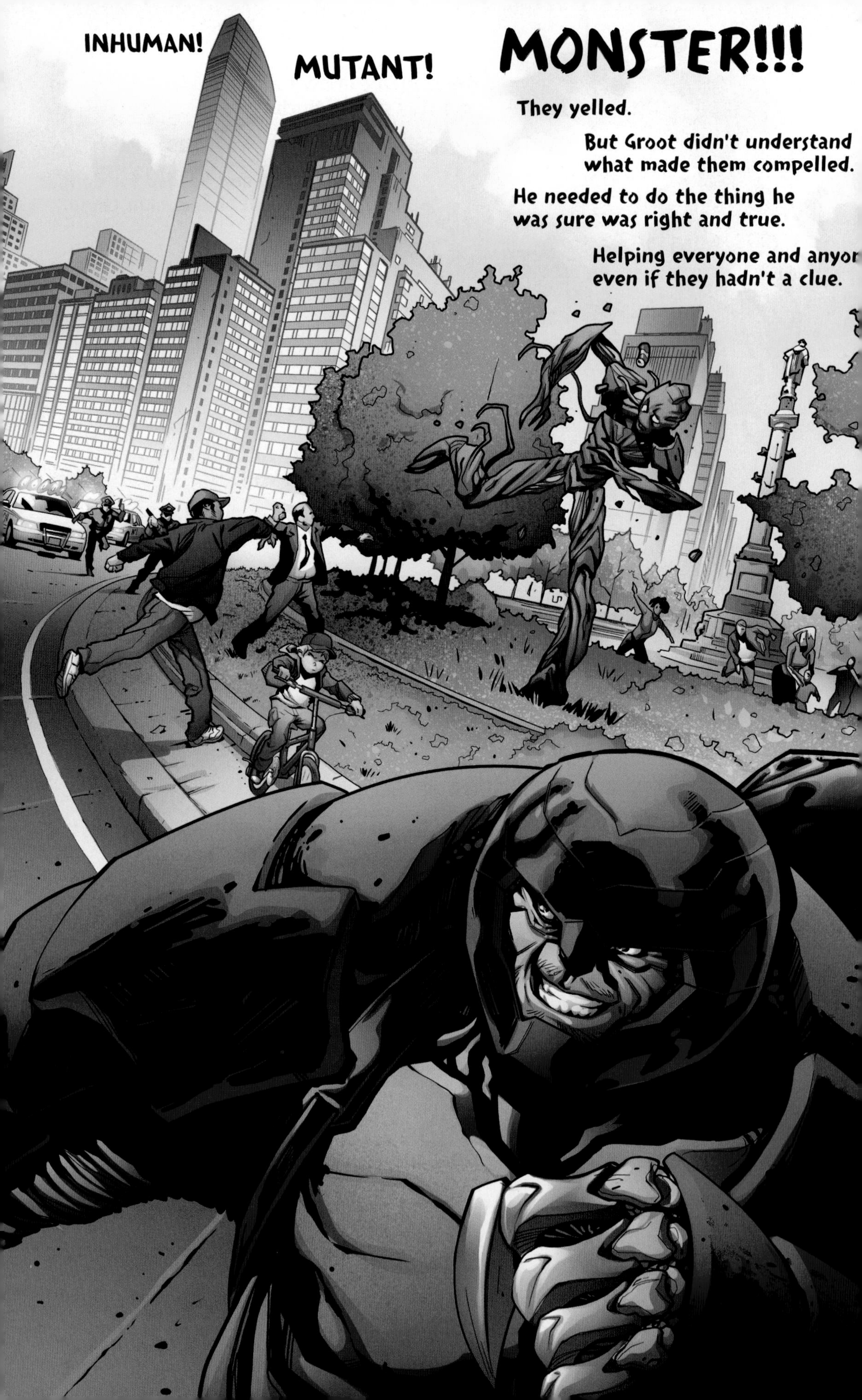
INHUMAN!
MUTANT!
MONSTER!!!
They yelled.
But Groot didn't understand what made them compelled.
He needed to do the thing he was sure was right and true.
Helping everyone and anyor even if they hadn't a clue.

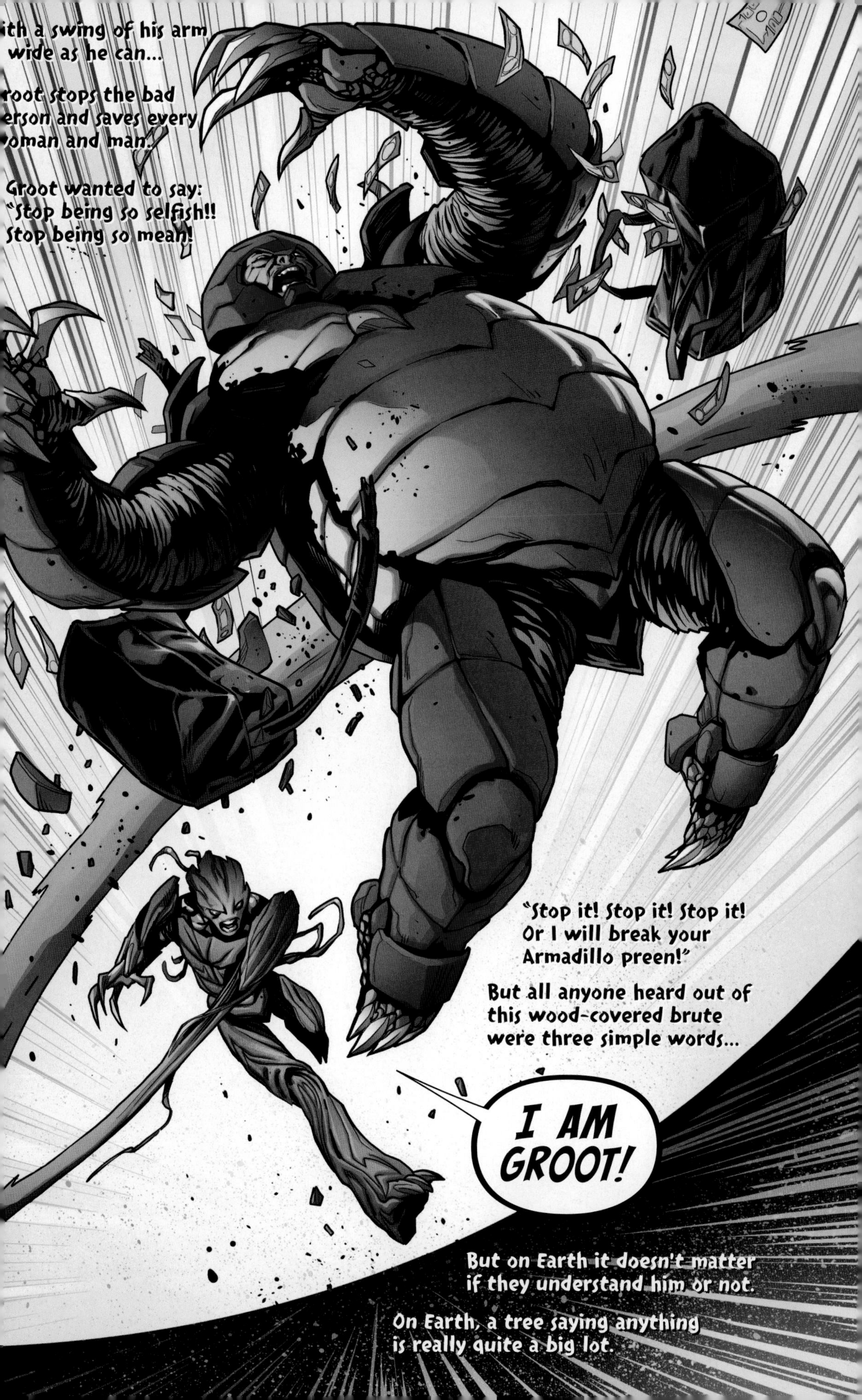
ith a swing of his arm
wide as he can...
root stops the bad
erson and saves every
oman and man.
Groot wanted to say:
"Stop being so selfish!!
Stop being so mean!
"Stop it! Stop it! Stop it!
Or I will break your
Armadillo preen!"
But all anyone heard out of
this wood-covered brute
were three simple words...
I AM GROOT!
But on Earth it doesn't matter
if they understand him or not.
On Earth, a tree saying anything
is really quite a big lot.

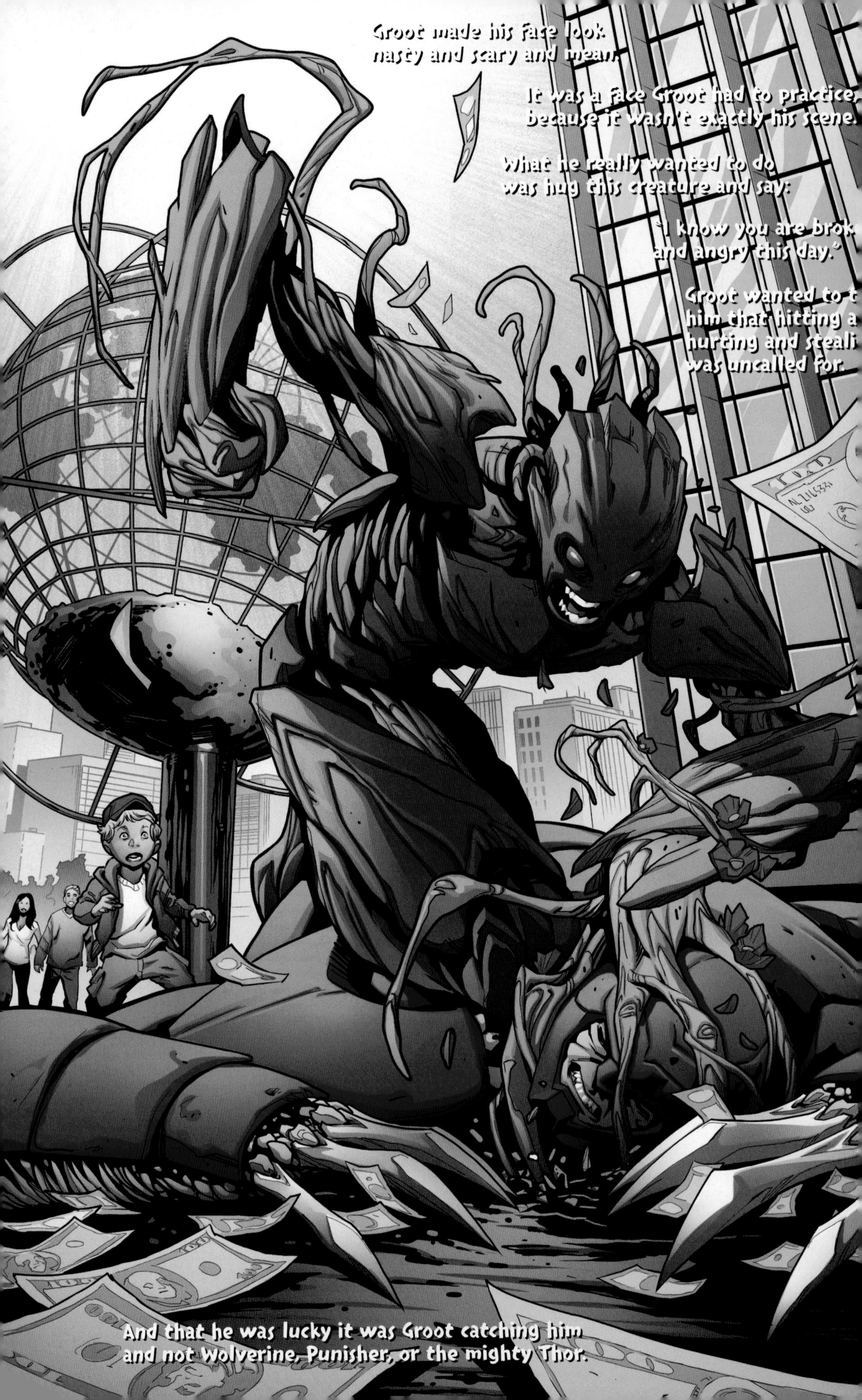
Groot made his face look
nasty and scary and mean.
It was a face Groot had to practice,
because it wasn't exactly his scene.
What he really wanted to do
was hug this creature and say:
"I know you are brok
and angry this day."
Groot wanted to t
him that hitting a
hurting and steali
was uncalled for.
And that he was lucky it was Groot catching him
and not Wolverine, Punisher, or the mighty Thor.

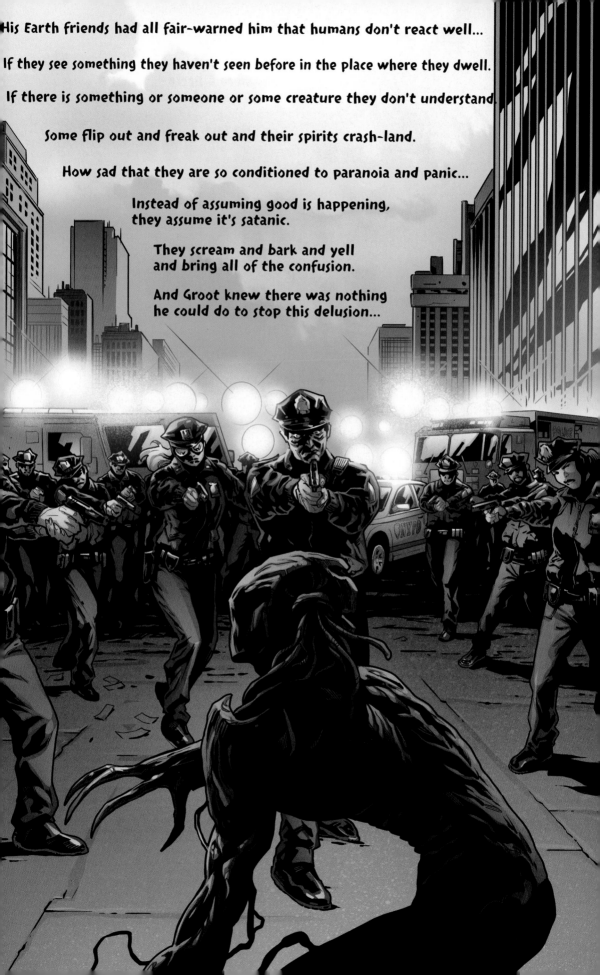

His Earth friends had all fair-warned him that humans don't react well...

If they see something they haven't seen before in the place where they dwell.

If there is something or someone or some creature they don't understand.

Some flip out and freak out and their spirits crash-land.

How sad that they are so conditioned to paranoia and panic...

Instead of assuming good is happening, they assume it's satanic.

They scream and bark and yell and bring all of the confusion.

And Groot knew there was nothing he could do to stop this delusion...

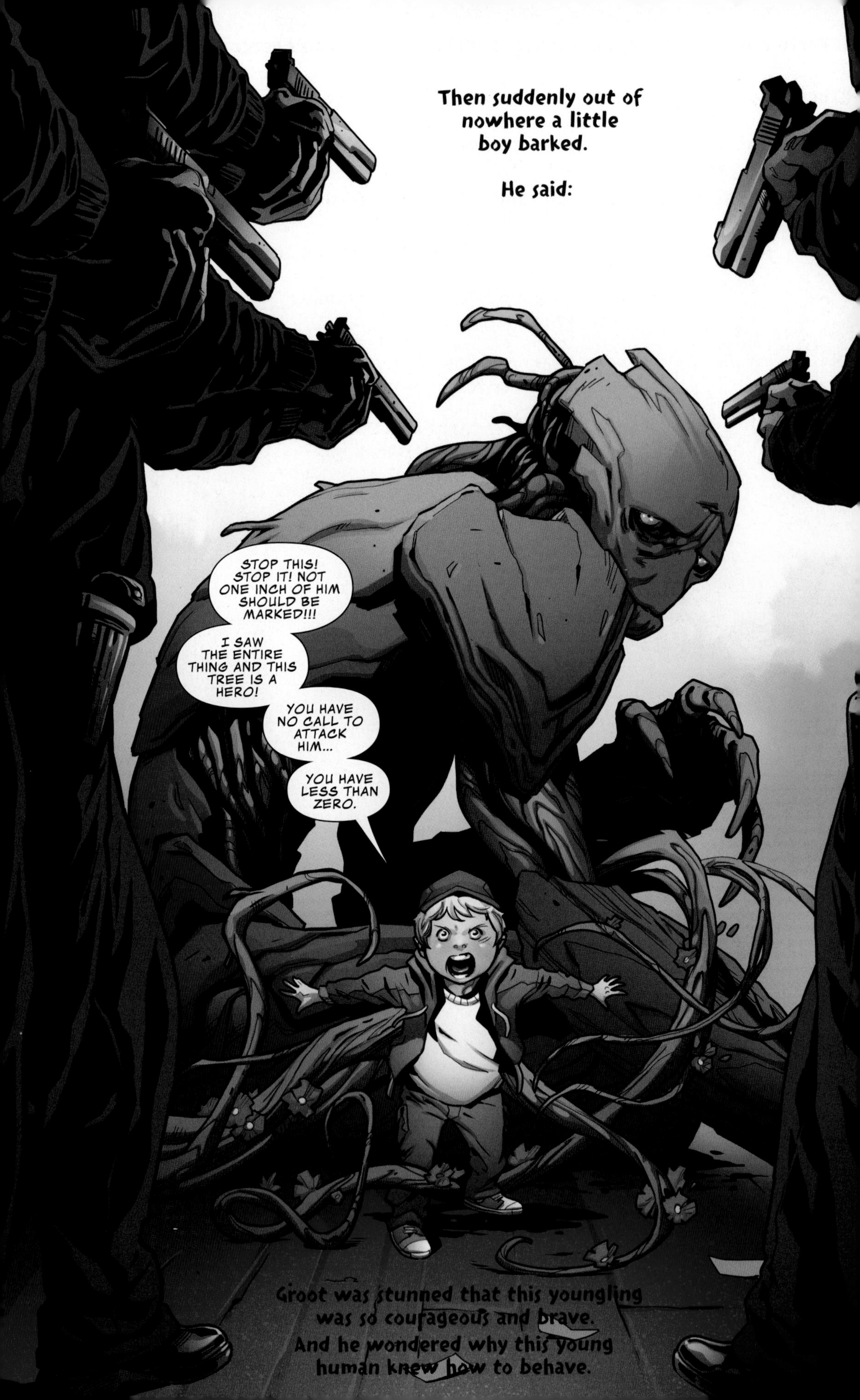
Then suddenly out of nowhere a little boy barked.
He said:
STOP THIS! STOP IT! NOT ONE INCH OF HIM SHOULD BE MARKED!!!
I SAW THE ENTIRE THING AND THIS TREE IS A HERO!
YOU HAVE NO CALL TO ATTACK HIM...
YOU HAVE LESS THAN ZERO.
Groot was stunned that this youngling was so courageous and brave.
And he wondered why this young human knew how to behave.

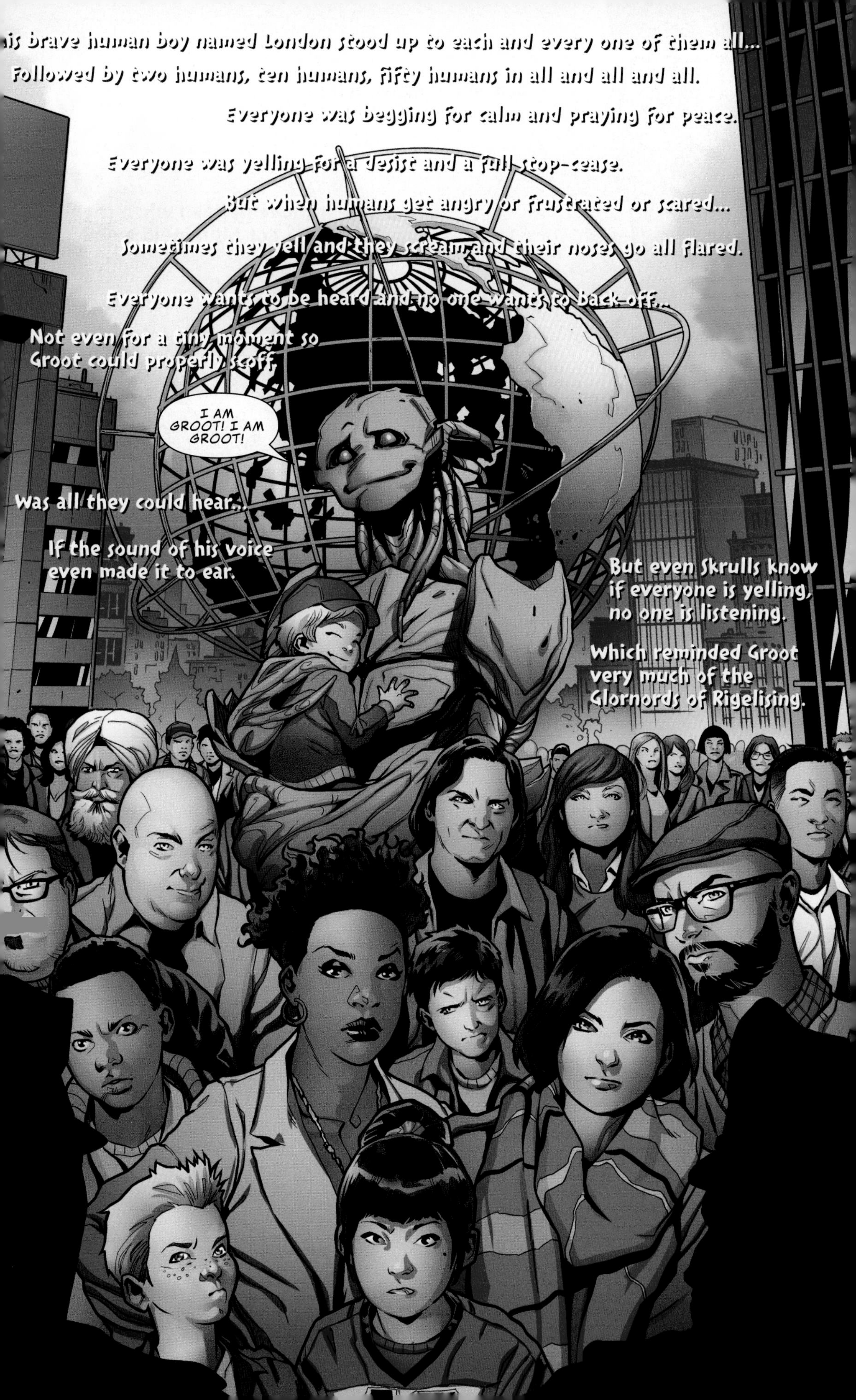
is brave human boy named London stood up to each and every one of them all...
Followed by two humans, ten humans, fifty humans in all and all and all.
Everyone was begging for calm and praying for peace.
Everyone was yelling for a desist and a full stop-cease.
But when humans get angry or frustrated or scared...
Sometimes they yell and they scream and their noses go all flared.
Everyone wants to be heard and no one wants to back off...
Not even for a tiny moment so Groot could properly scoff.
I AM GROOT! I AM GROOT!
Was all they could hear...
If the sound of his voice even made it to ear.
But even Skrulls know if everyone is yelling, no one is listening.
Which reminded Groot very much of the Glornords of Rigelising.

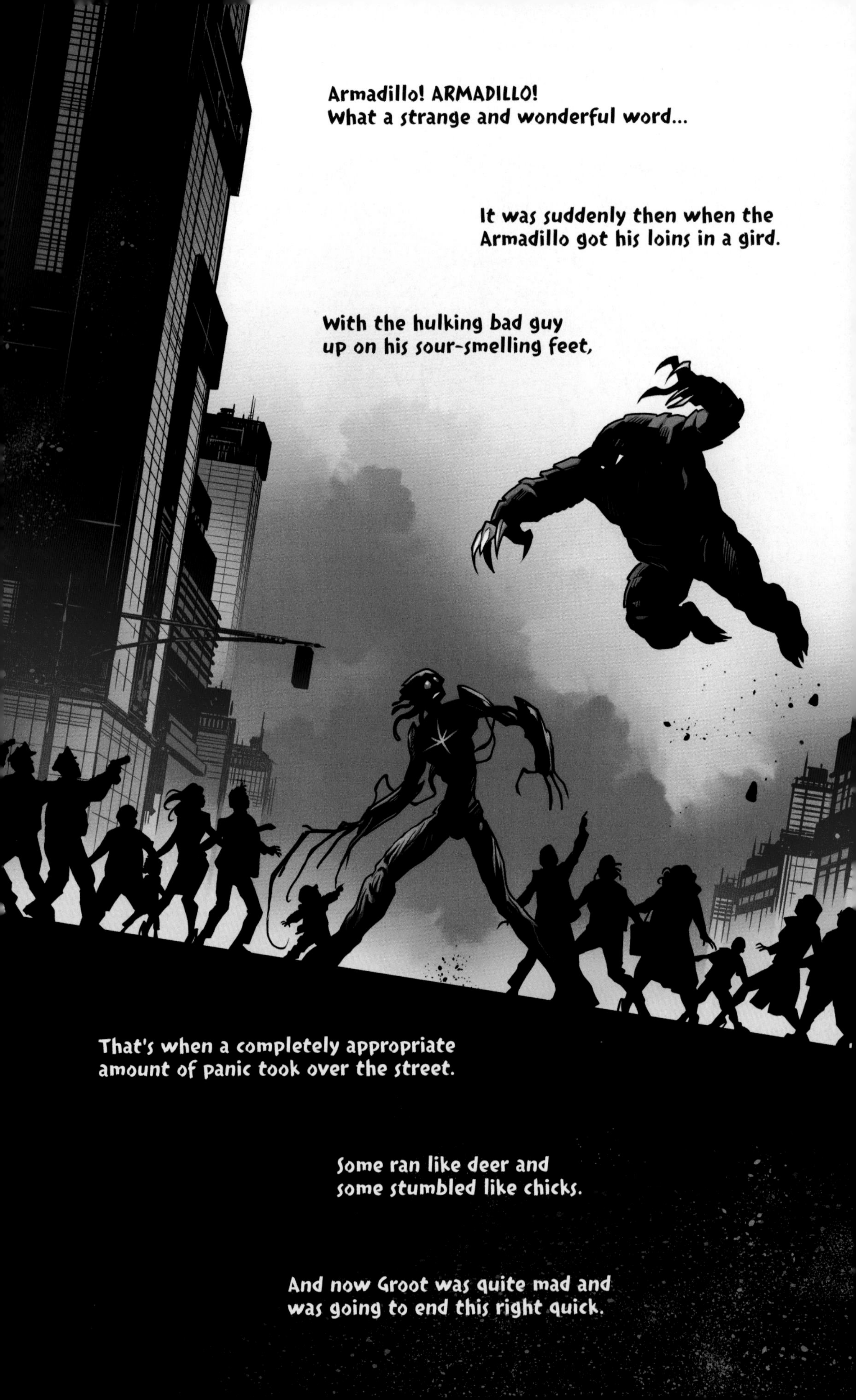
Armadillo! ARMADILLO!
What a strange and wonderful word...
It was suddenly then when the
Armadillo got his loins in a gird.
With the hulking bad guy
up on his sour-smelling feet,
That's when a completely appropriate
amount of panic took over the street.
Some ran like deer and
some stumbled like chicks.
And now Groot was quite mad and
was going to end this right quick.

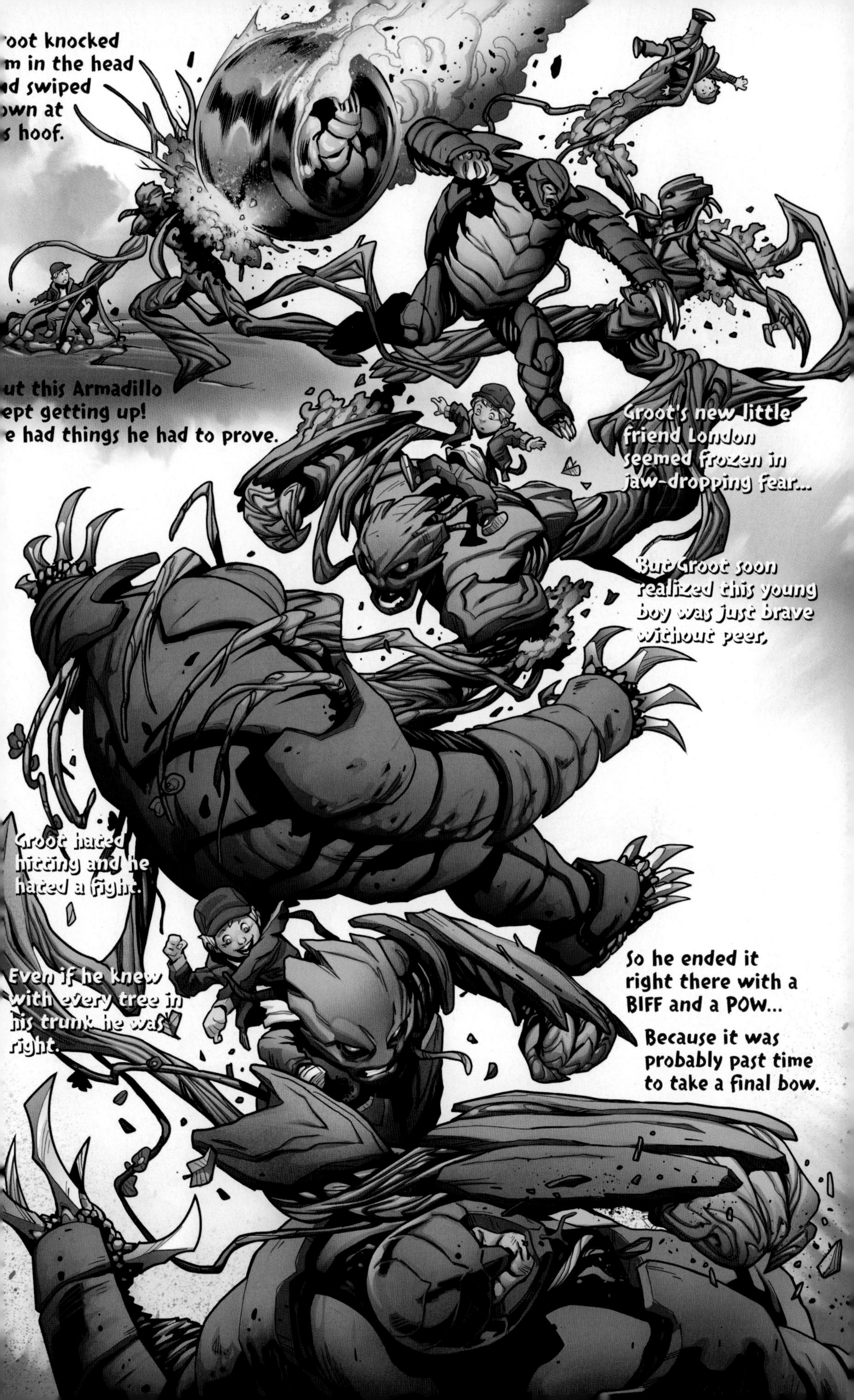

root knocked
m in the head
d swiped
own at
s hoof.
ut this Armadillo
ept getting up!
e had things he had to prove.
Groot's new little
friend London
seemed frozen in
jaw-dropping fear...
But Groot soon
realized this young
boy was just brave
without peer,
Groot hated
hitting and he
hated a fight.
Even if he knew
with every tree in
his trunk he was
right.
So he ended it
right there with a
BIFF and a POW...
Because it was
probably past time
to take a final bow.

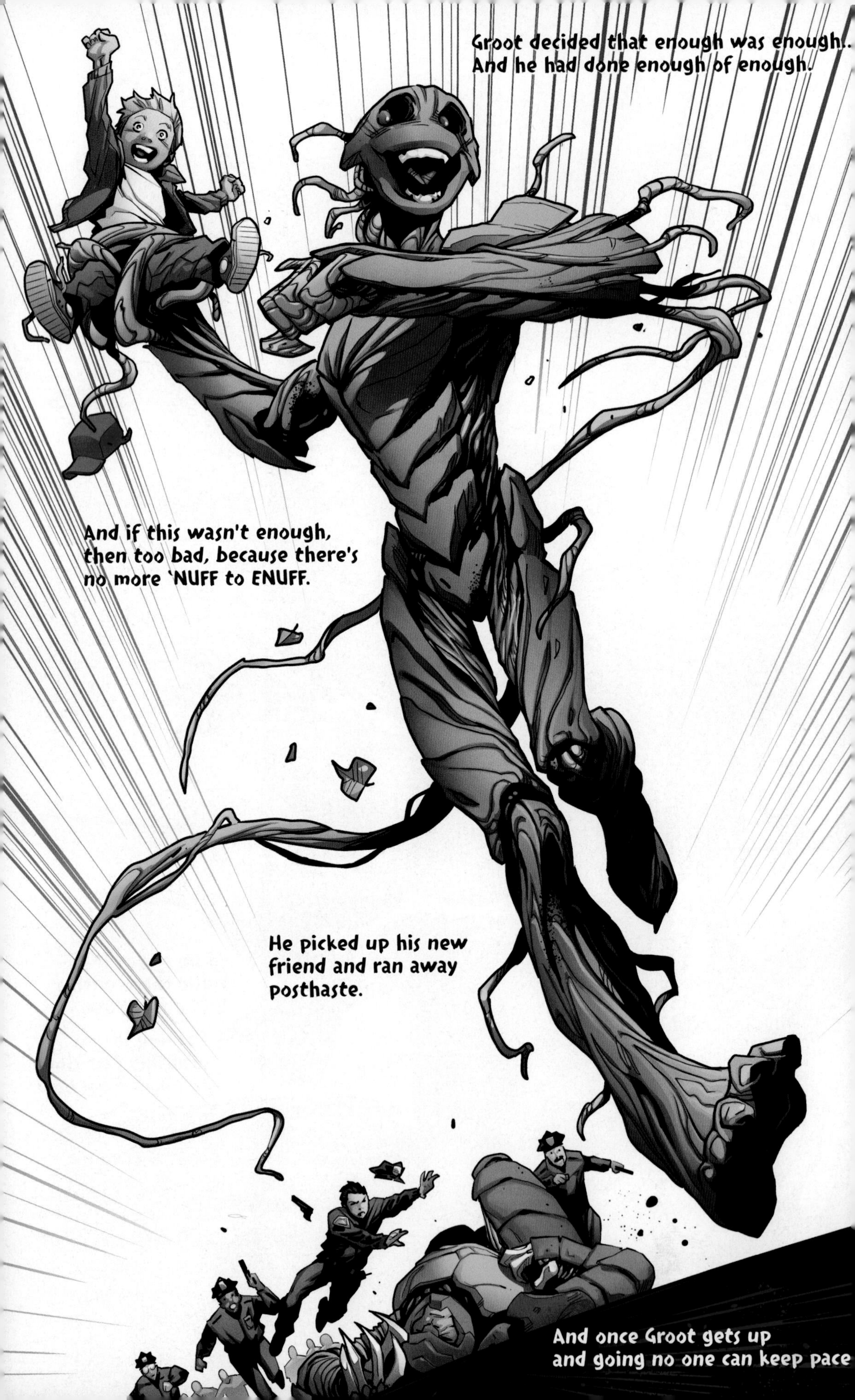
Groot decided that enough was enough.
And he had done enough of enough.
And if this wasn't enough, then too bad, because there's no more 'NUFF to ENUFF.
He picked up his new friend and ran away posthaste.
And once Groot gets up and going no one can keep pace

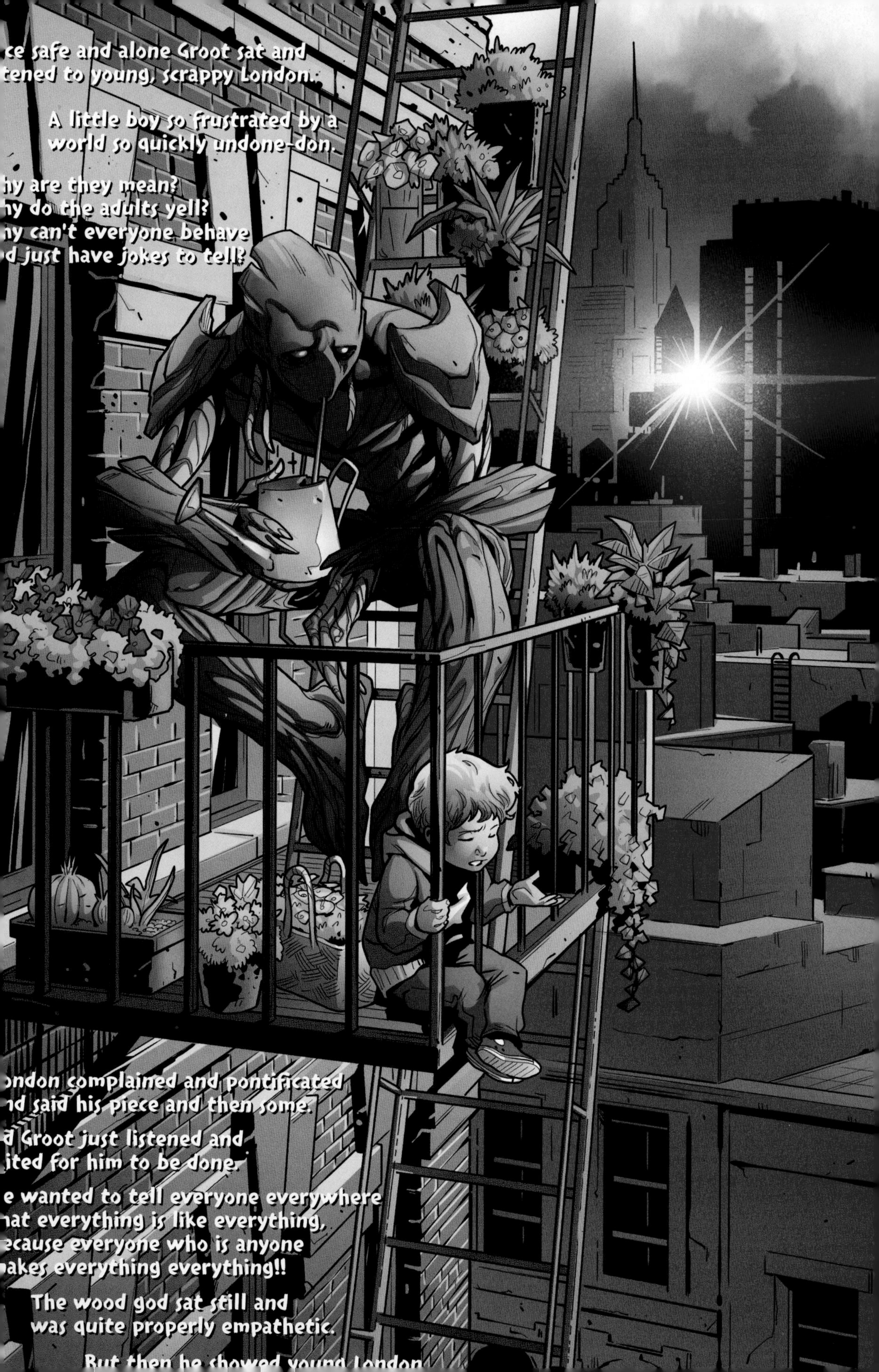
ce safe and alone Groot sat and
tened to young, scrappy London.
A little boy so frustrated by a
world so quickly undone-don.
hy are they mean?
hy do the adults yell?
hy can't everyone behave
d just have jokes to tell?
ondon complained and pontificated
nd said his piece and then some.
d Groot just listened and
ited for him to be done.
e wanted to tell everyone everywhere
hat everything is like everything,
ecause everyone who is anyone
akes everything everything!!
The wood god sat still and
was quite properly empathetic.
But then he showed young London

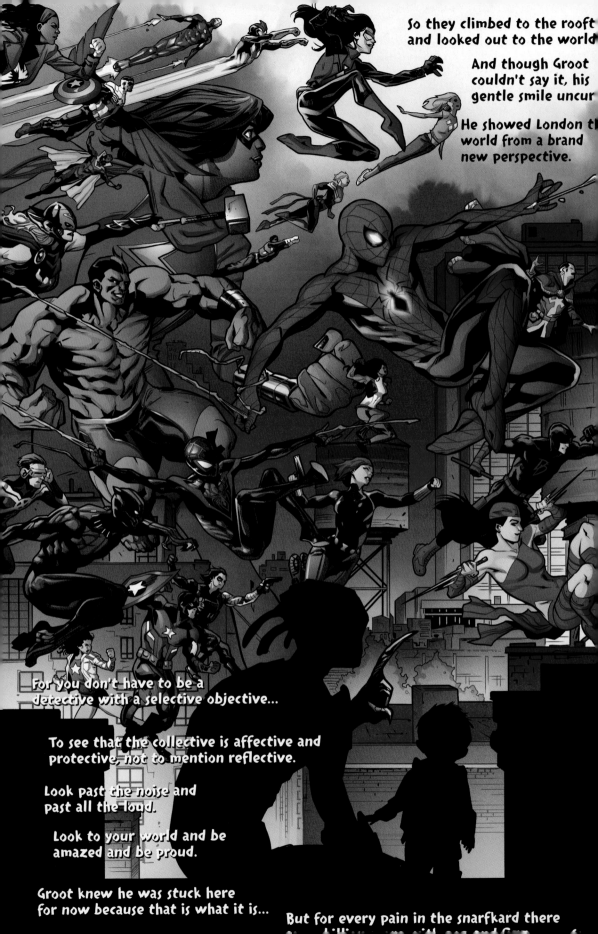

So they climbed to the rooft
and looked out to the world

And though Groot
couldn't say it, his
gentle smile uncur

He showed London tl
world from a brand
new perspective.

For you don't have to be a
detective with a selective objective...

To see that the collective is affective and
protective, not to mention reflective.

Look past the noise and
past all the loud.

Look to your world and be
amazed and be proud.

Groot knew he was stuck here
for now because that is what it is...

But for every pain in the snarfkard there

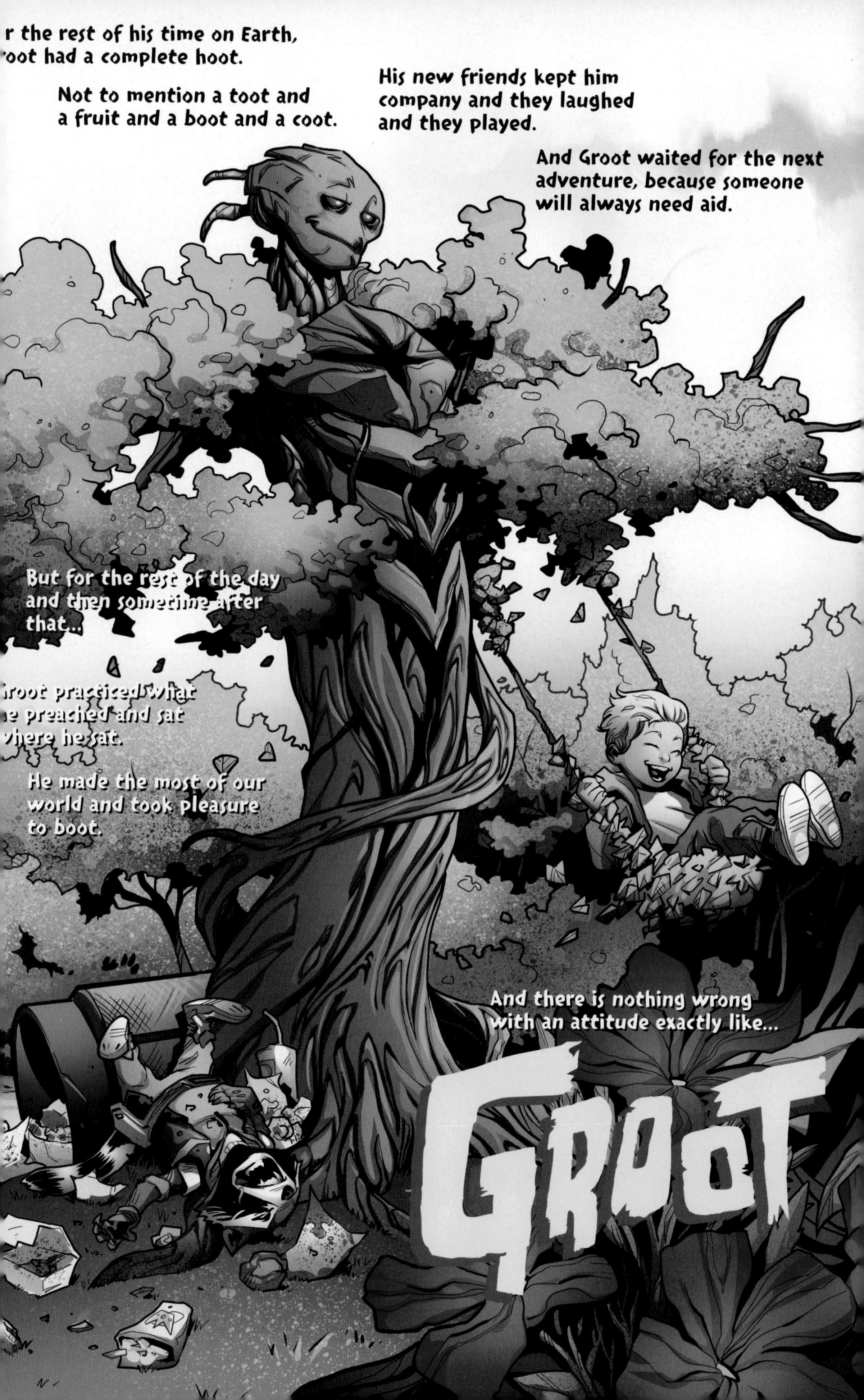
r the rest of his time on Earth,
'oot had a complete hoot.
Not to mention a toot and
a fruit and a boot and a coot.
His new friends kept him
company and they laughed
and they played.
And Groot waited for the next
adventure, because someone
will always need aid.
But for the rest of the day
and then sometime after
that...
iroot practiced what
e preached and sat
vhere he sat.
He made the most of our
world and took pleasure
to boot.
And there is nothing wrong
with an attitude exactly like...
GROOT

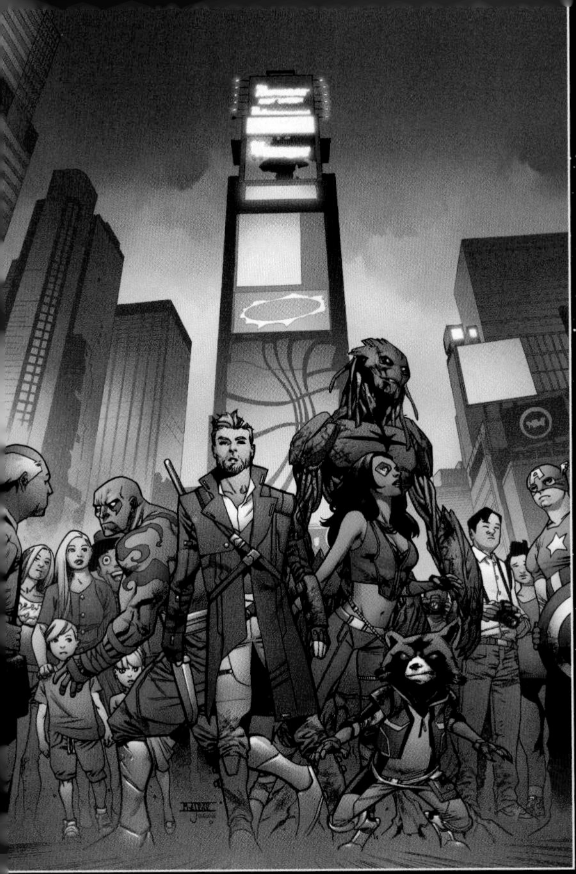

#15 SDCC VARIANT BY
MAHMUD ASRAR & RICHARD ISANOVE

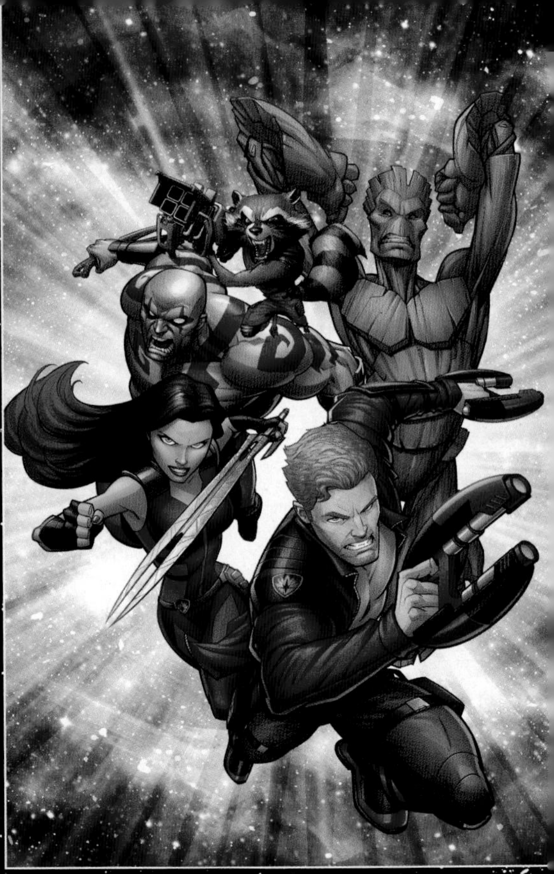

#15 ANIMATION VARIANT

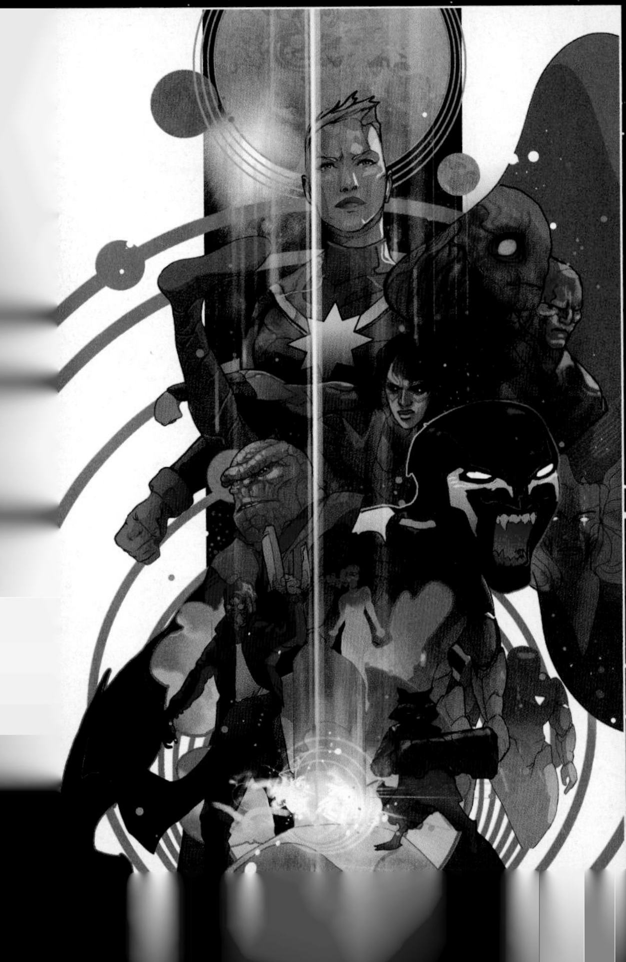

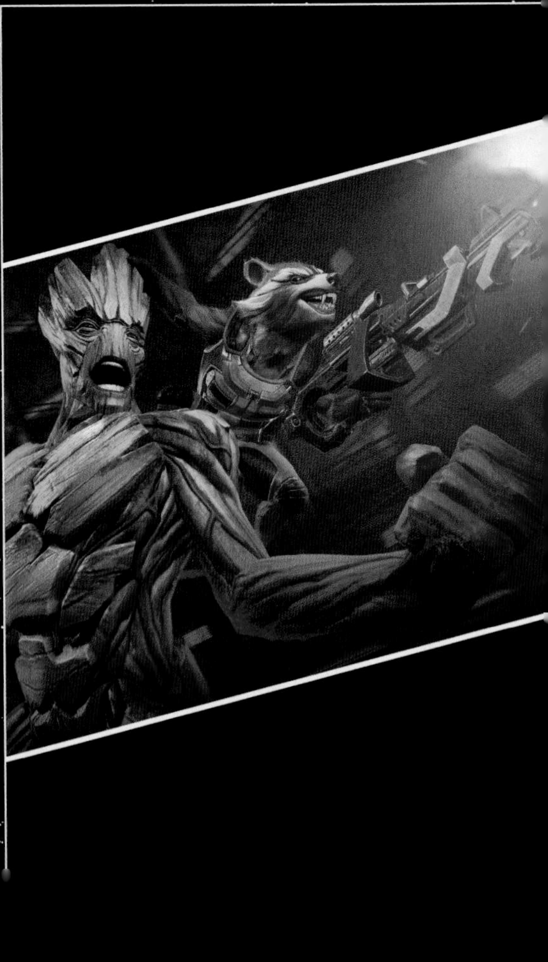

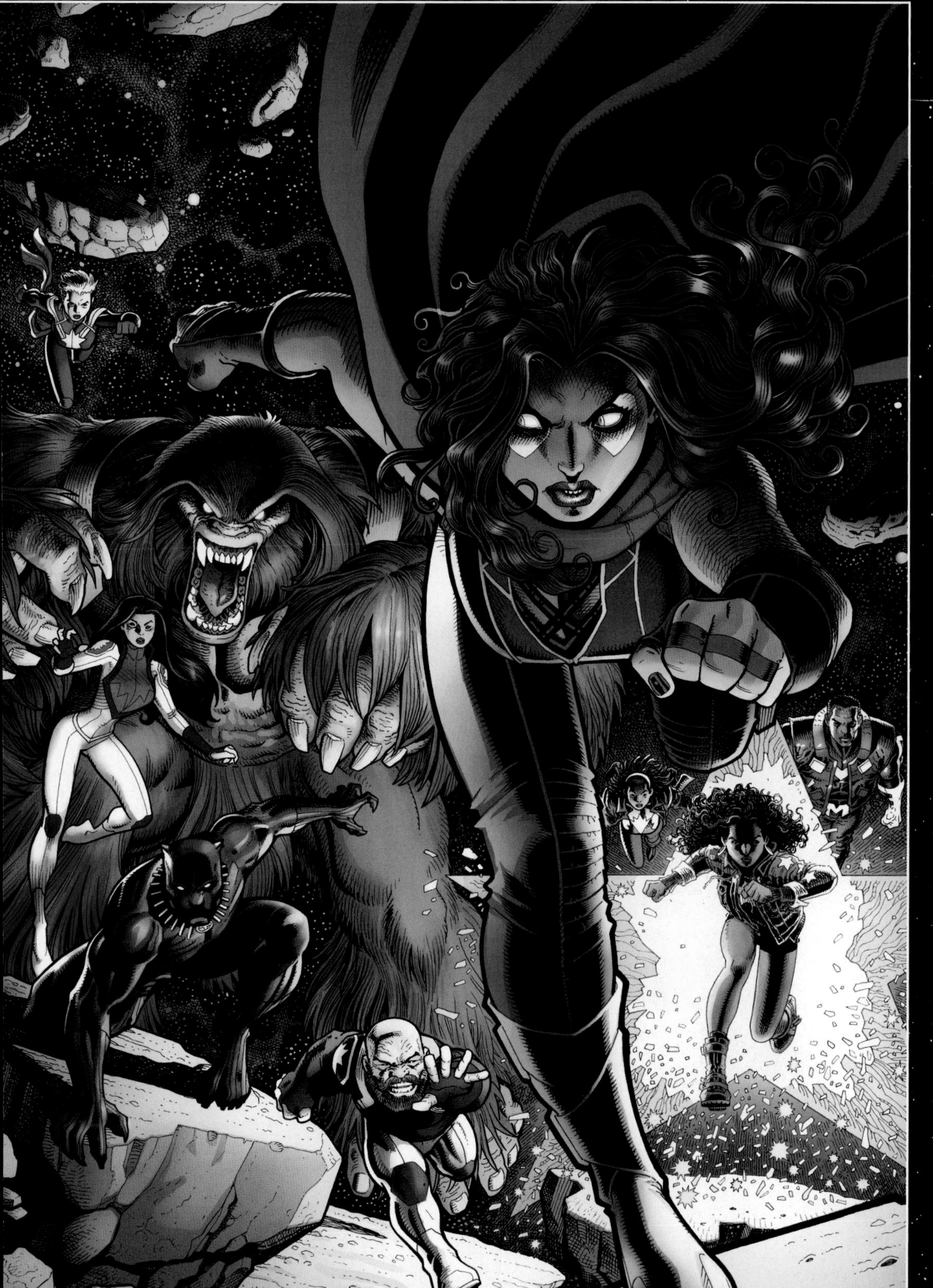
ARTHUR ADAMS
12-5-2016

# 17

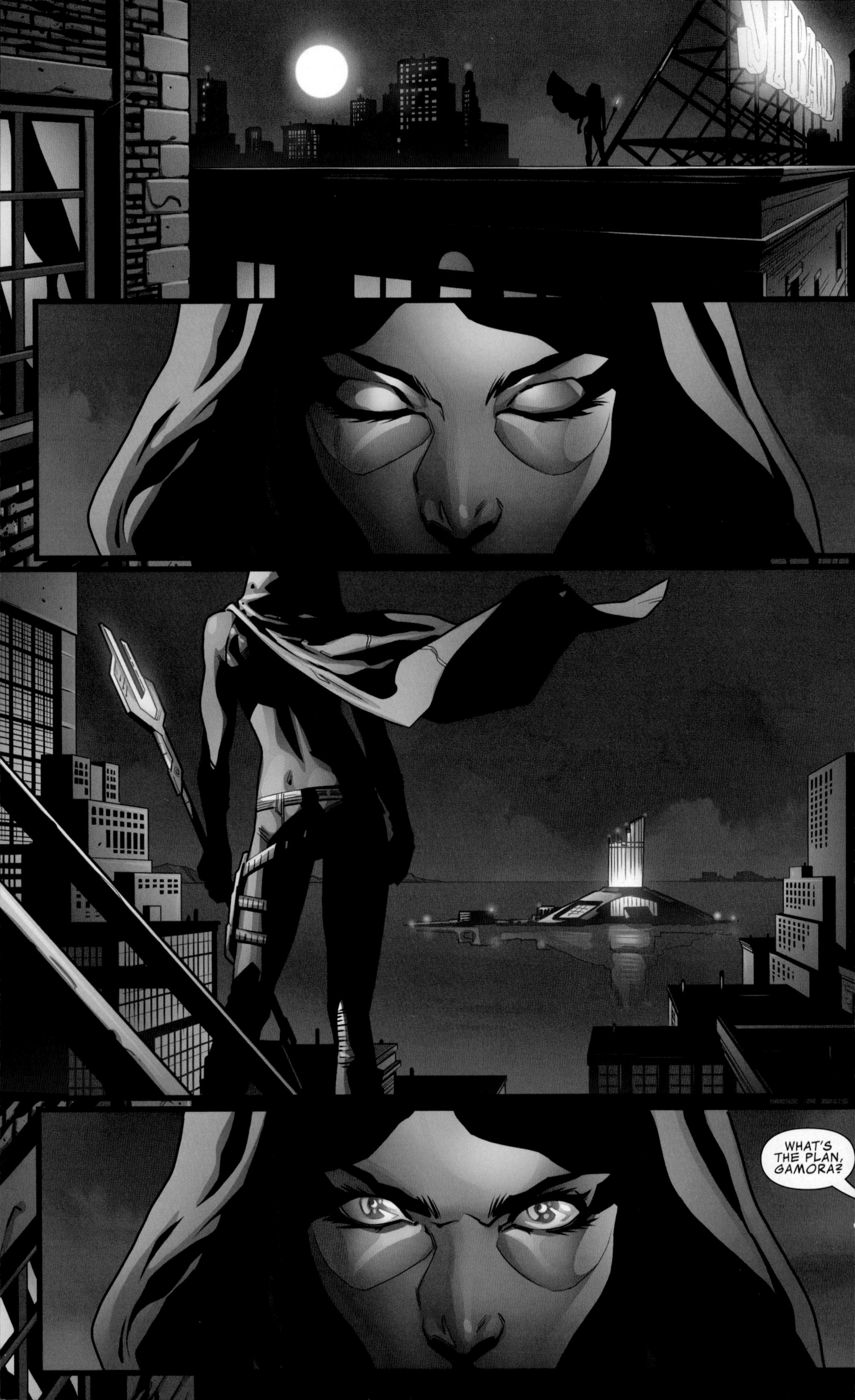
WHAT'S THE PLAN, GAMORA?

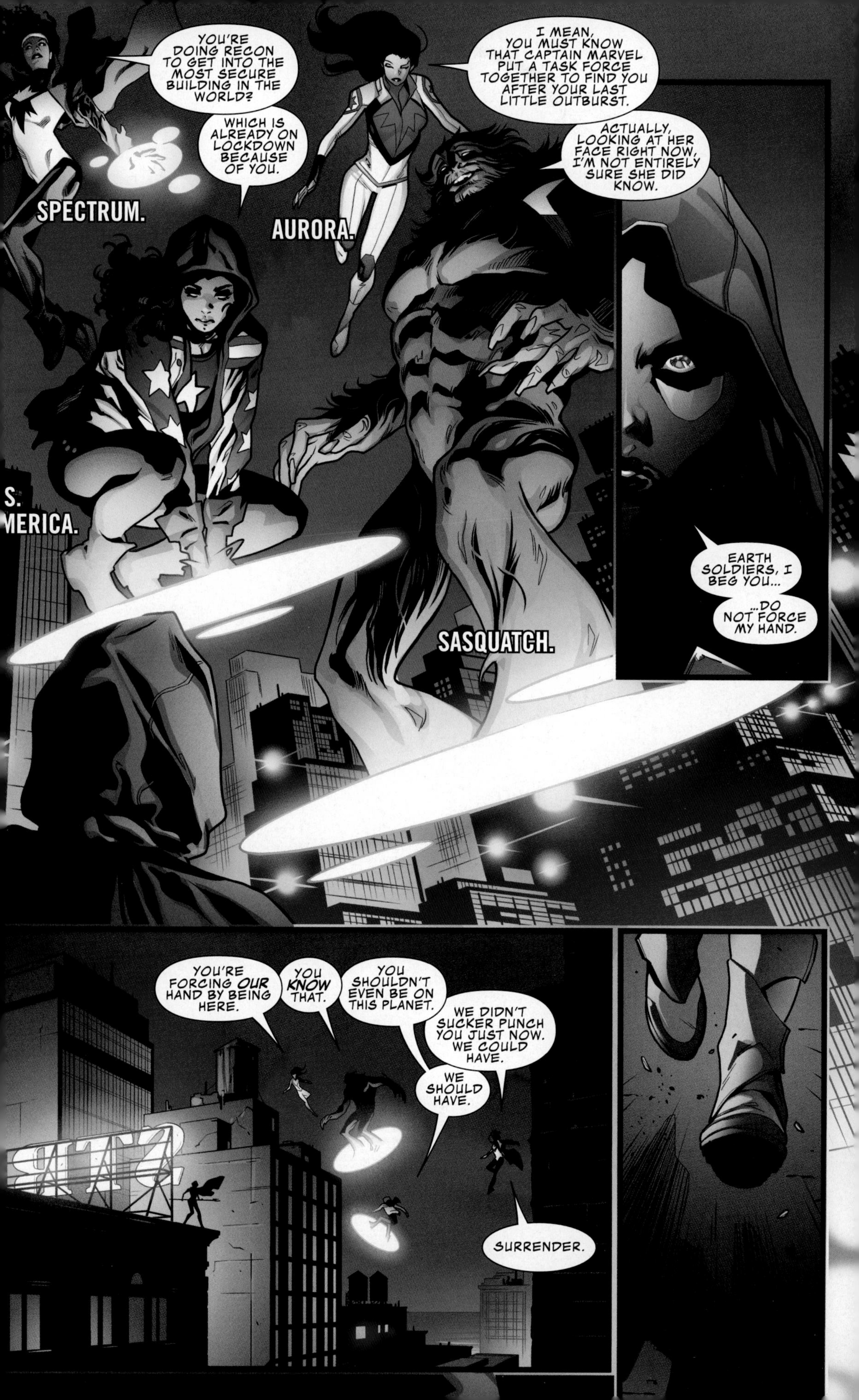

YOU'RE DOING RECON TO GET INTO THE MOST SECURE BUILDING IN THE WORLD?
WHICH IS ALREADY ON LOCKDOWN BECAUSE OF YOU.
I MEAN, YOU MUST KNOW THAT CAPTAIN MARVEL PUT A TASK FORCE TOGETHER TO FIND YOU AFTER YOUR LAST LITTLE OUTBURST.
ACTUALLY, LOOKING AT HER FACE RIGHT NOW, I'M NOT ENTIRELY SURE SHE DID KNOW.
SPECTRUM.
AURORA.
S.
MERICA.
SASQUATCH.
EARTH SOLDIERS, I BEG YOU...
...DO NOT FORCE MY HAND.
YOU'RE FORCING OUR HAND BY BEING HERE.
YOU KNOW THAT.
YOU SHOULDN'T EVEN BE ON THIS PLANET.
WE DIDN'T SUCKER PUNCH YOU JUST NOW. WE COULD HAVE.
WE SHOULD HAVE.
SURRENDER.

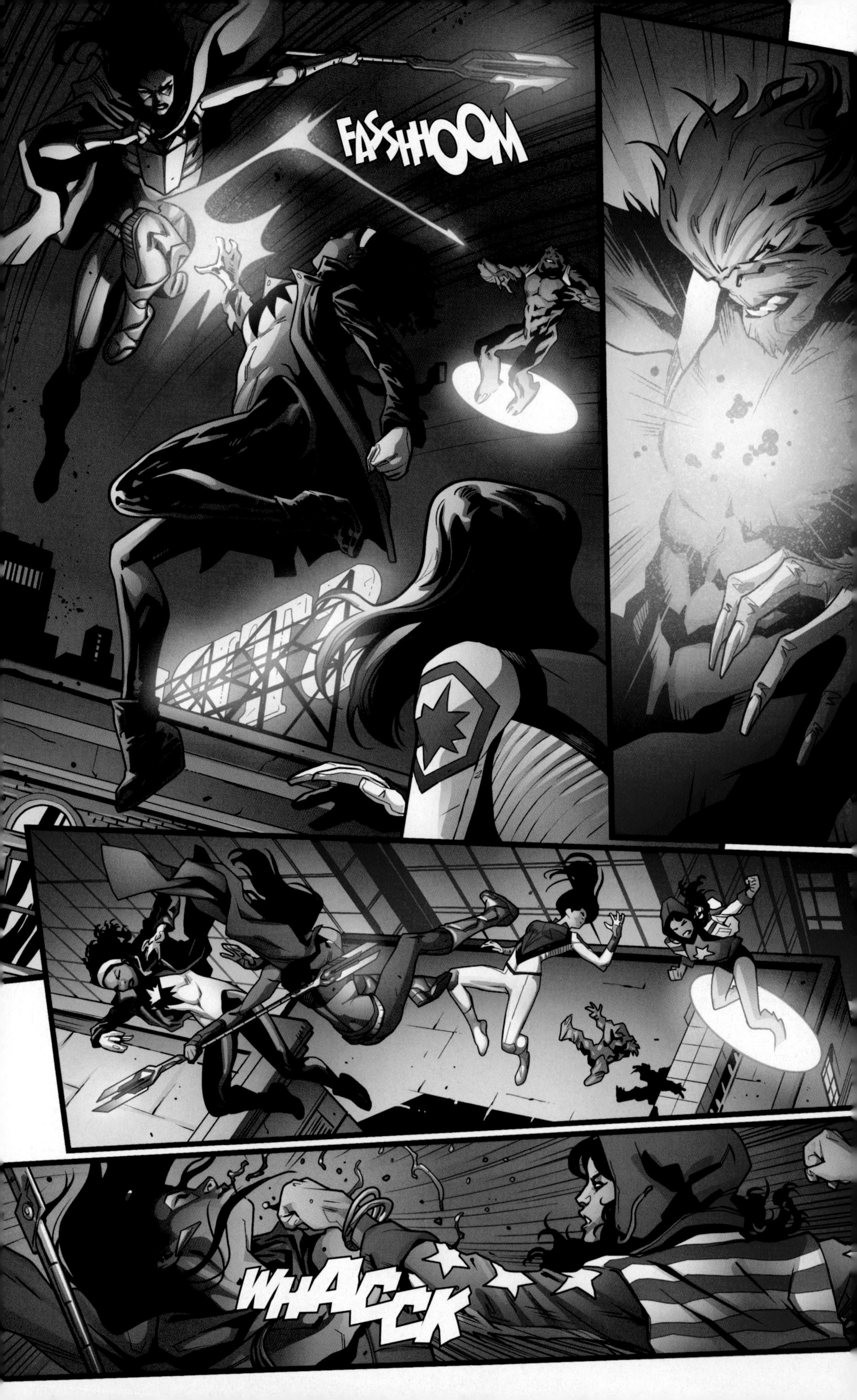
FASSHOOM
WHACCK

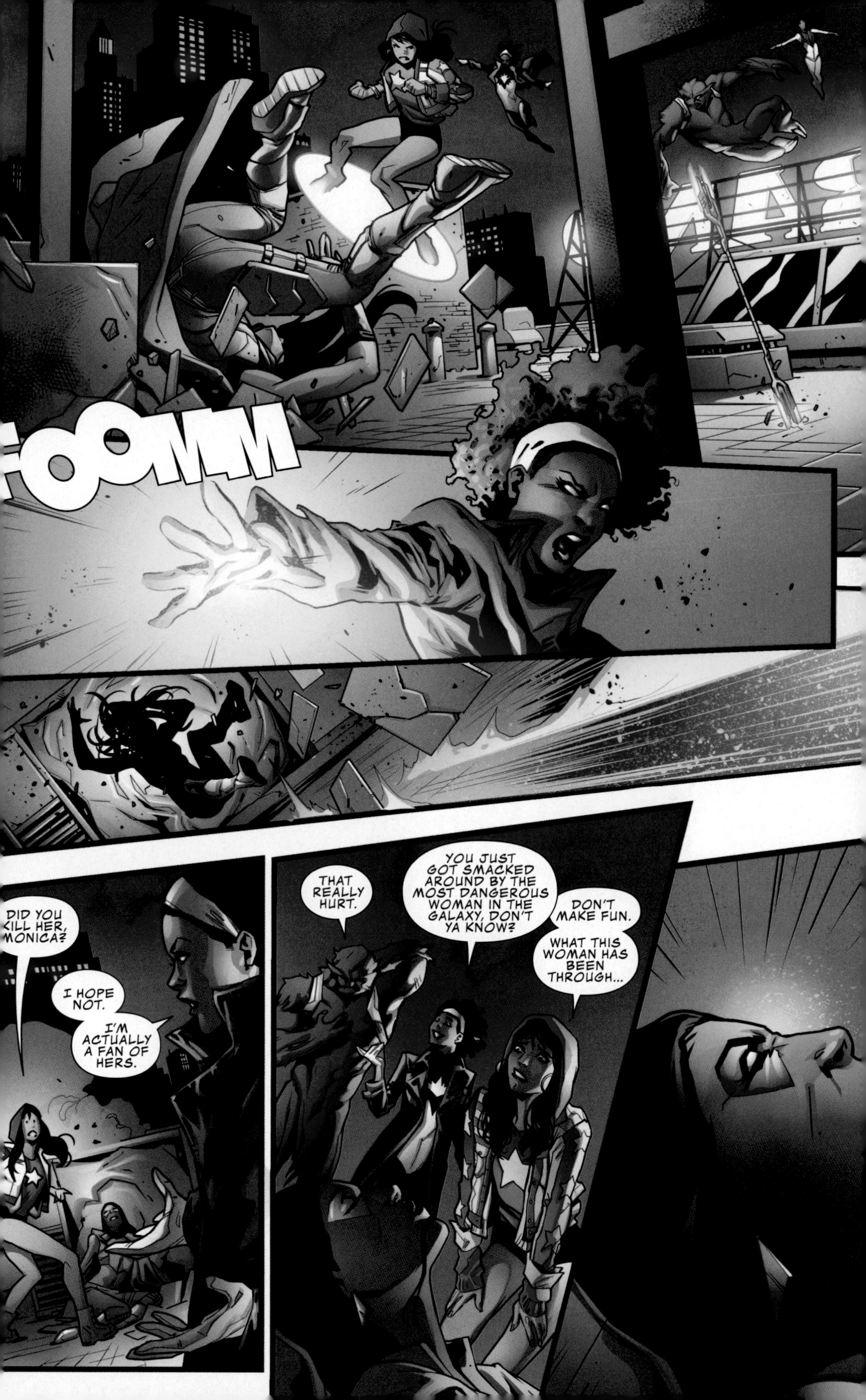
FOOMMM
DID YOU KILL HER, MONICA?
I HOPE NOT.
I'M ACTUALLY A FAN OF HERS.
THAT REALLY HURT.
YOU JUST GOT SMACKED AROUND BY THE MOST DANGEROUS WOMAN IN THE GALAXY, DON'T YA KNOW?
DON'T MAKE FUN.
WHAT THIS WOMAN HAS BEEN THROUGH...

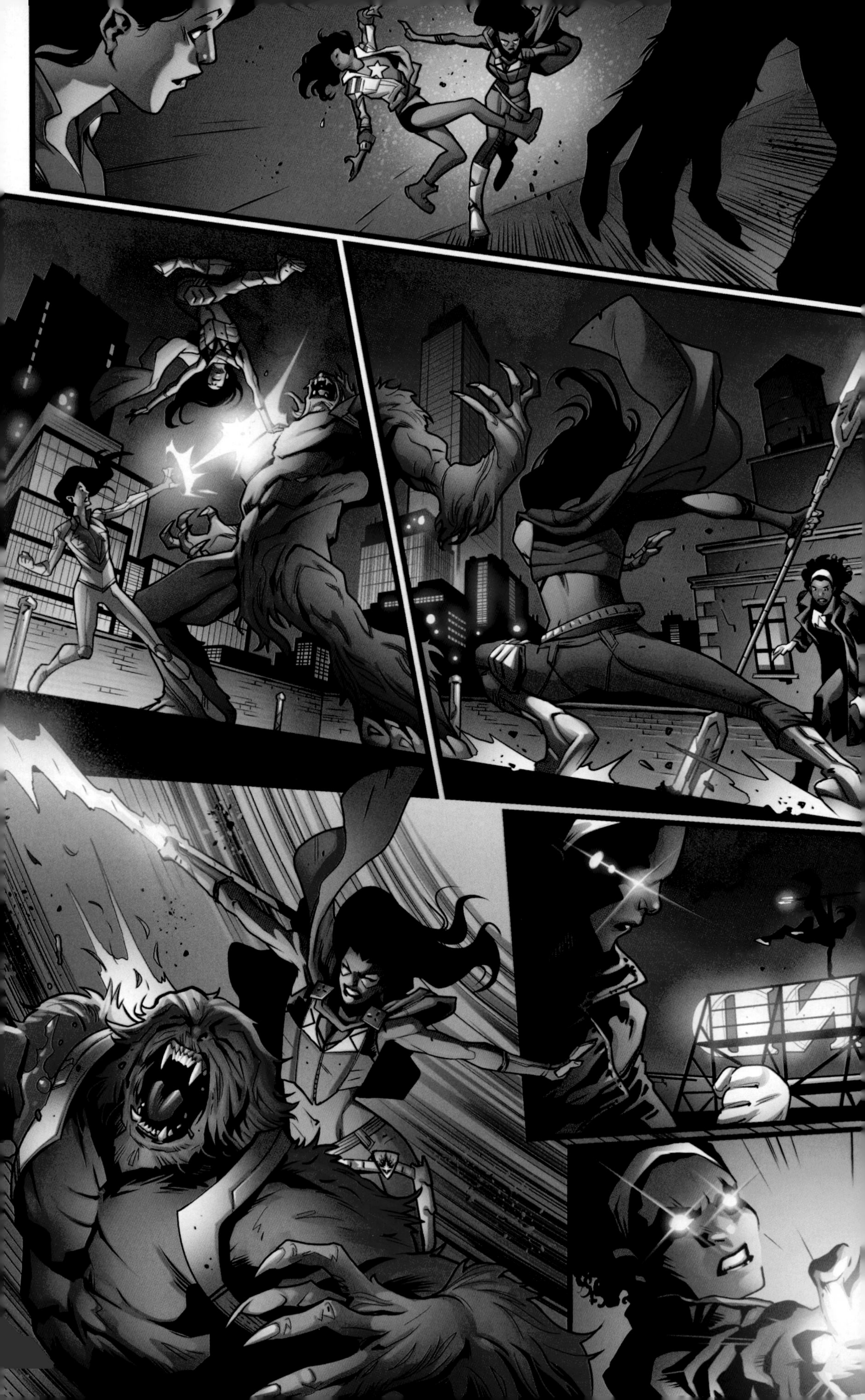

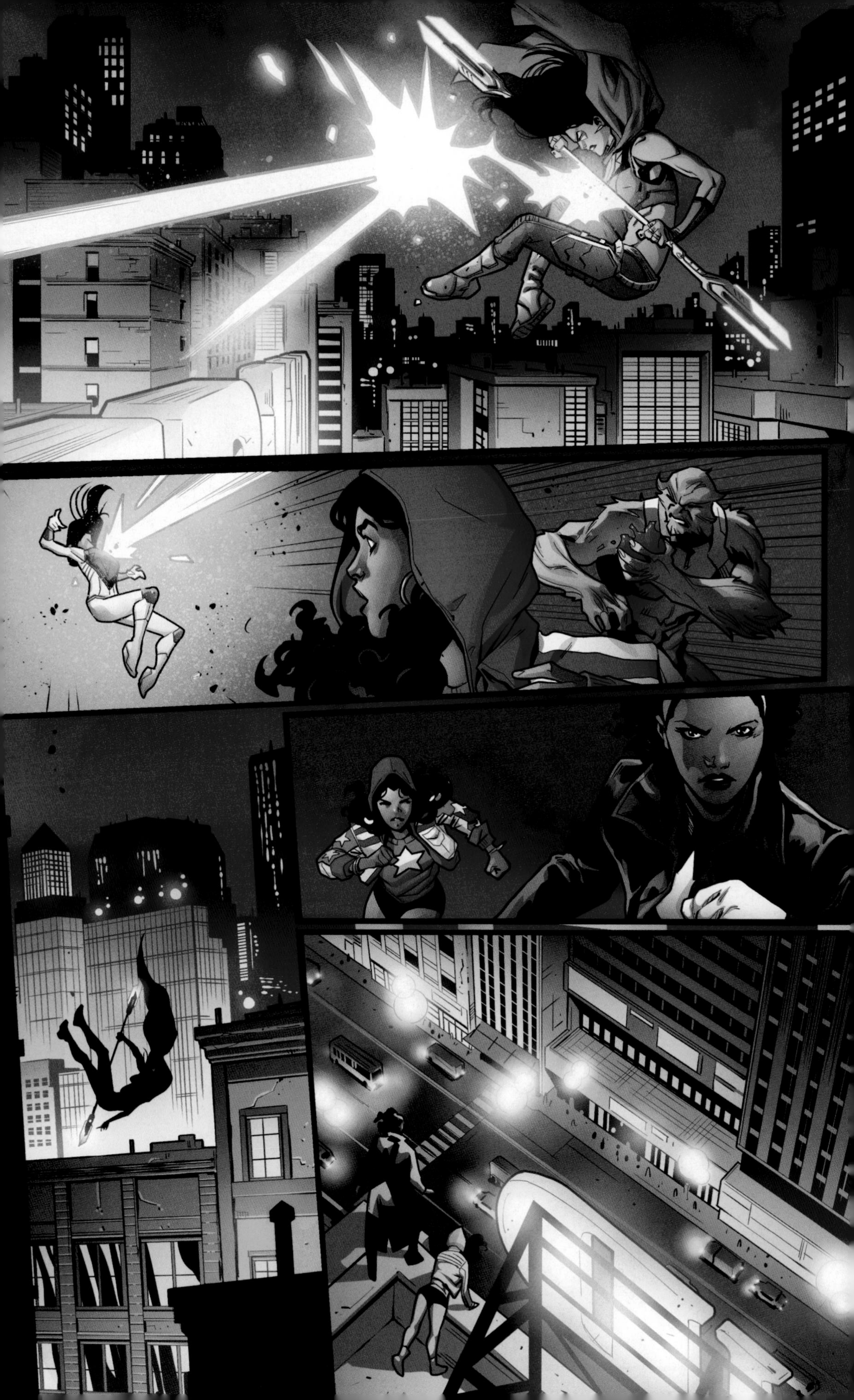

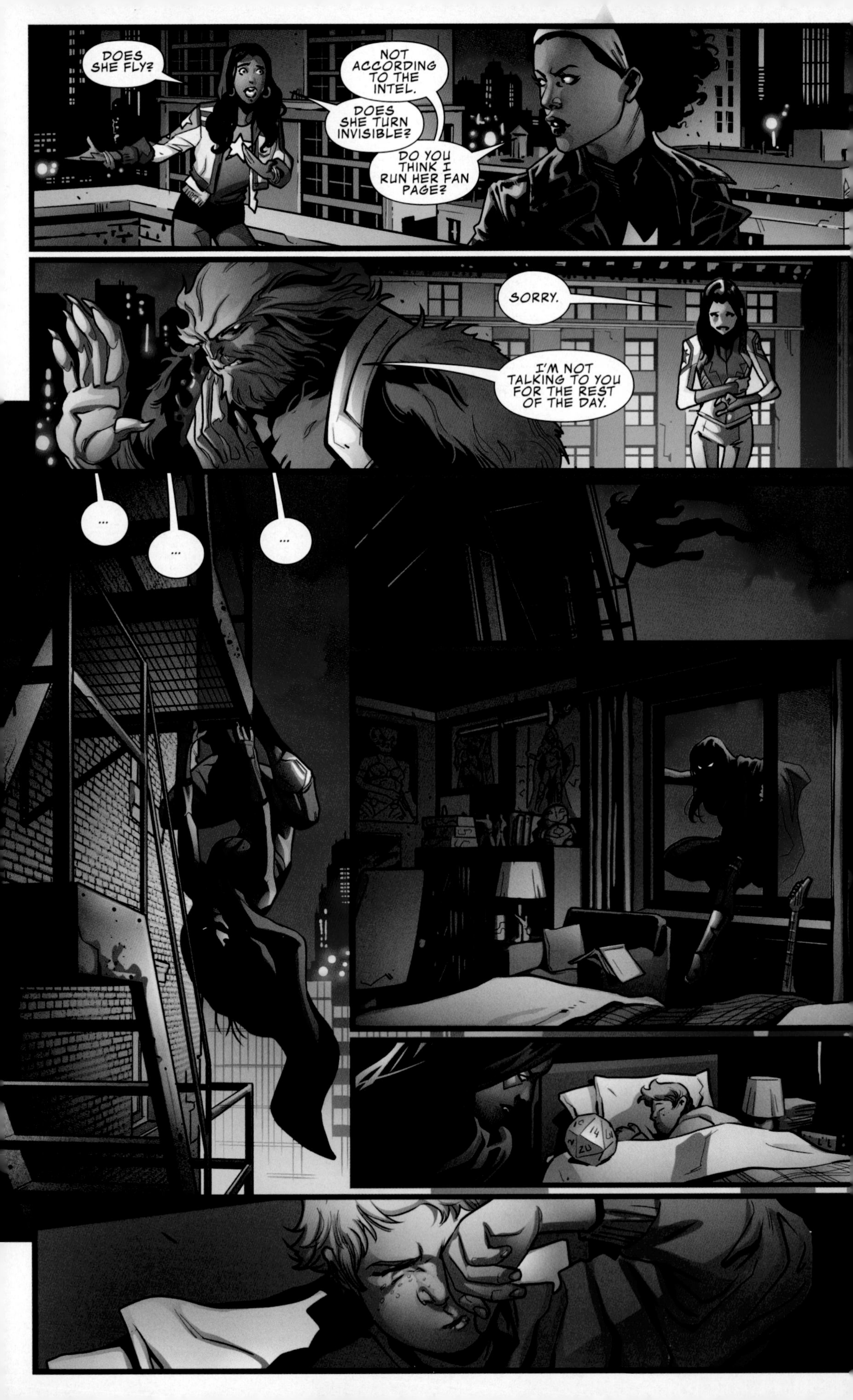

DOES SHE FLY?
NOT ACCORDING TO THE INTEL.
DOES SHE TURN INVISIBLE?
DO YOU THINK I RUN HER FAN PAGE?
SORRY.
I'M NOT TALKING TO YOU FOR THE REST OF THE DAY.
...
...
...

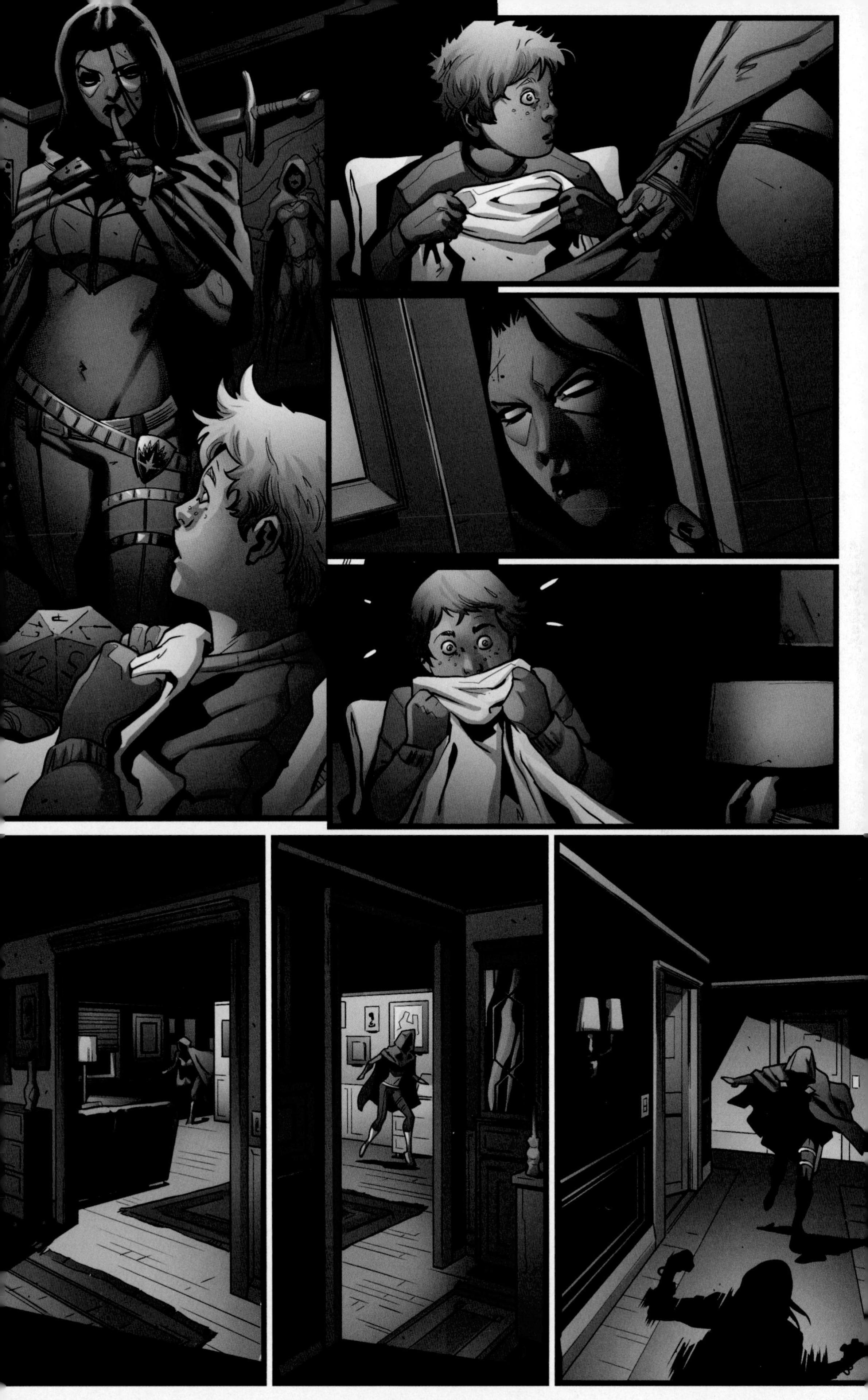

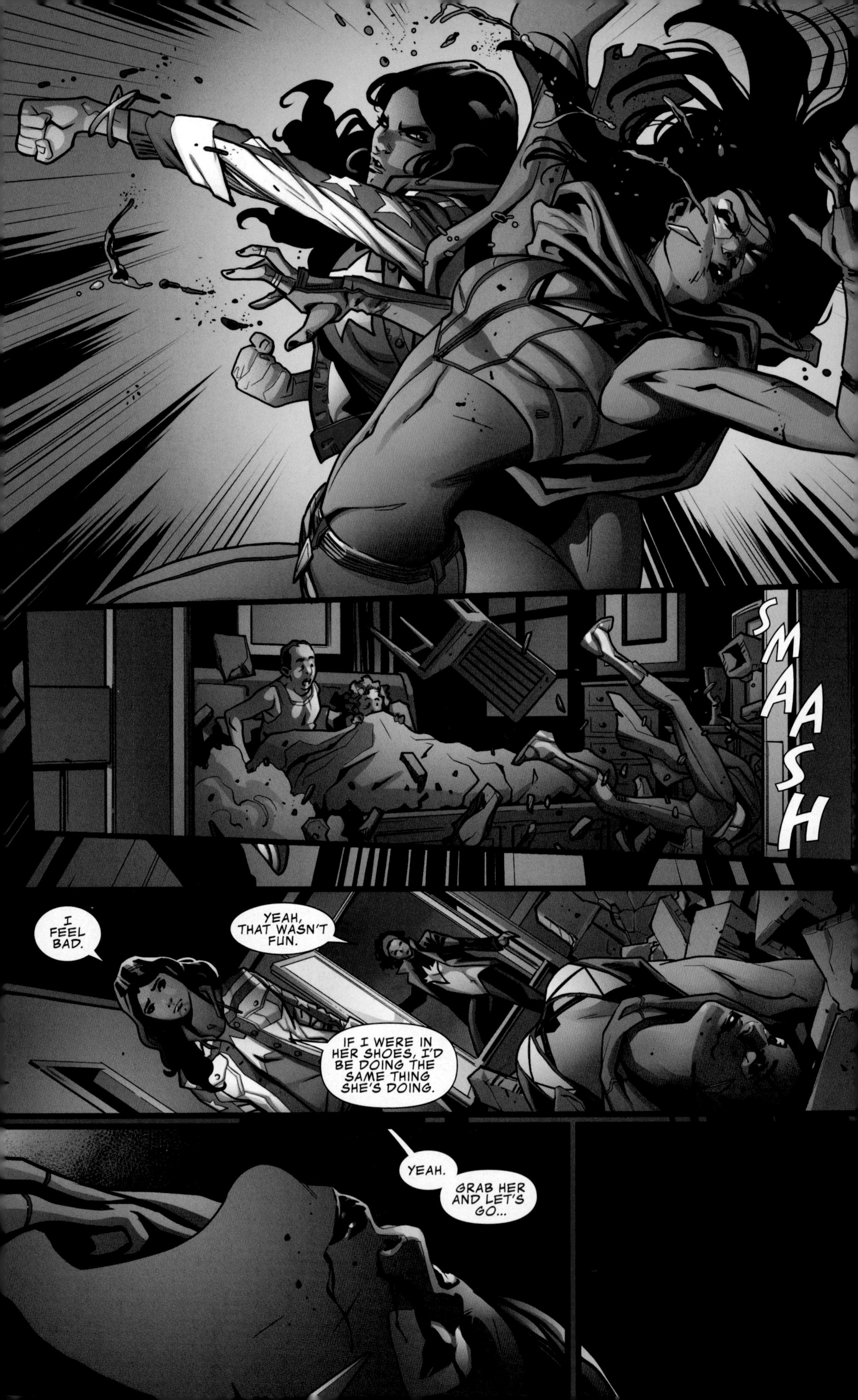
SMAASH
I FEEL BAD.
YEAH, THAT WASN'T FUN.
IF I WERE IN HER SHOES, I'D BE DOING THE SAME THING SHE'S DOING.
YEAH.
GRAB HER AND LET'S GO...

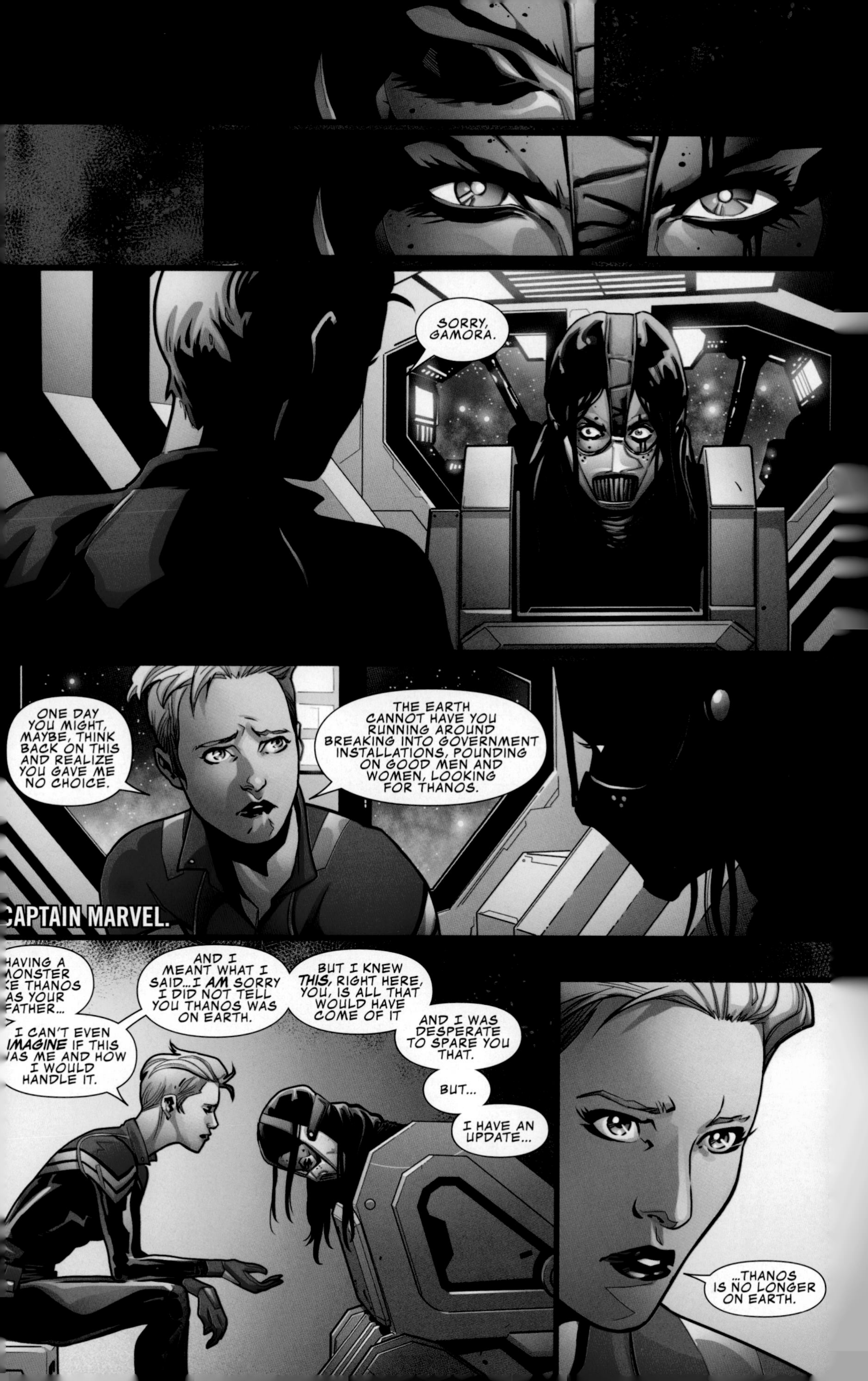
SORRY, GAMORA.
ONE DAY YOU MIGHT, MAYBE, THINK BACK ON THIS AND REALIZE YOU GAVE ME NO CHOICE.
THE EARTH CANNOT HAVE YOU RUNNING AROUND BREAKING INTO GOVERNMENT INSTALLATIONS, POUNDING ON GOOD MEN AND WOMEN, LOOKING FOR THANOS.
CAPTAIN MARVEL.
HAVING A MONSTER KE THANOS AS YOUR FATHER...
I CAN'T EVEN IMAGINE IF THIS AS ME AND HOW I WOULD HANDLE IT.
AND I MEANT WHAT I SAID...I AM SORRY I DID NOT TELL YOU THANOS WAS ON EARTH.
BUT I KNEW THIS, RIGHT HERE, YOU, IS ALL THAT WOULD HAVE COME OF IT
AND I WAS DESPERATE TO SPARE YOU THAT.
BUT...
I HAVE AN UPDATE...
...THANOS IS NO LONGER ON EARTH.

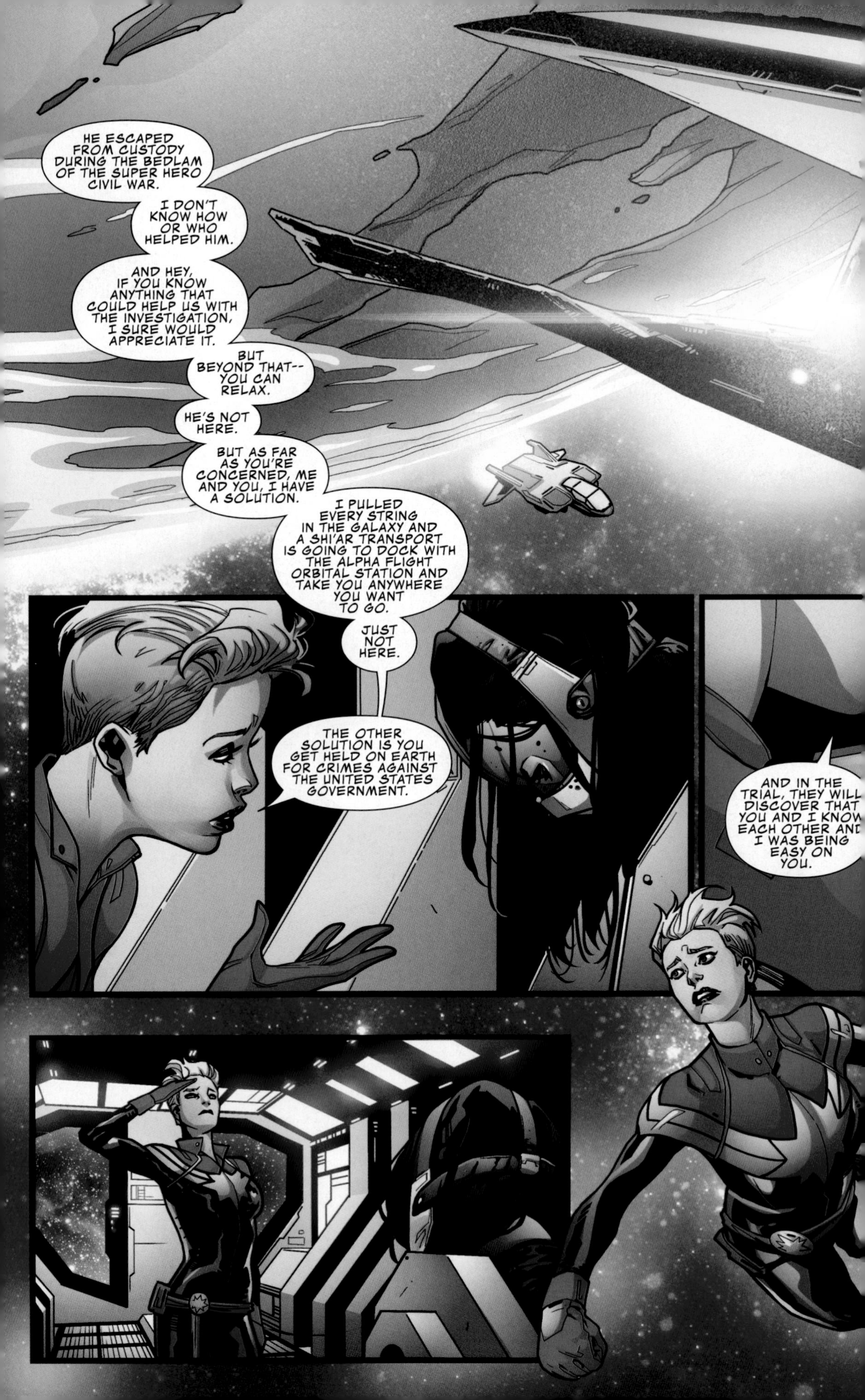
HE ESCAPED FROM CUSTODY DURING THE BEDLAM OF THE SUPER HERO CIVIL WAR.
I DON'T KNOW HOW OR WHO HELPED HIM.
AND HEY, IF YOU KNOW ANYTHING THAT COULD HELP US WITH THE INVESTIGATION, I SURE WOULD APPRECIATE IT.
BUT BEYOND THAT-- YOU CAN RELAX.
HE'S NOT HERE.
BUT AS FAR AS YOU'RE CONCERNED, ME AND YOU, I HAVE A SOLUTION.
I PULLED EVERY STRING IN THE GALAXY AND A SHI'AR TRANSPORT IS GOING TO DOCK WITH THE ALPHA FLIGHT ORBITAL STATION AND TAKE YOU ANYWHERE YOU WANT TO GO.
JUST NOT HERE.
THE OTHER SOLUTION IS YOU GET HELD ON EARTH FOR CRIMES AGAINST THE UNITED STATES GOVERNMENT.
AND IN THE TRIAL, THEY WILL DISCOVER THAT YOU AND I KNOW EACH OTHER AND I WAS BEING EASY ON YOU.

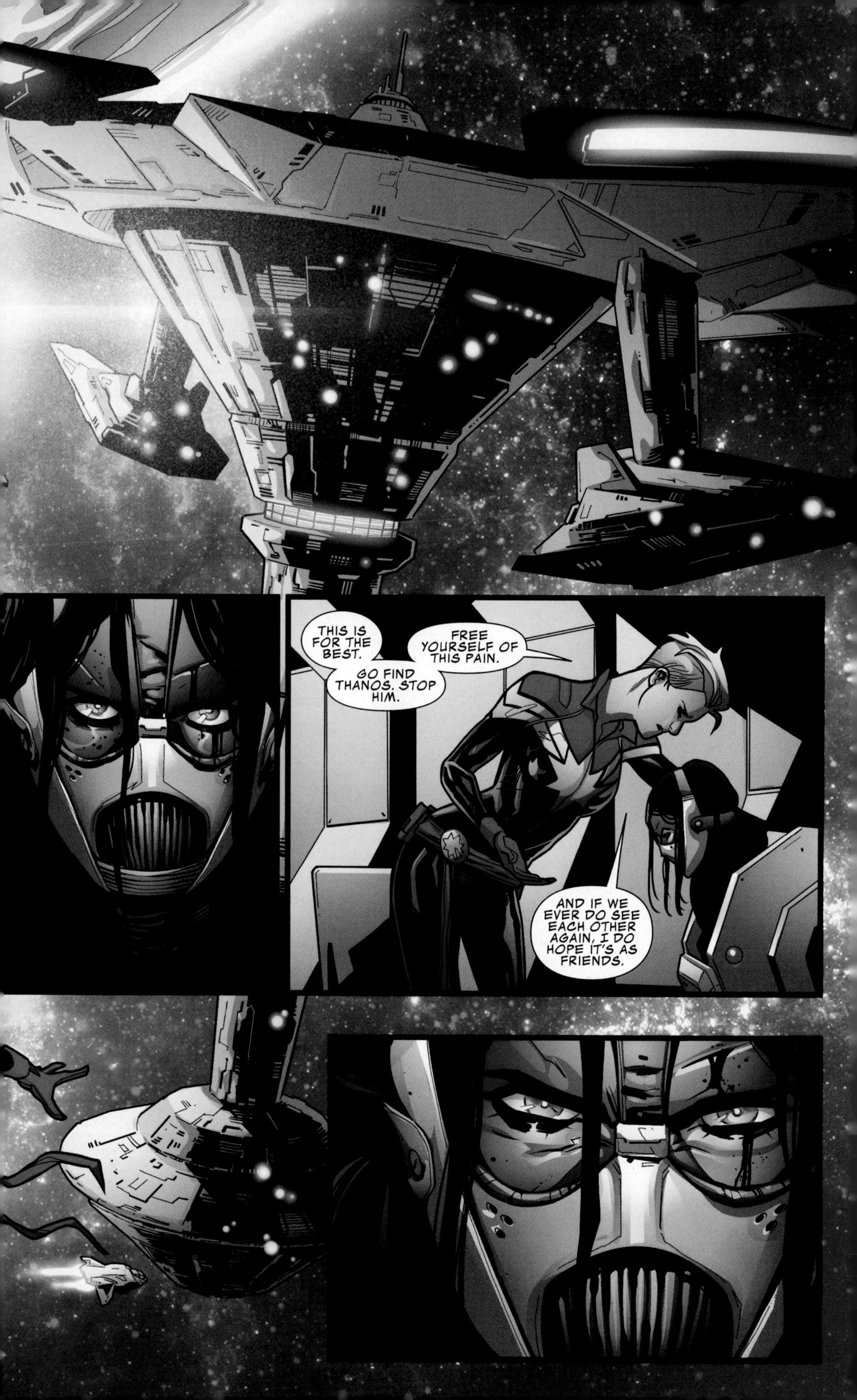
THIS IS FOR THE BEST.
FREE YOURSELF OF THIS PAIN.
GO FIND THANOS. STOP HIM.
AND IF WE EVER DO SEE EACH OTHER AGAIN, I DO HOPE IT'S AS FRIENDS.

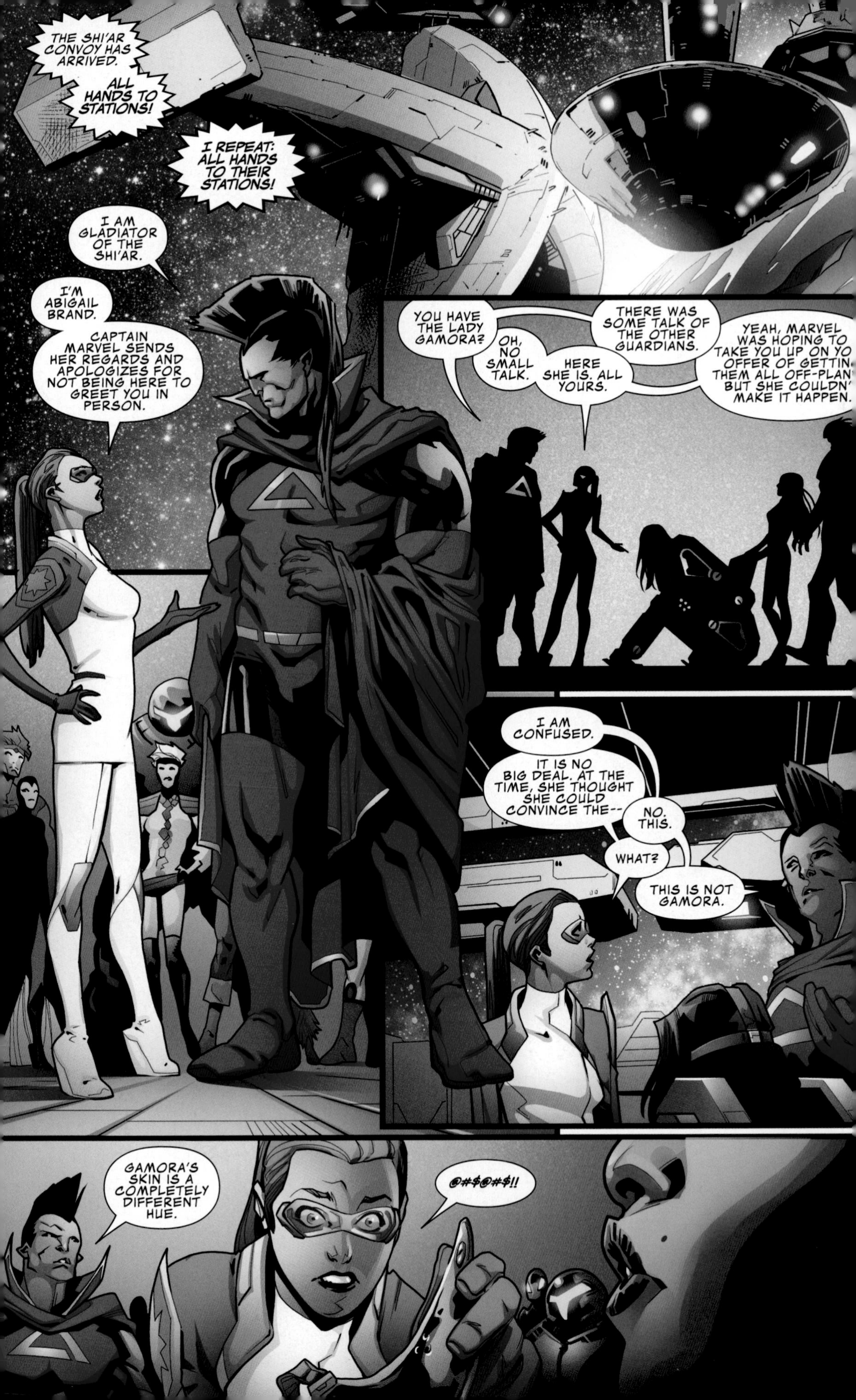
THE SHI'AR CONVOY HAS ARRIVED.
ALL HANDS TO STATIONS!
I REPEAT: ALL HANDS TO THEIR STATIONS!
I AM GLADIATOR OF THE SHI'AR.
I'M ABIGAIL BRAND.
CAPTAIN MARVEL SENDS HER REGARDS AND APOLOGIZES FOR NOT BEING HERE TO GREET YOU IN PERSON.
YOU HAVE THE LADY GAMORA?
OH, NO SMALL TALK.
THERE WAS SOME TALK OF THE OTHER GUARDIANS.
HERE SHE IS. ALL YOURS.
YEAH, MARVEL WAS HOPING TO TAKE YOU UP ON YO OFFER OF GETTIN THEM ALL OFF-PLAN BUT SHE COULDN' MAKE IT HAPPEN.
I AM CONFUSED.
IT IS NO BIG DEAL. AT THE TIME, SHE THOUGHT SHE COULD CONVINCE THE--
NO. THIS.
WHAT?
THIS IS NOT GAMORA.
GAMORA'S SKIN IS A COMPLETELY DIFFERENT HUE.
@#$@#$!!

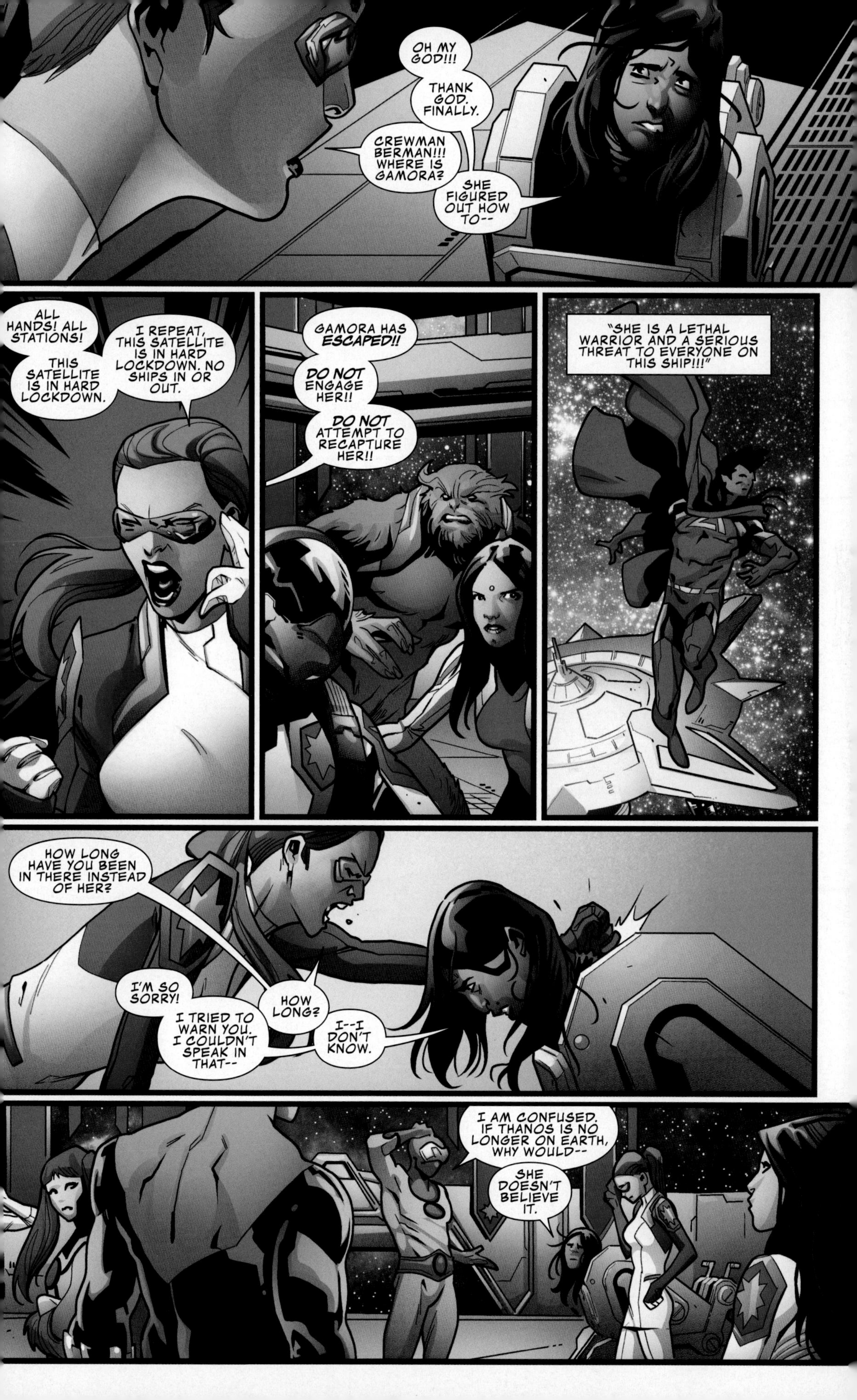
OH MY GOD!!!
THANK GOD. FINALLY.
CREWMAN BERMAN!!! WHERE IS GAMORA?
SHE FIGURED OUT HOW TO--
ALL HANDS! ALL STATIONS!
THIS SATELLITE IS IN HARD LOCKDOWN.
I REPEAT, THIS SATELLITE IS IN HARD LOCKDOWN. NO SHIPS IN OR OUT.
GAMORA HAS ESCAPED!!
DO NOT ENGAGE HER!!
DO NOT ATTEMPT TO RECAPTURE HER!!
"SHE IS A LETHAL WARRIOR AND A SERIOUS THREAT TO EVERYONE ON THIS SHIP!!!"
HOW LONG HAVE YOU BEEN IN THERE INSTEAD OF HER?
I'M SO SORRY!
I TRIED TO WARN YOU. I COULDN'T SPEAK IN THAT--
HOW LONG?
I--I DON'T KNOW.
I AM CONFUSED. IF THANOS IS NO LONGER ON EARTH, WHY WOULD--
SHE DOESN'T BELIEVE IT.

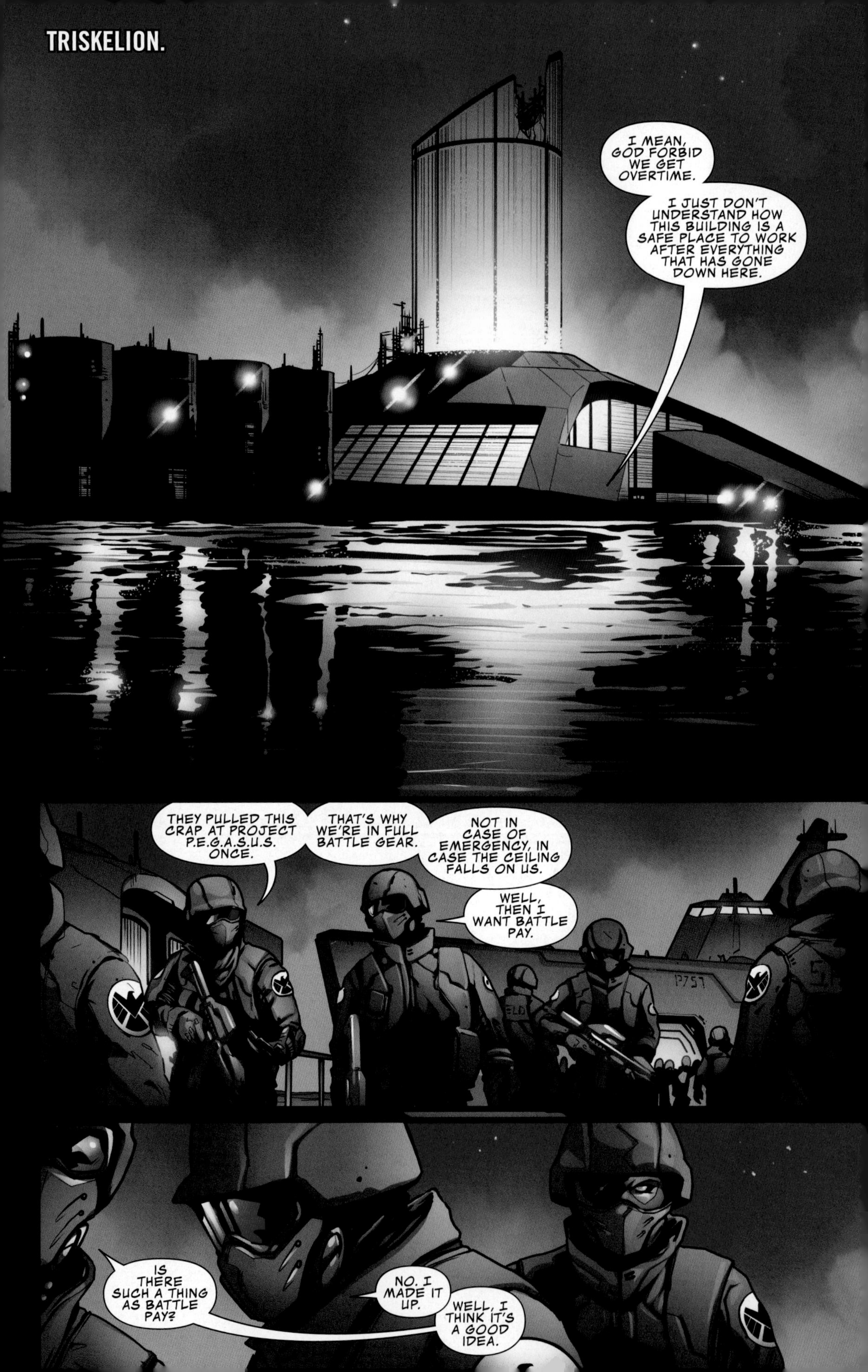
TRISKELION.
I MEAN, GOD FORBID WE GET OVERTIME.
I JUST DON'T UNDERSTAND HOW THIS BUILDING IS A SAFE PLACE TO WORK AFTER EVERYTHING THAT HAS GONE DOWN HERE.
THEY PULLED THIS CRAP AT PROJECT P.E.G.A.S.U.S. ONCE.
THAT'S WHY WE'RE IN FULL BATTLE GEAR.
NOT IN CASE OF EMERGENCY, IN CASE THE CEILING FALLS ON US.
WELL, THEN I WANT BATTLE PAY.
IS THERE SUCH A THING AS BATTLE PAY?
NO. I MADE IT UP.
WELL, I THINK IT'S A GOOD IDEA.

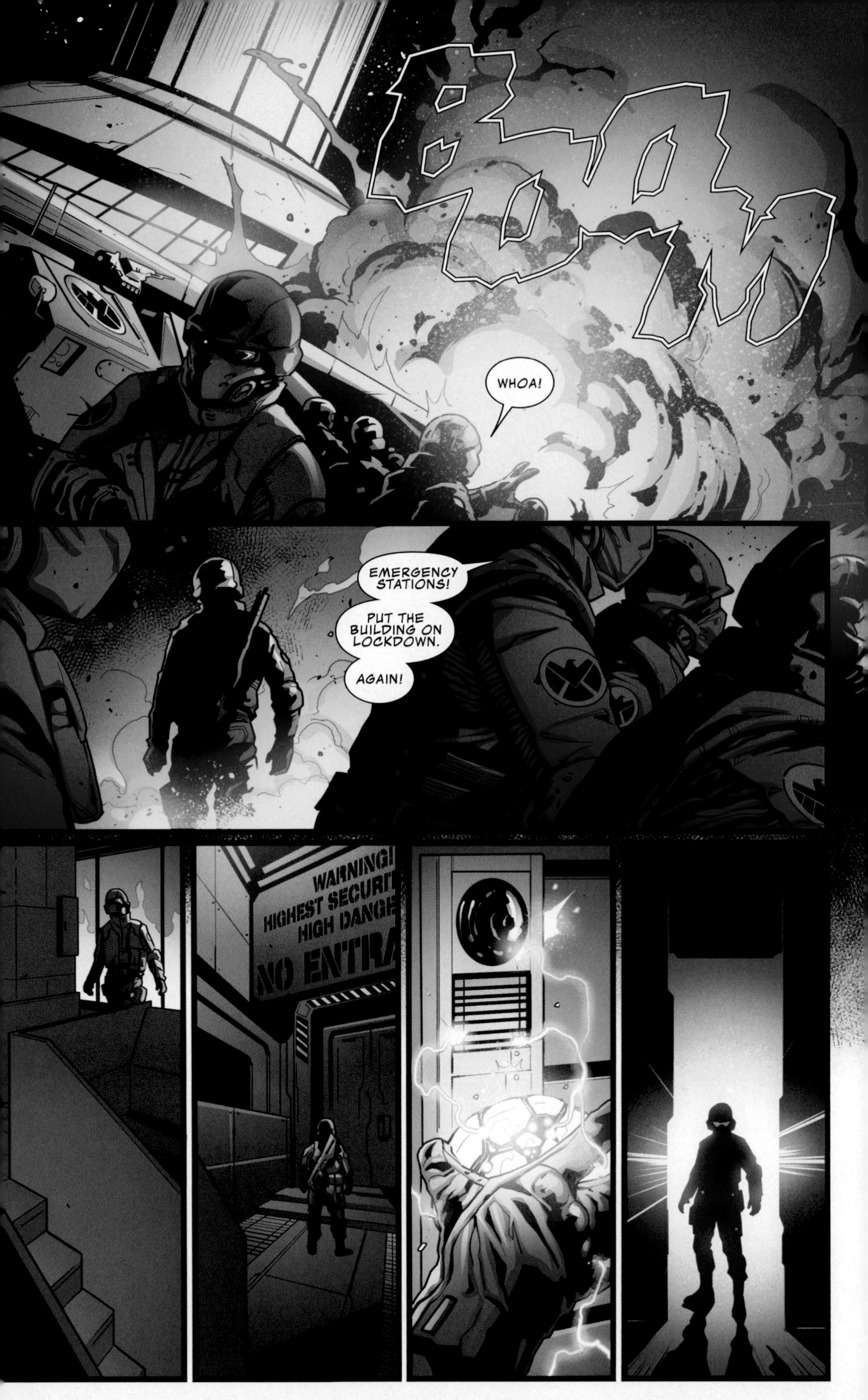
BOOM
WHOA!
EMERGENCY STATIONS!
PUT THE BUILDING ON LOCKDOWN.
AGAIN!
WARNING!

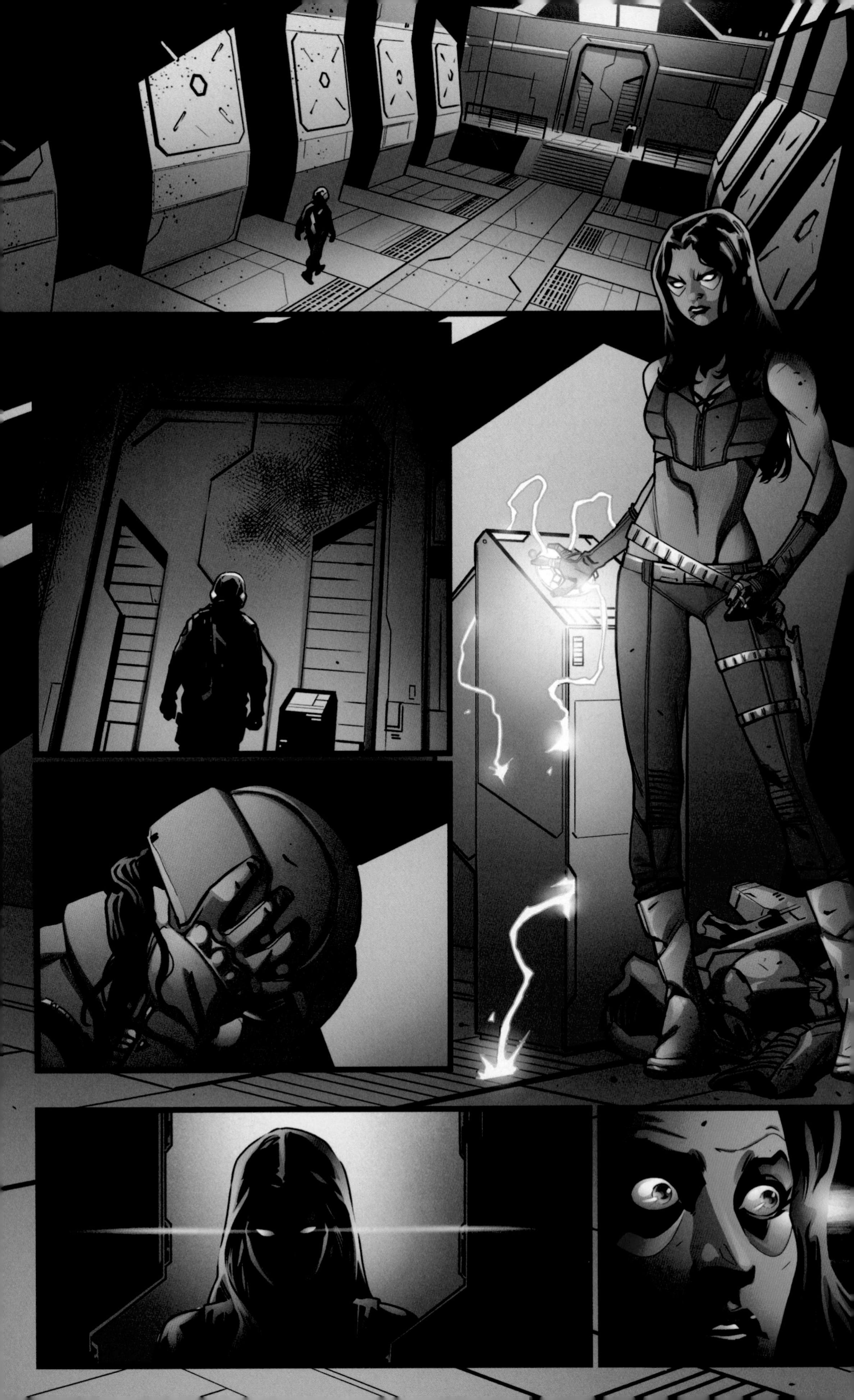

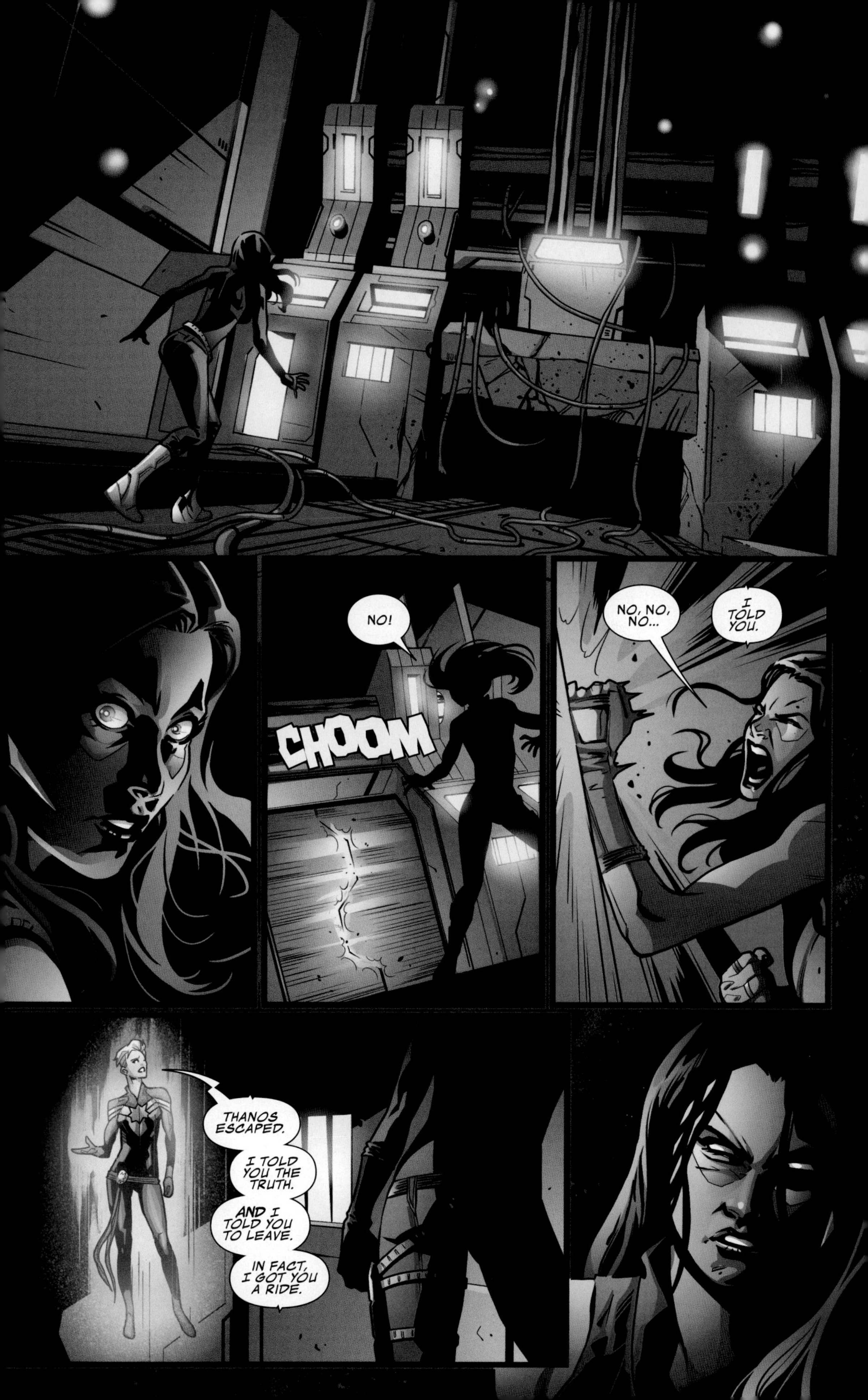
CHOOM
NO!
NO, NO, NO...
I TOLD YOU.
THANOS ESCAPED.
I TOLD YOU THE TRUTH.
AND I TOLD YOU TO LEAVE.
IN FACT, I GOT YOU A RIDE.

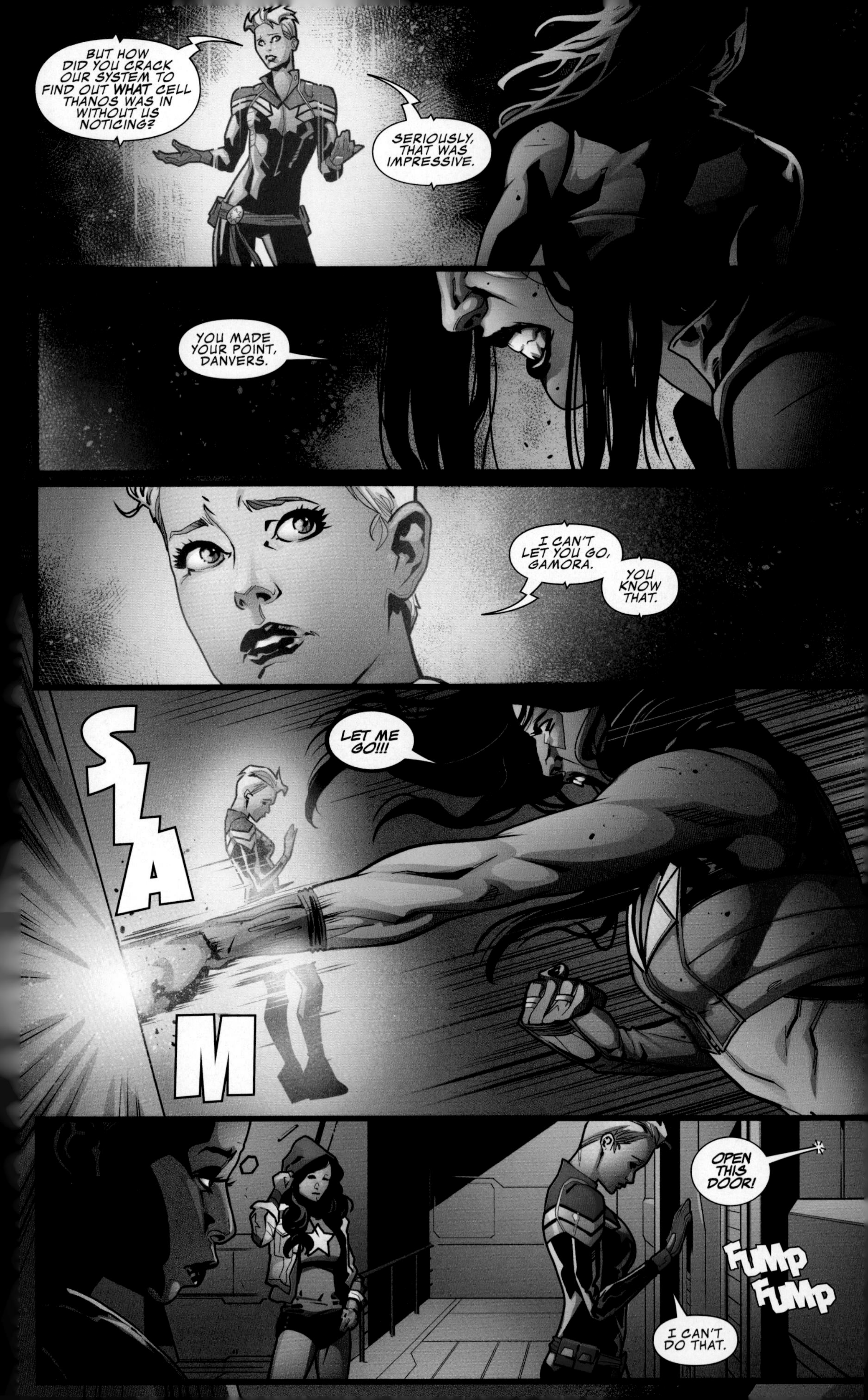
BUT HOW DID YOU CRACK OUR SYSTEM TO FIND OUT WHAT CELL THANOS WAS IN WITHOUT US NOTICING?
SERIOUSLY, THAT WAS IMPRESSIVE.
YOU MADE YOUR POINT, DANVERS.
I CAN'T LET YOU GO, GAMORA.
YOU KNOW THAT.
SLAM
LET ME GO!!!
OPEN THIS DOOR!
FUMP FUMP
I CAN'T DO THAT.

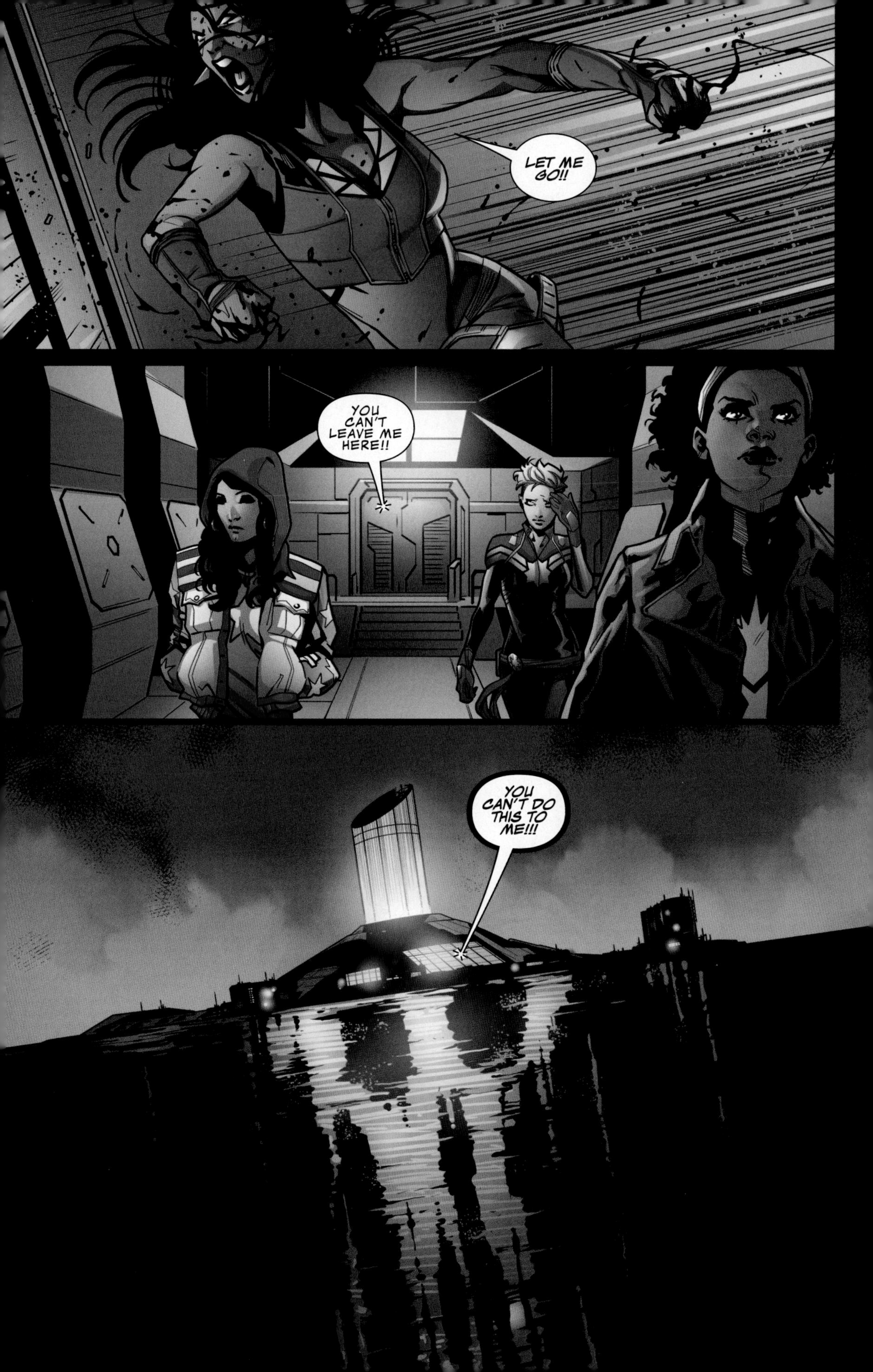
LET ME GO!!
YOU CAN'T LEAVE ME HERE!!
YOU CAN'T DO THIS TO ME!!!

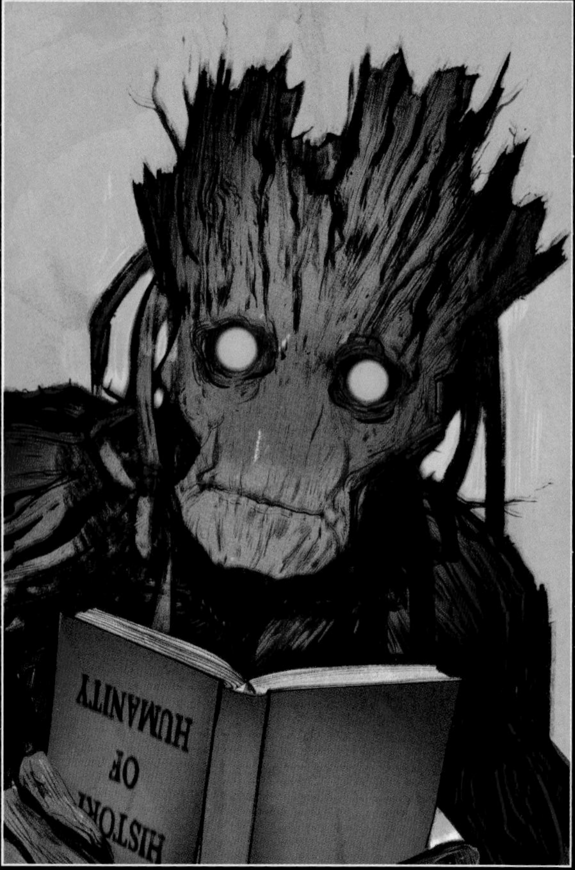

#16 VARIANT BY
TULA LOTAY

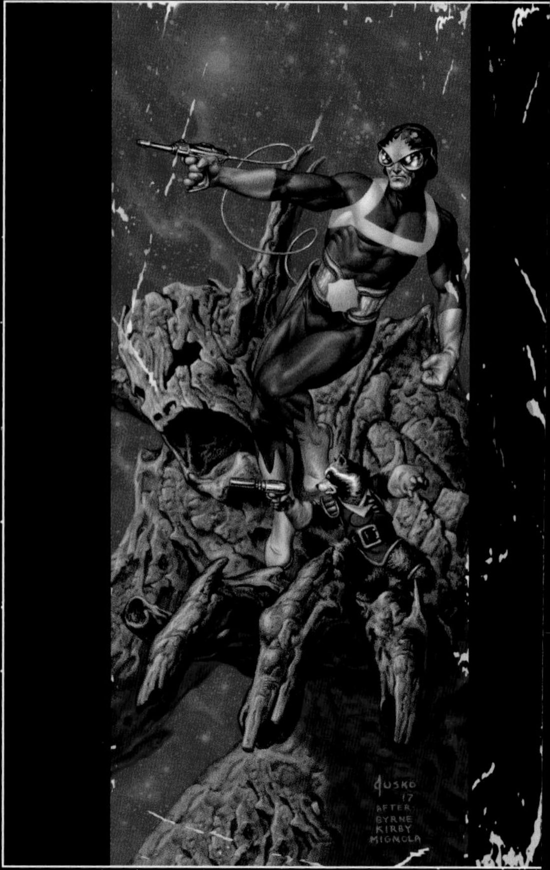
JUSKO
17
AFTER
BYRNE
KIRBY
MIGNOLA

#17 CORNER BOX VARIANT BY
JOE JUSKO

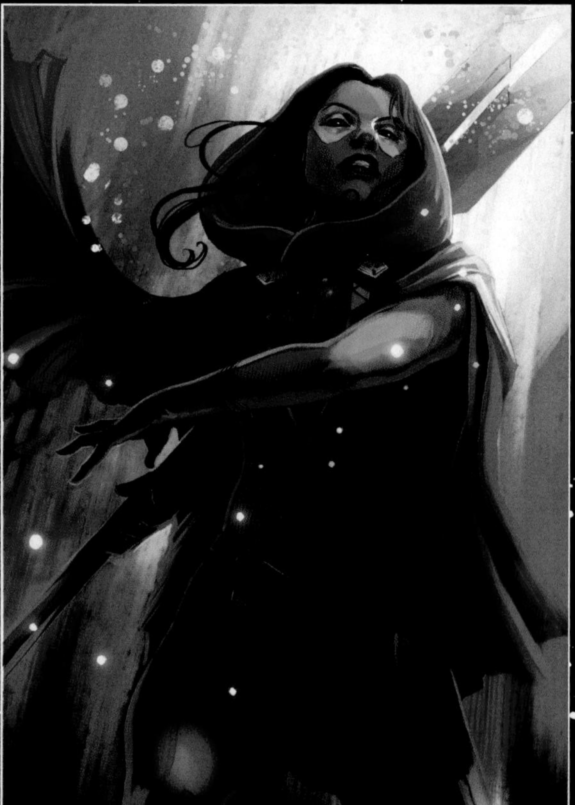

#17 VARIANT BY
STEPHANIE HANS

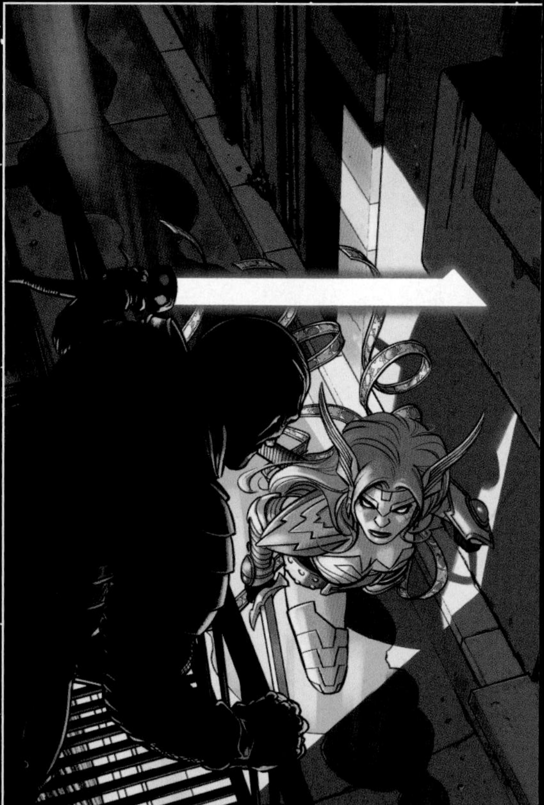

#18 VARIANT BY
DAVID LOPEZ

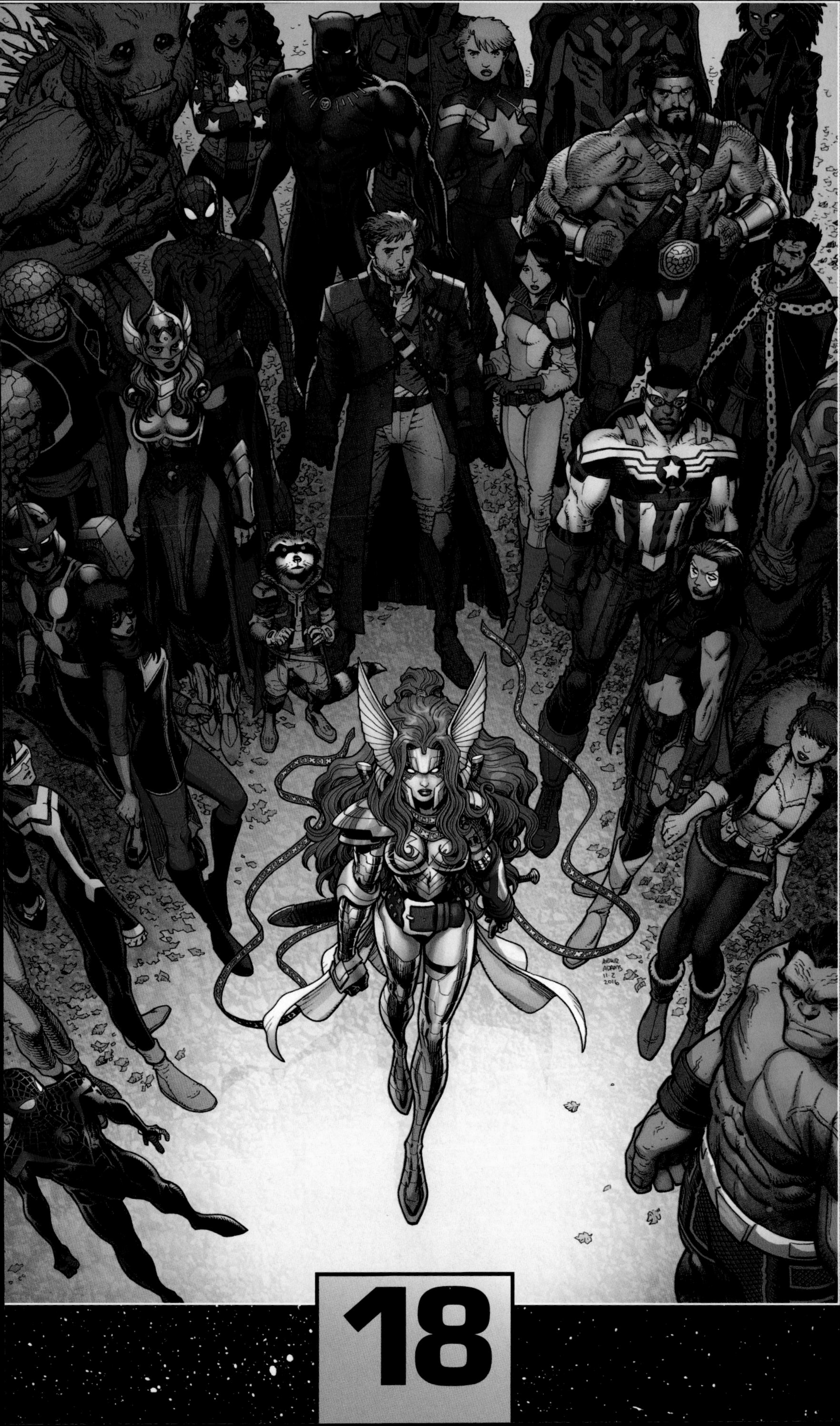

# 18

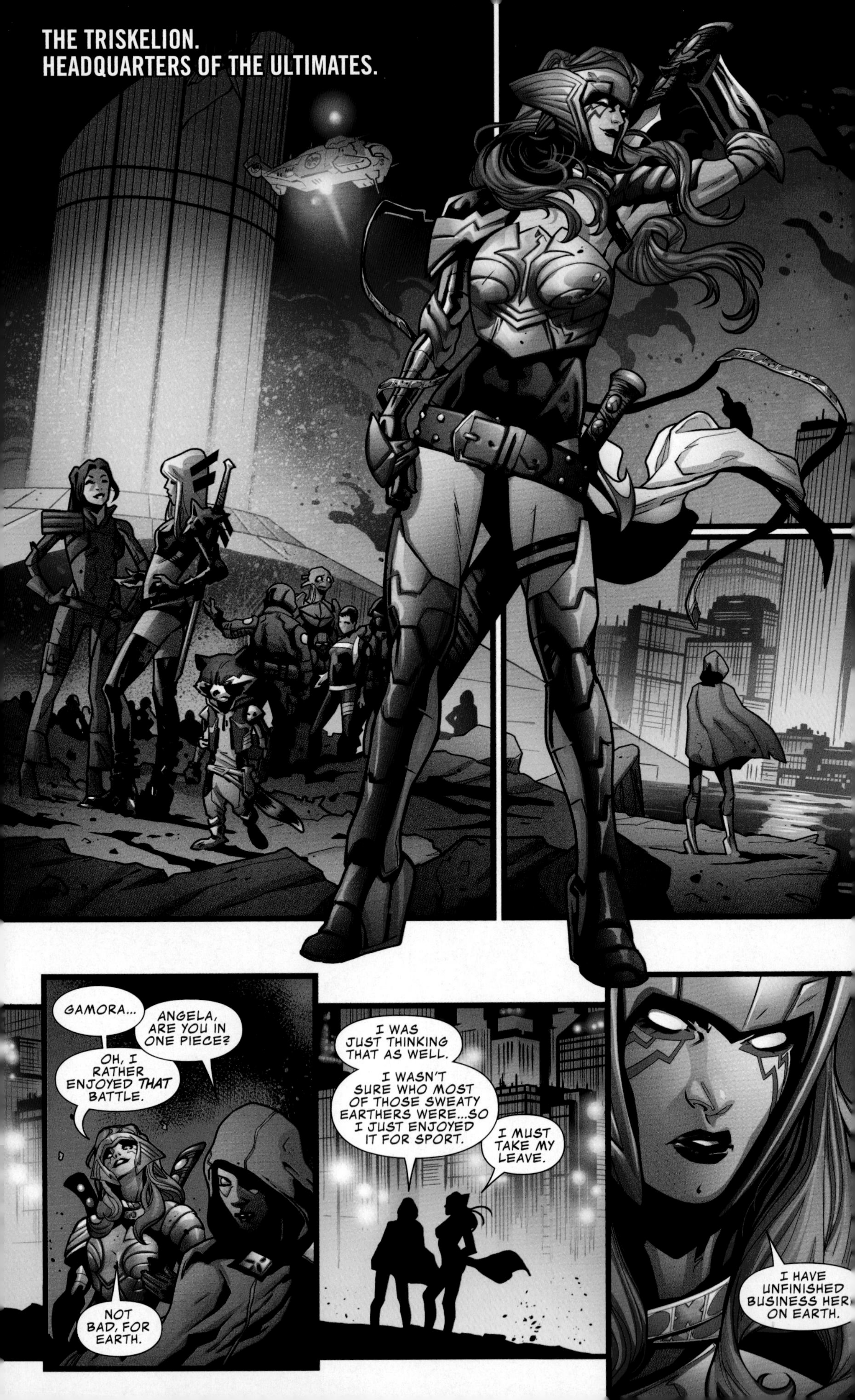
THE TRISKELION.
HEADQUARTERS OF THE ULTIMATES.
GAMORA...
ANGELA, ARE YOU IN ONE PIECE?
OH, I RATHER ENJOYED THAT BATTLE.
NOT BAD, FOR EARTH.
I WAS JUST THINKING THAT AS WELL.
I WASN'T SURE WHO MOST OF THOSE SWEATY EARTHERS WERE...SO I JUST ENJOYED IT FOR SPORT.
I MUST TAKE MY LEAVE.
I HAVE UNFINISHED BUSINESS HER ON EARTH.

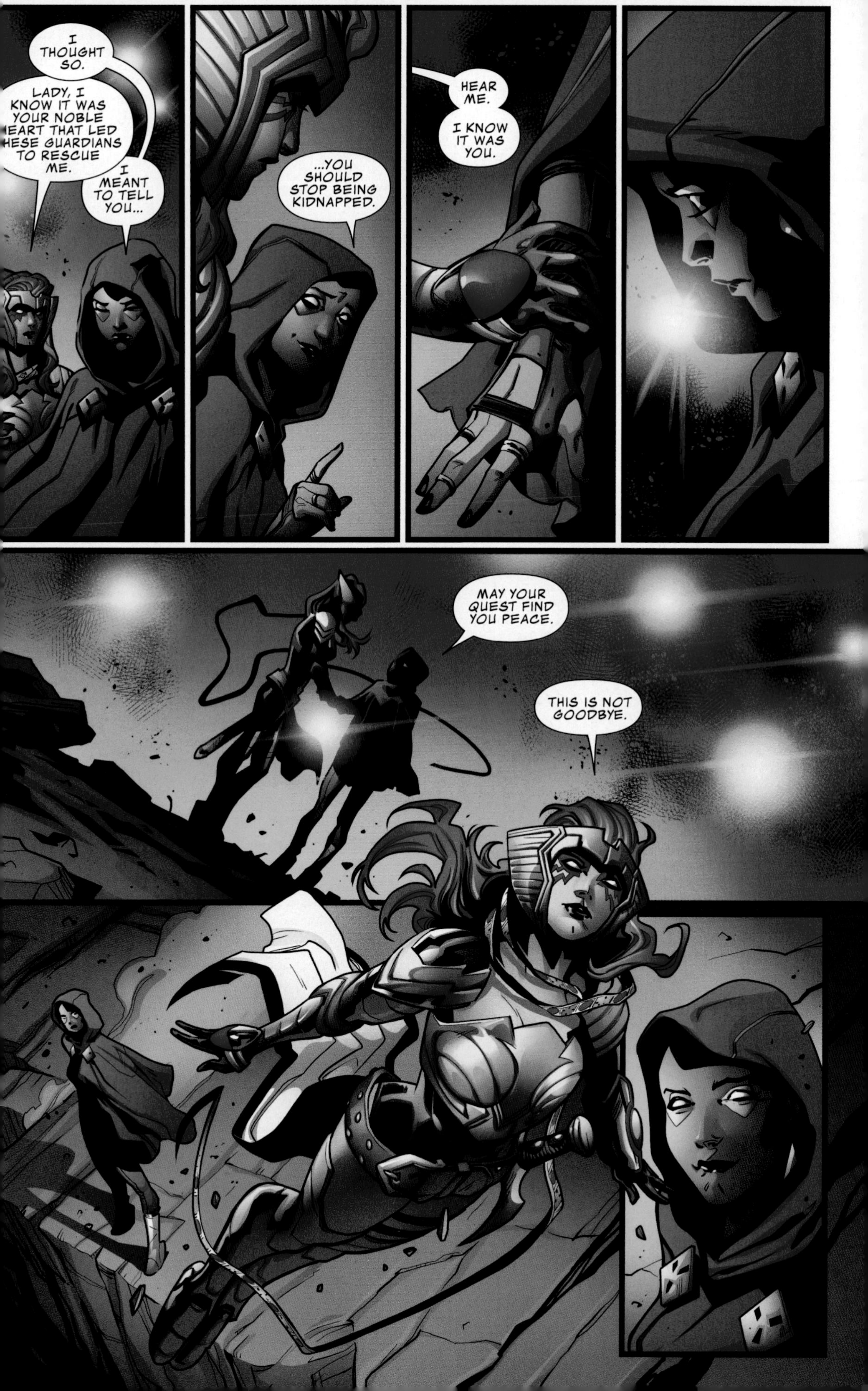
I THOUGHT SO.
LADY, I KNOW IT WAS YOUR NOBLE HEART THAT LED THESE GUARDIANS TO RESCUE ME.
I MEANT TO TELL YOU...
...YOU SHOULD STOP BEING KIDNAPPED.
HEAR ME.
I KNOW IT WAS YOU.
MAY YOUR QUEST FIND YOU PEACE.
THIS IS NOT GOODBYE.

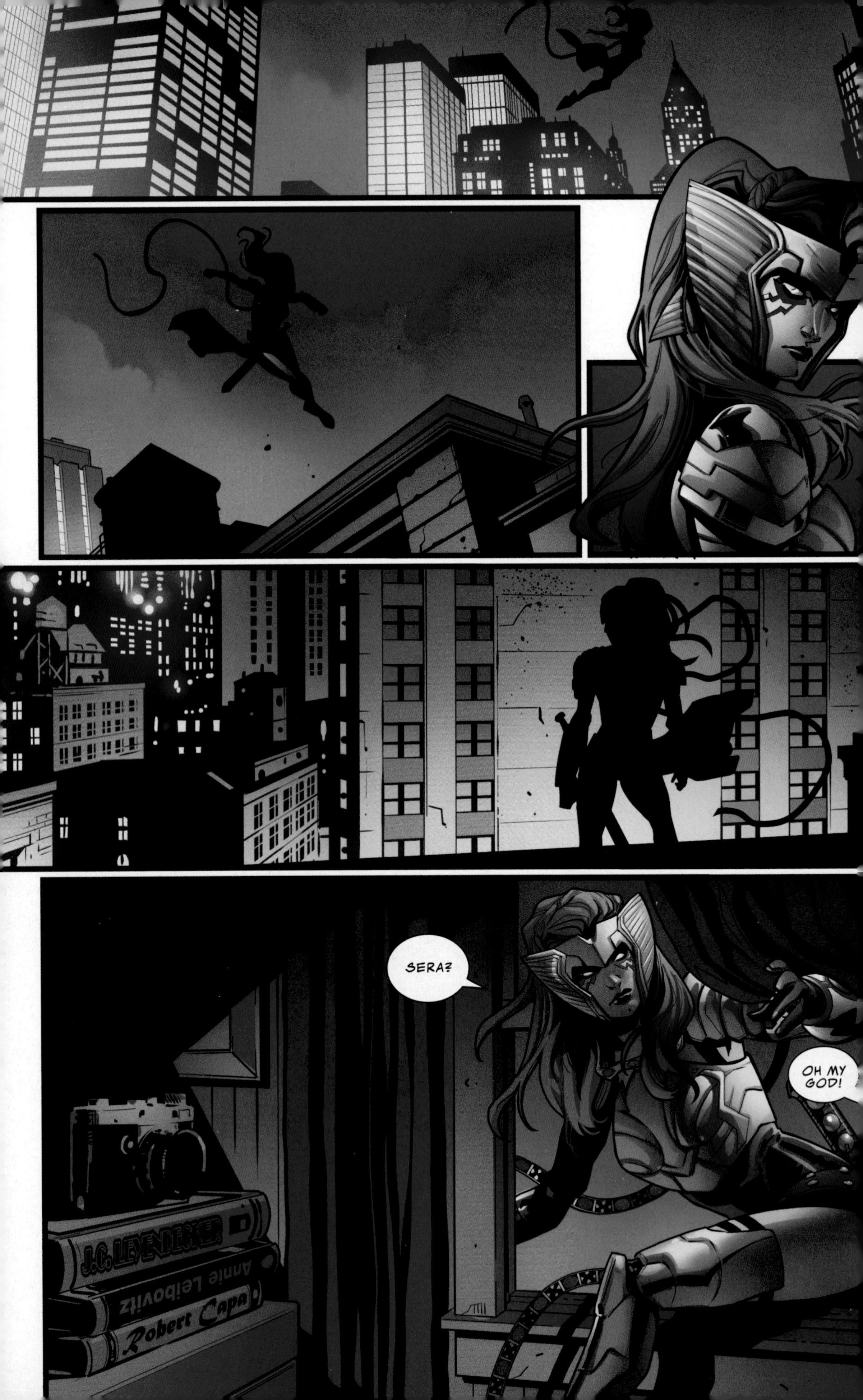
SERA?
OH MY GOD!
J.C. LEYENDECKER
Annie Leibovitz
Robert Capa

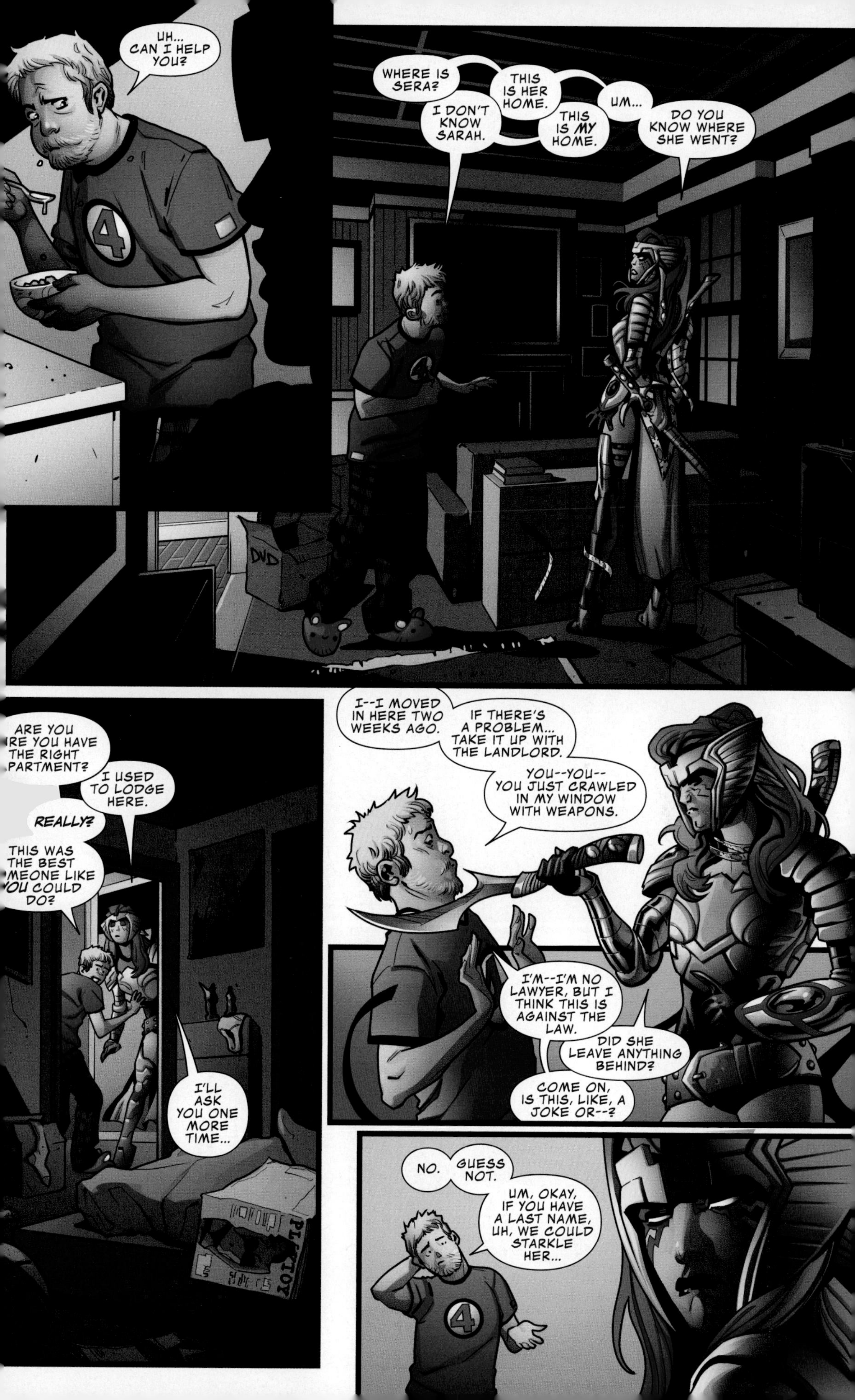
UH... CAN I HELP YOU?
WHERE IS SERA?
I DON'T KNOW SARAH.
THIS IS HER HOME.
THIS IS *MY* HOME.
UM...
DO YOU KNOW WHERE SHE WENT?
ARE YOU
RE YOU HAVE THE RIGHT PARTMENT?
I USED TO LODGE HERE.
*REALLY?*
THIS WAS THE BEST MEONE LIKE *YOU* COULD DO?
I'LL ASK YOU ONE MORE TIME...
I--I MOVED IN HERE TWO WEEKS AGO.
IF THERE'S A PROBLEM... TAKE IT UP WITH THE LANDLORD.
YOU--YOU-- YOU JUST CRAWLED IN MY WINDOW WITH WEAPONS.
I'M--I'M NO LAWYER, BUT I THINK THIS IS AGAINST THE LAW.
DID SHE LEAVE ANYTHING BEHIND?
COME ON, IS THIS, LIKE, A JOKE OR--?
NO.
GUESS NOT.
UM, OKAY, IF YOU HAVE A LAST NAME, UH, WE COULD STARKLE HER...
DVD

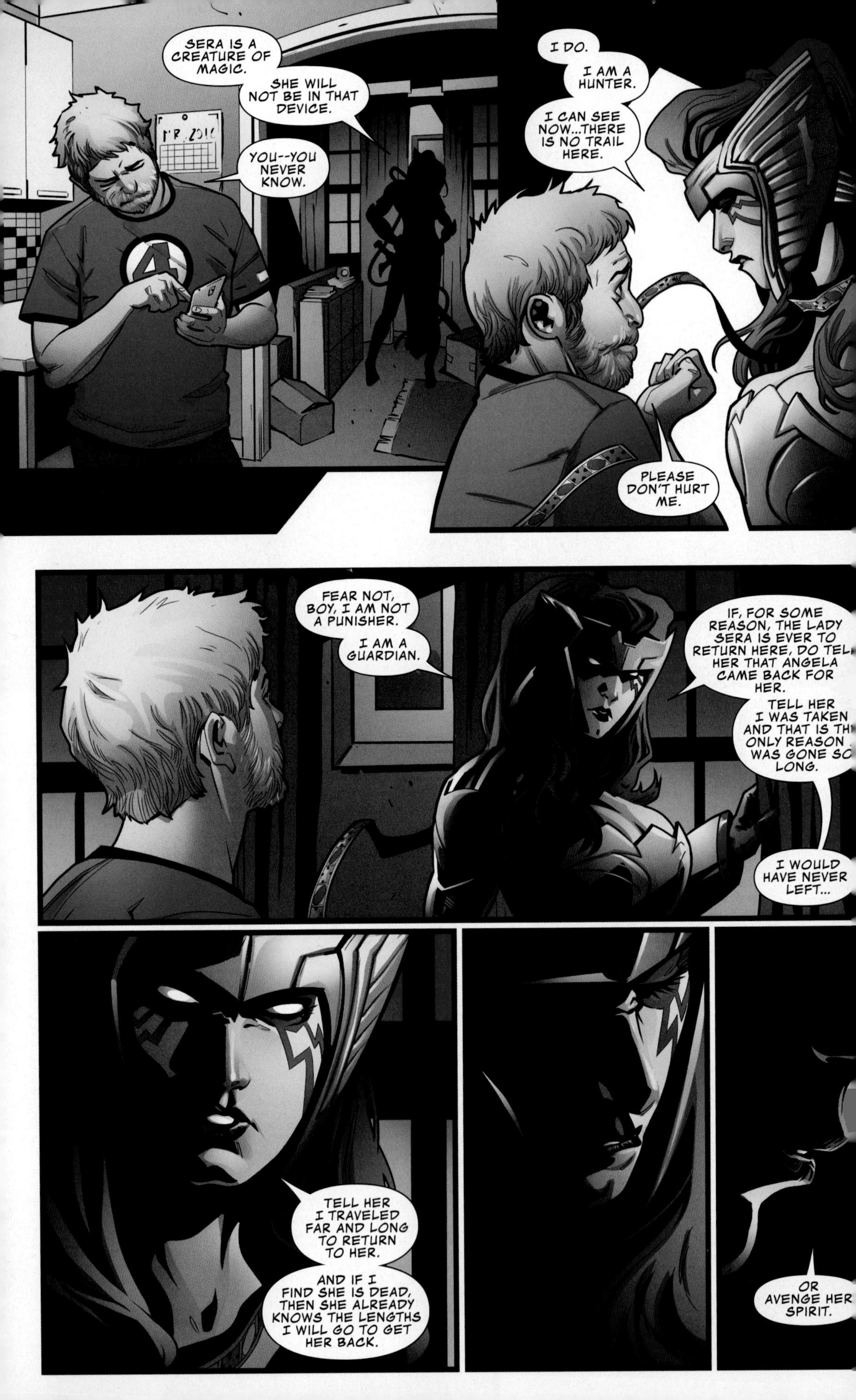
SERA IS A CREATURE OF MAGIC.
SHE WILL NOT BE IN THAT DEVICE.
YOU--YOU NEVER KNOW.
I DO.
I AM A HUNTER.
I CAN SEE NOW...THERE IS NO TRAIL HERE.
PLEASE DON'T HURT ME.
FEAR NOT, BOY, I AM NOT A PUNISHER.
I AM A GUARDIAN.
IF, FOR SOME REASON, THE LADY SERA IS EVER TO RETURN HERE, DO TEL HER THAT ANGELA CAME BACK FOR HER.
TELL HER I WAS TAKEN AND THAT IS TH ONLY REASON WAS GONE SO LONG.
I WOULD HAVE NEVER LEFT...
TELL HER I TRAVELED FAR AND LONG TO RETURN TO HER.
AND IF I FIND SHE IS DEAD, THEN SHE ALREADY KNOWS THE LENGTHS I WILL GO TO GET HER BACK.
OR AVENGE HER SPIRIT.

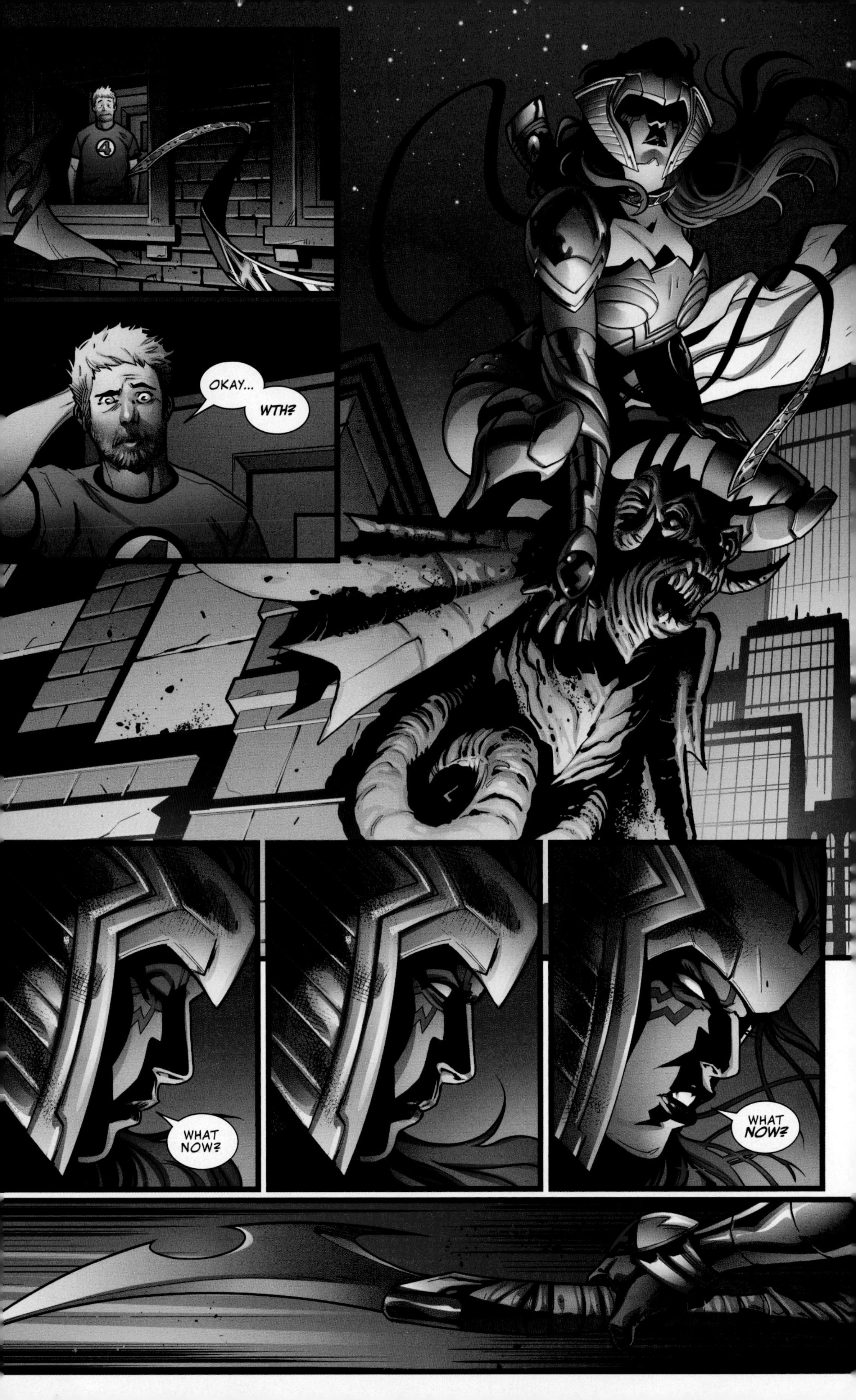

OKAY...
WTH?
WHAT NOW?
WHAT NOW?

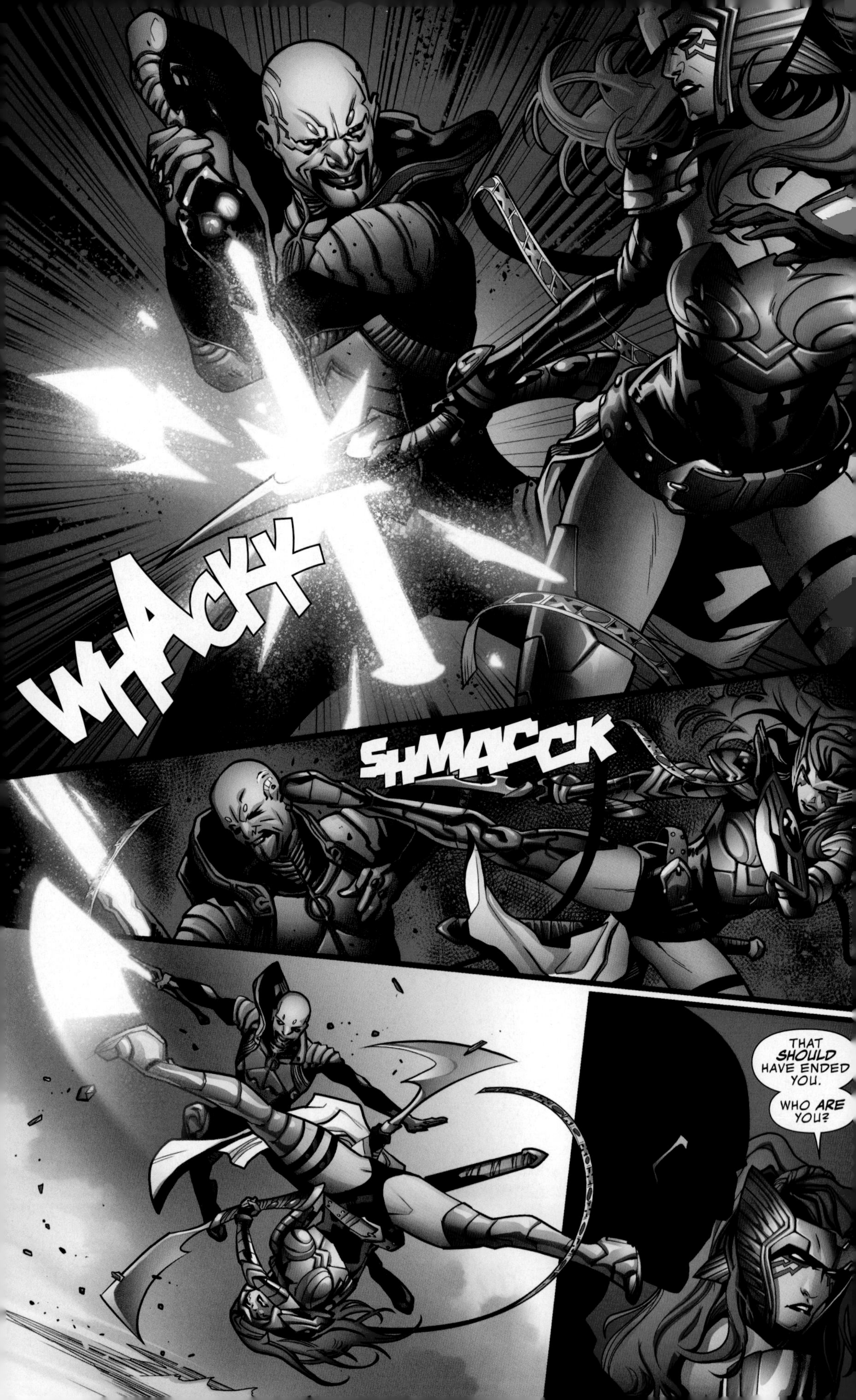
WHACK
SHMACCK
THAT SHOULD HAVE ENDED YOU.
WHO ARE YOU?

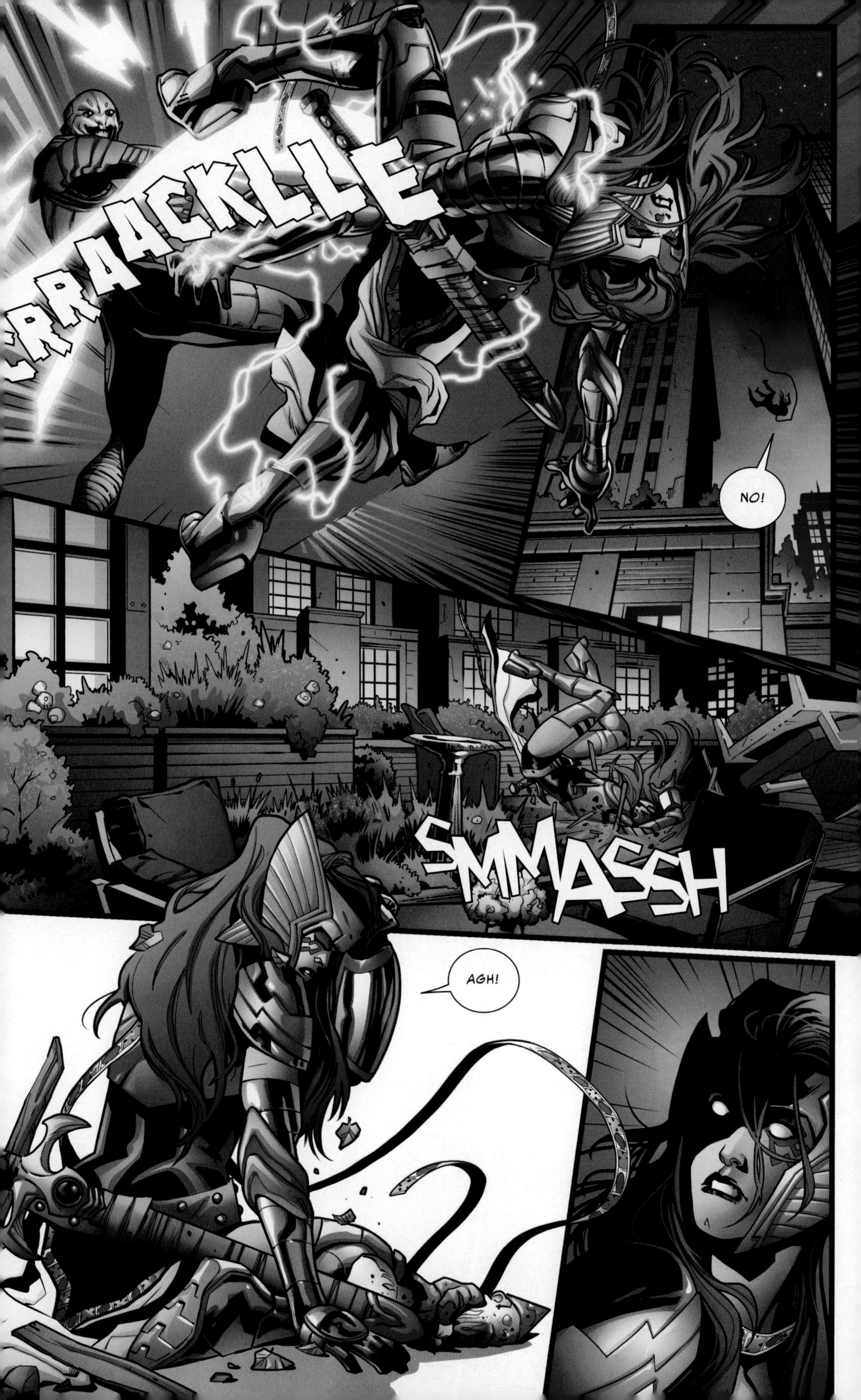
CRRAACKLLE
NO!
SMMASSH
AGH!

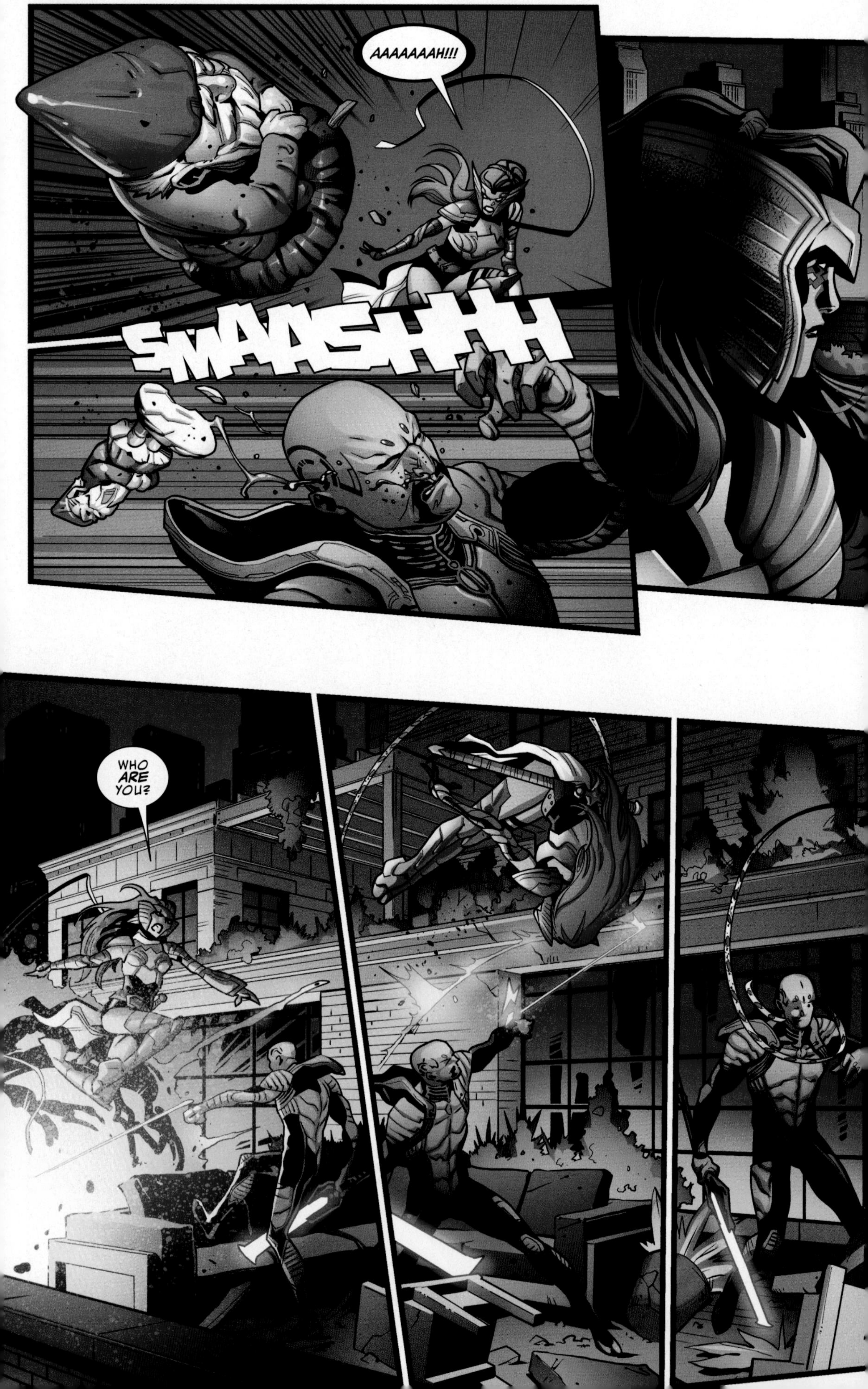
AAAAAAAH!!!
SMAASHHH
WHO ARE YOU?

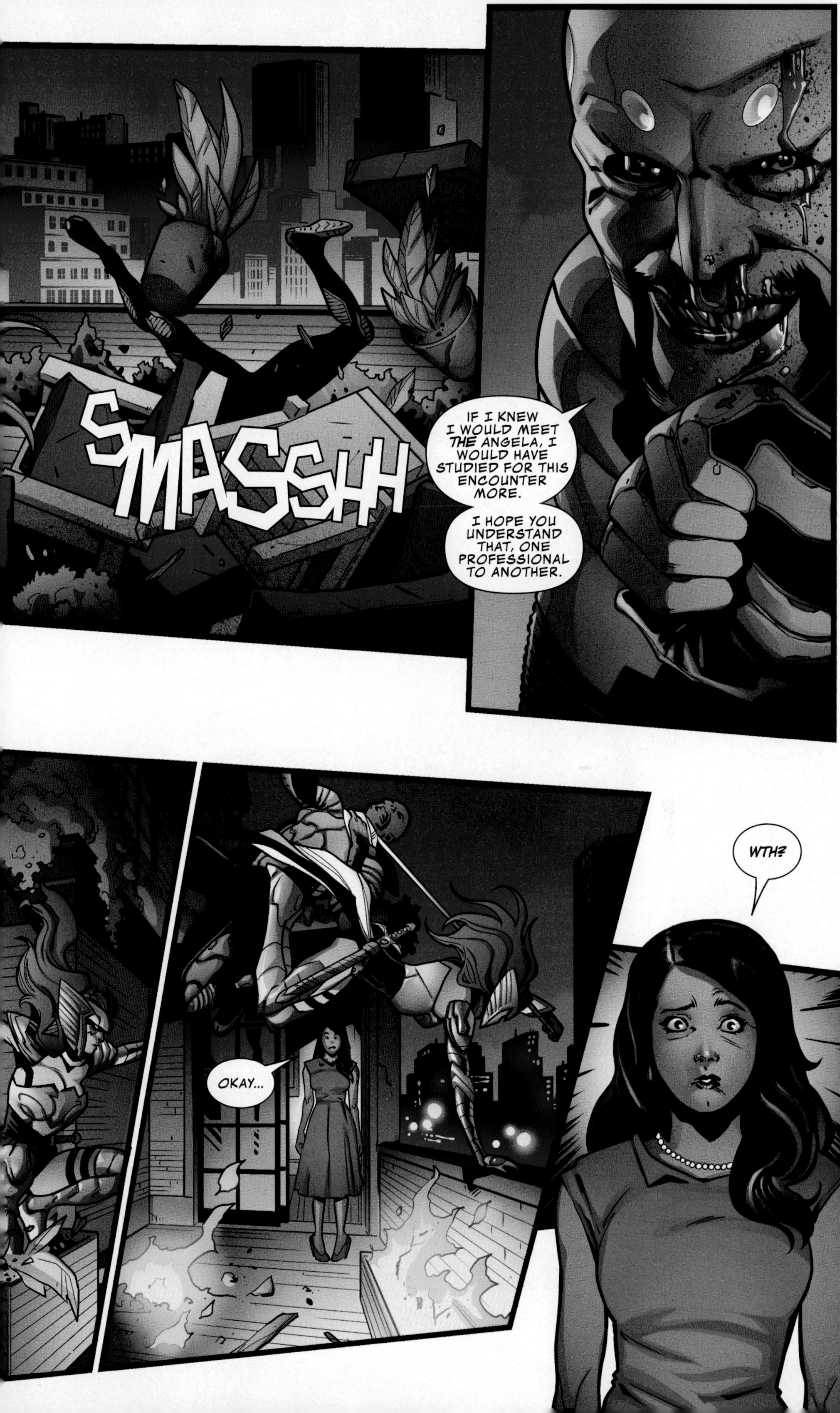
SMASSHH
IF I KNEW I WOULD MEET THE ANGELA, I WOULD HAVE STUDIED FOR THIS ENCOUNTER MORE.
I HOPE YOU UNDERSTAND THAT, ONE PROFESSIONAL TO ANOTHER.
OKAY...
WTH?

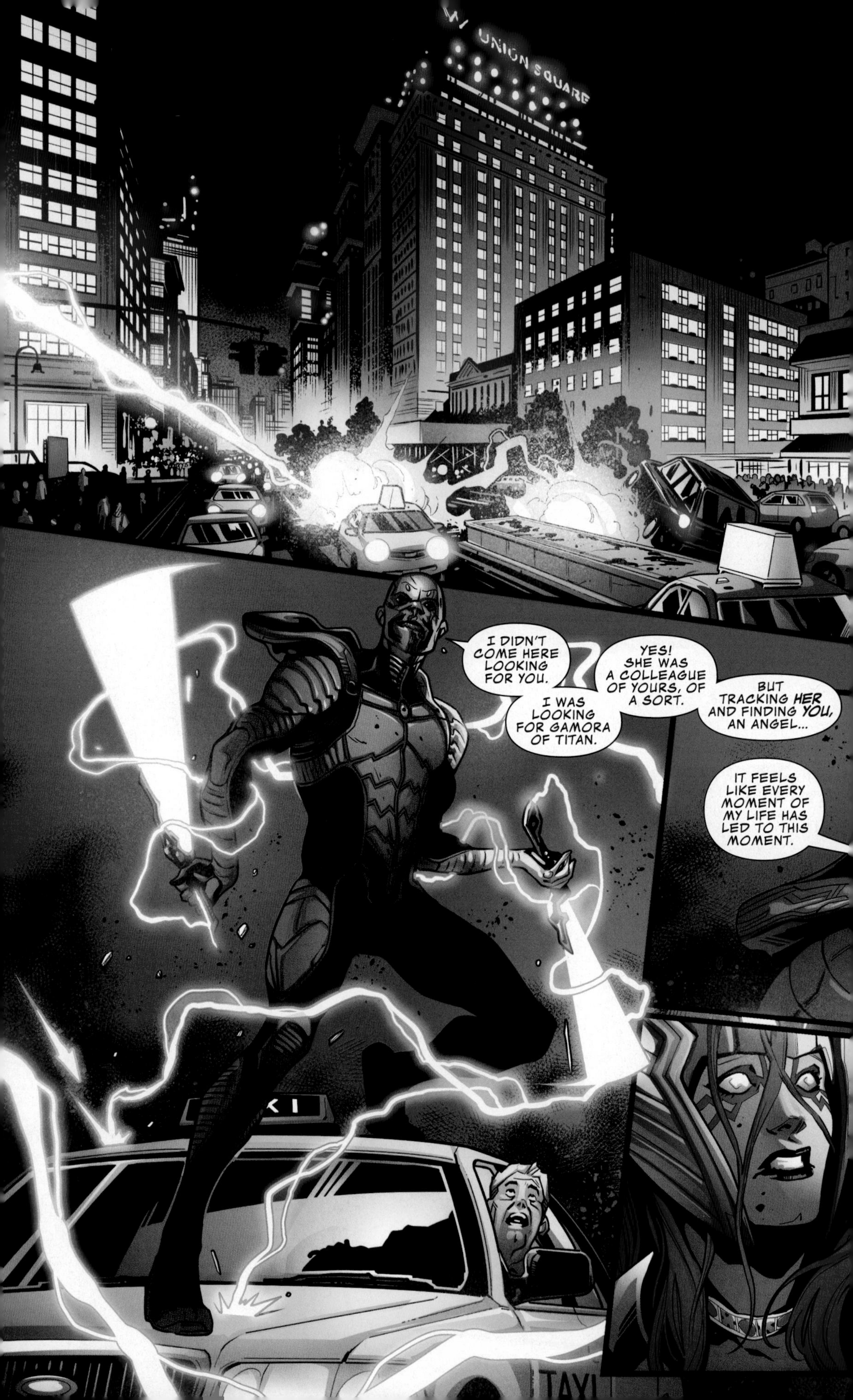
W UNION SQUARE
I DIDN'T COME HERE LOOKING FOR YOU.
I WAS LOOKING FOR GAMORA OF TITAN.
YES! SHE WAS A COLLEAGUE OF YOURS, OF A SORT.
BUT TRACKING HER AND FINDING YOU, AN ANGEL...
IT FEELS LIKE EVERY MOMENT OF MY LIFE HAS LED TO THIS MOMENT.

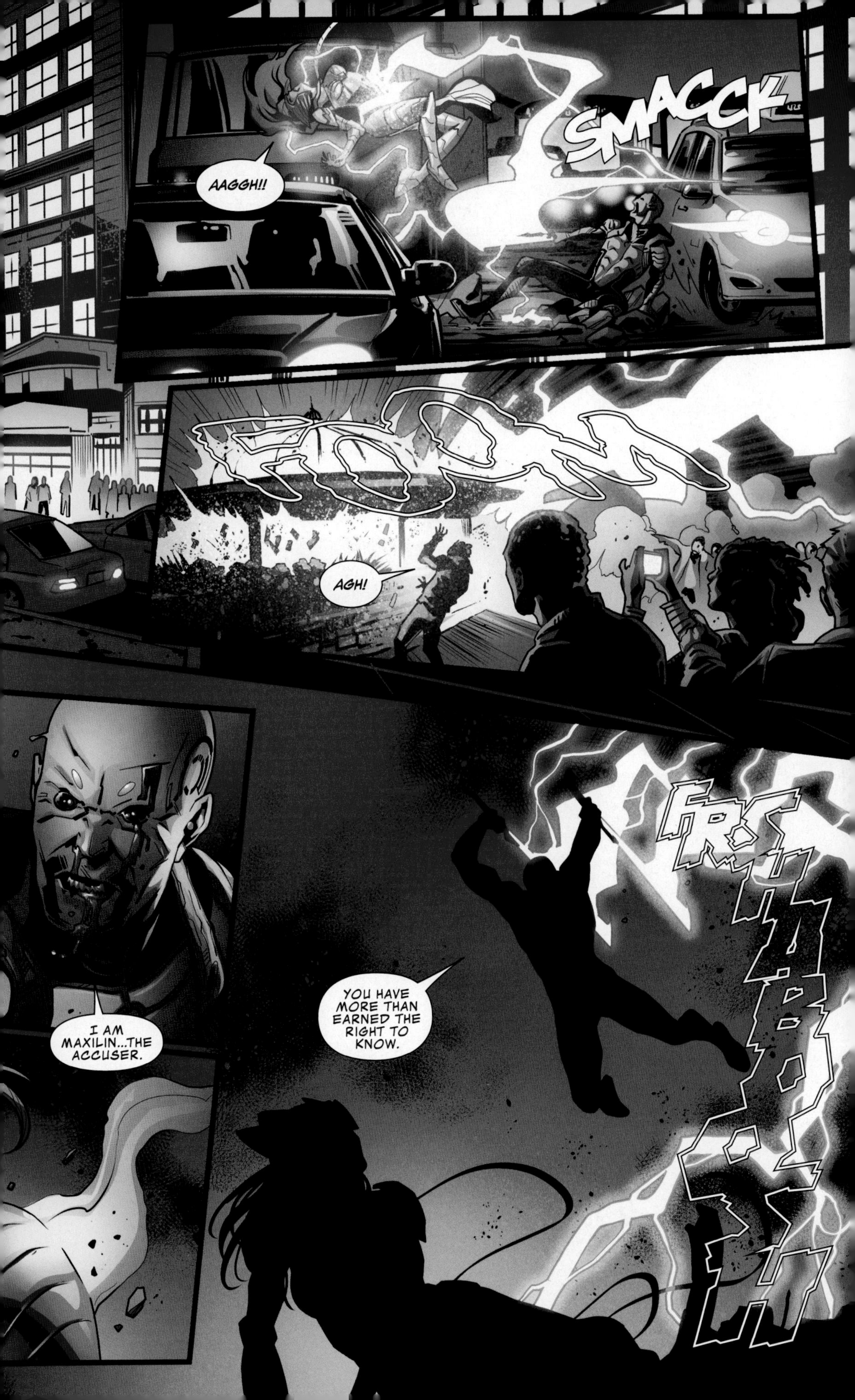
SMACCK
AAGGH!!
AGH!
I AM MAXILIN...THE ACCUSER.
YOU HAVE MORE THAN EARNED THE RIGHT TO KNOW.

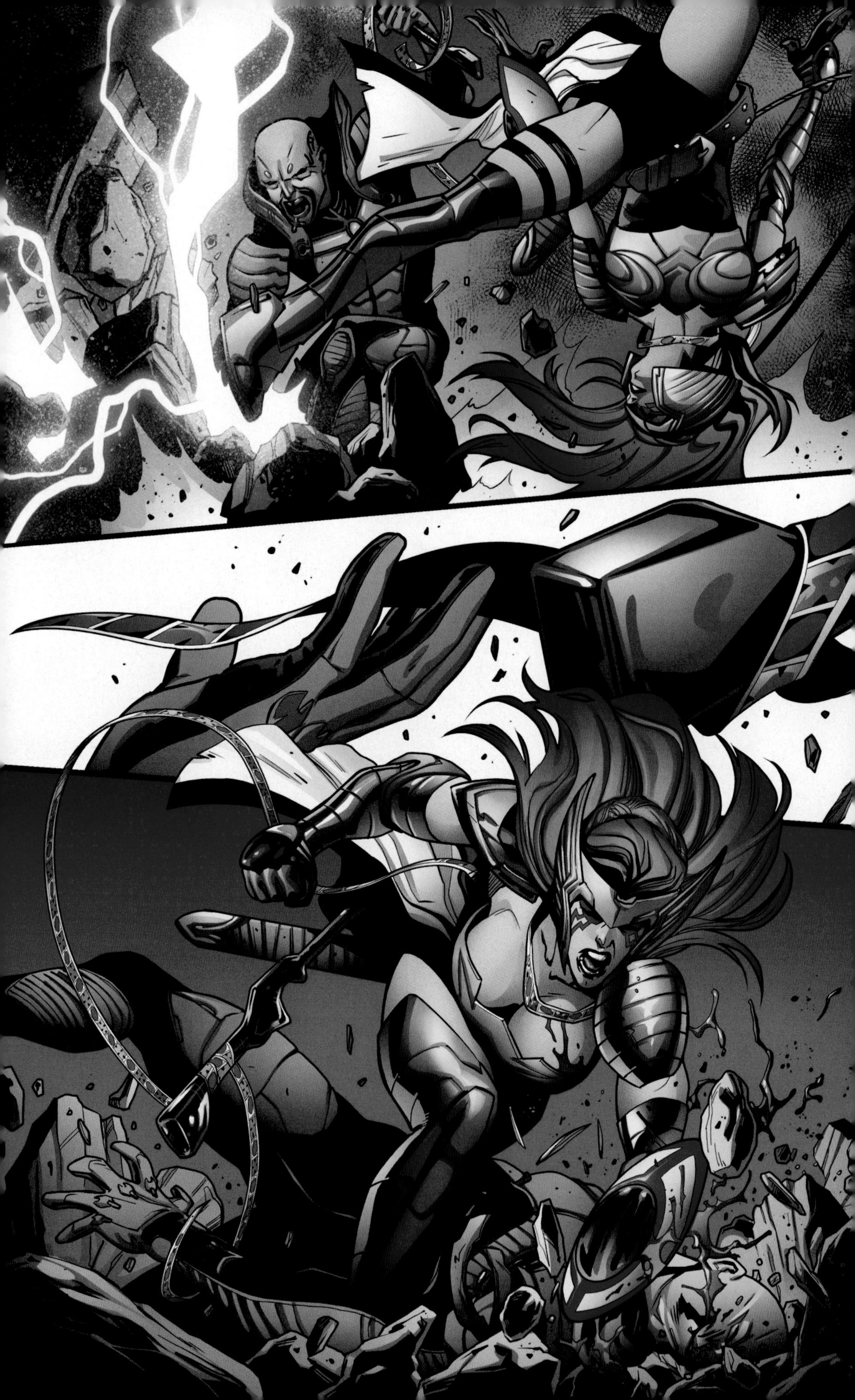

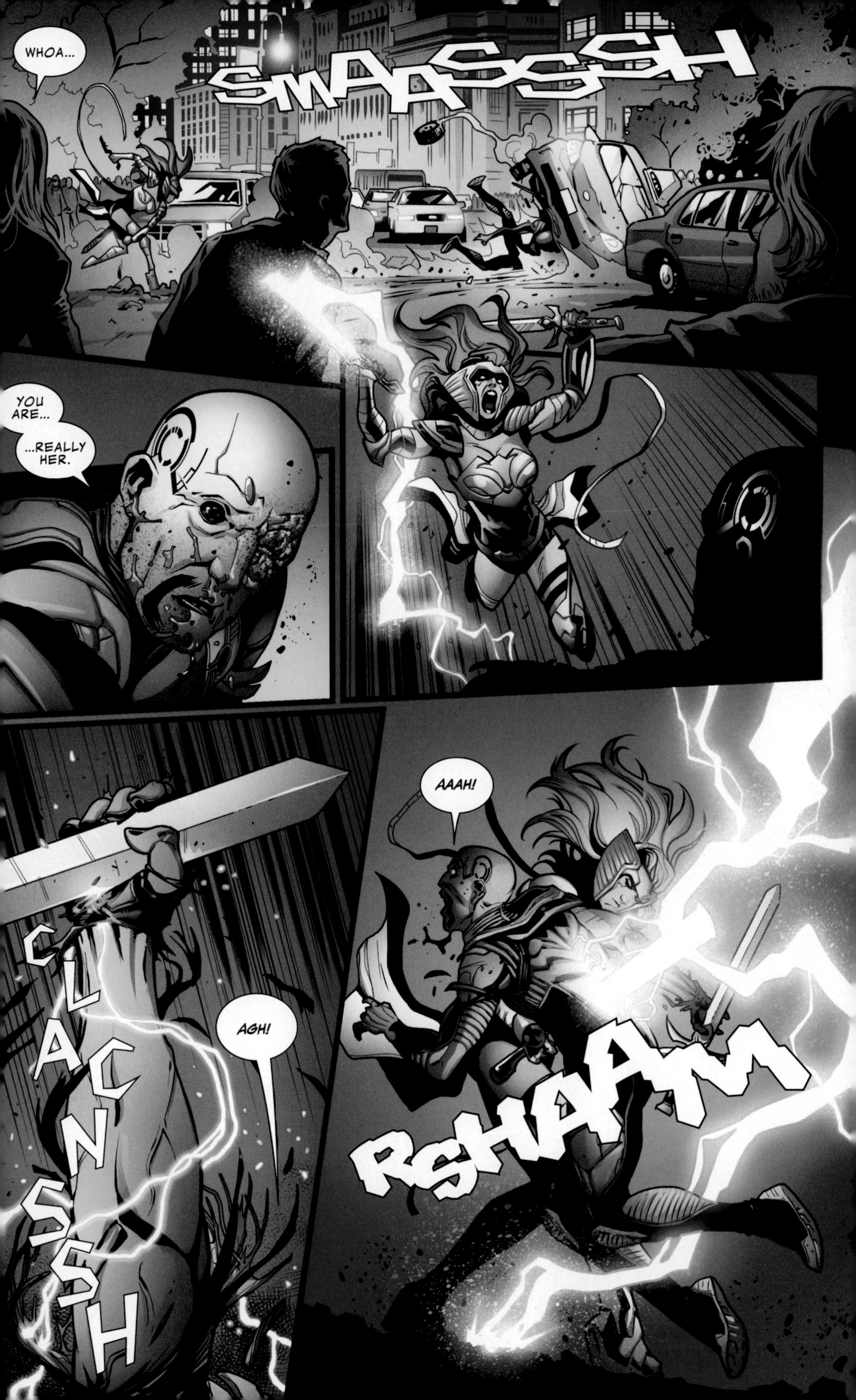
WHOA...
SMAASCH
YOU ARE...
...REALLY HER.
CLLACNSSH
AGH!
AAAH!
RSHAAM

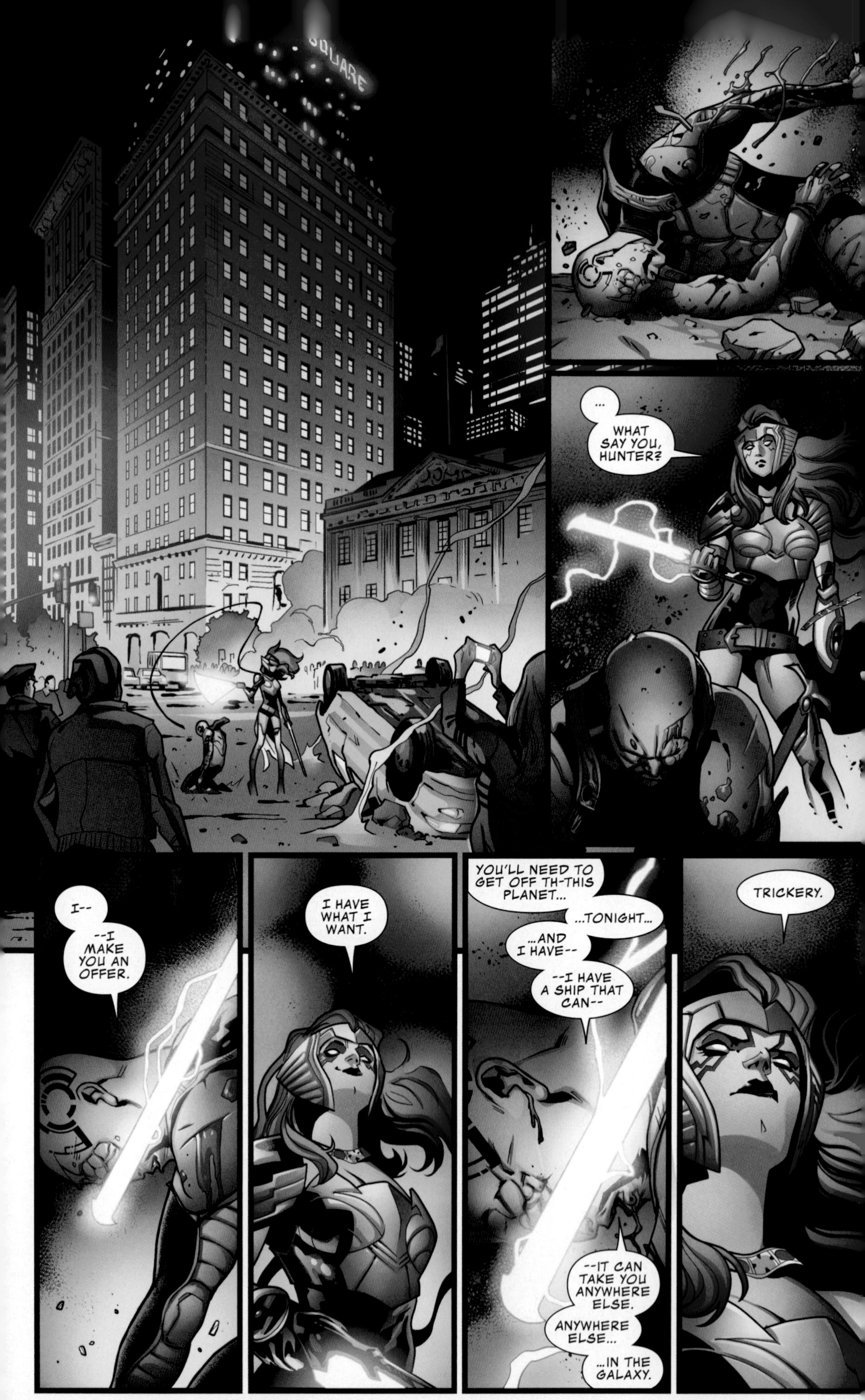
SQUARE
...
WHAT SAY YOU, HUNTER?
I--
--I MAKE YOU AN OFFER.
I HAVE WHAT I WANT.
YOU'LL NEED TO GET OFF TH-THIS PLANET...
...TONIGHT...
...AND I HAVE--
--I HAVE A SHIP THAT CAN--
--IT CAN TAKE YOU ANYWHERE ELSE.
ANYWHERE ELSE...
...IN THE GALAXY.
TRICKERY.

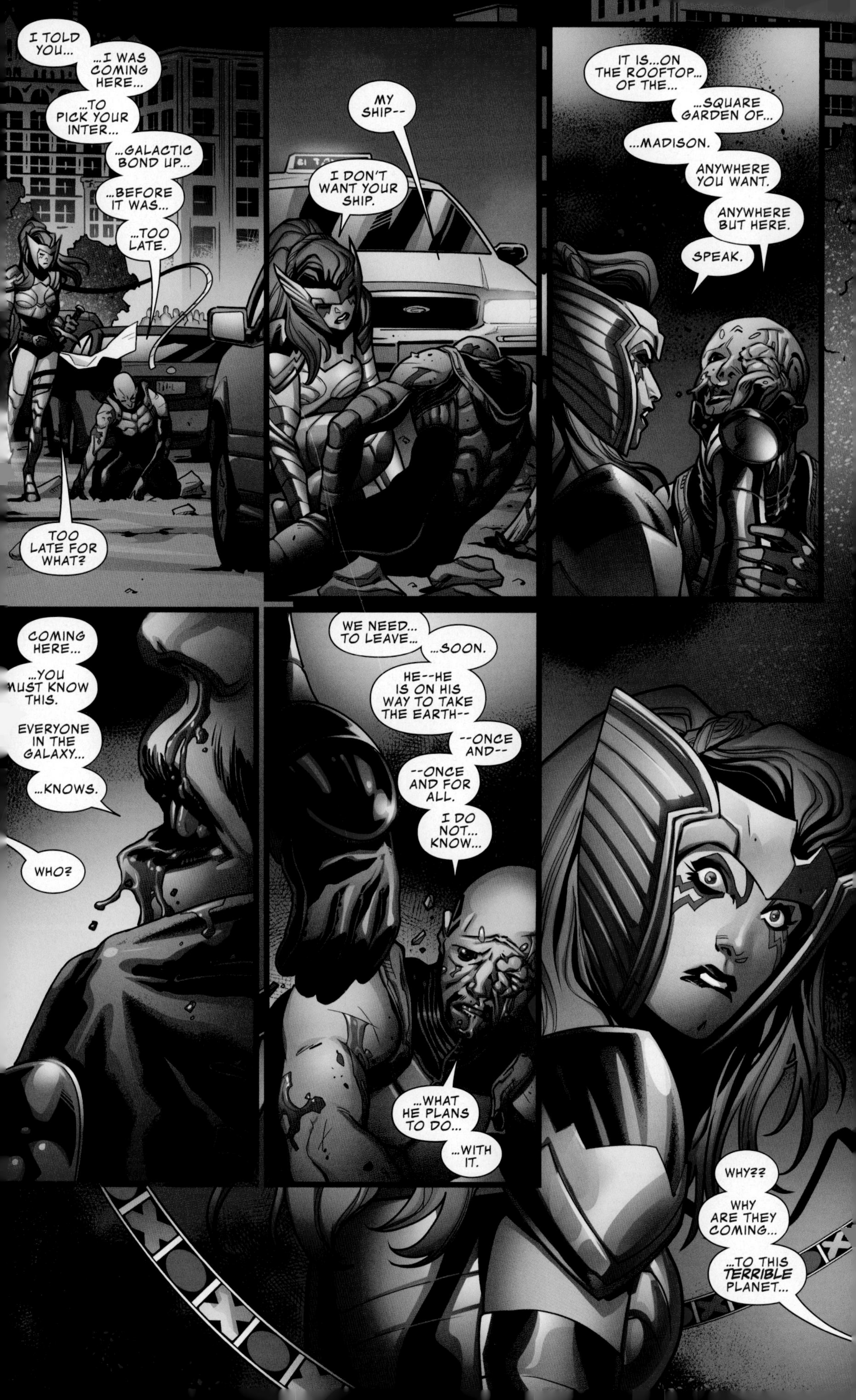
I TOLD YOU...
...I WAS COMING HERE...
...TO PICK YOUR INTER...
...GALACTIC BOND UP...
...BEFORE IT WAS...
...TOO LATE.
TOO LATE FOR WHAT?
MY SHIP--
I DON'T WANT YOUR SHIP.
IT IS...ON THE ROOFTOP... OF THE...
...SQUARE GARDEN OF...
...MADISON.
ANYWHERE YOU WANT.
ANYWHERE BUT HERE.
SPEAK.
COMING HERE...
...YOU MUST KNOW THIS.
EVERYONE IN THE GALAXY...
...KNOWS.
WHO?
WE NEED... TO LEAVE...
...SOON.
HE--HE IS ON HIS WAY TO TAKE THE EARTH--
--ONCE AND--
--ONCE AND FOR ALL.
I DO NOT... KNOW...
...WHAT HE PLANS TO DO...
...WITH IT.
WHY??
WHY ARE THEY COMING...
...TO THIS *TERRIBLE* PLANET...

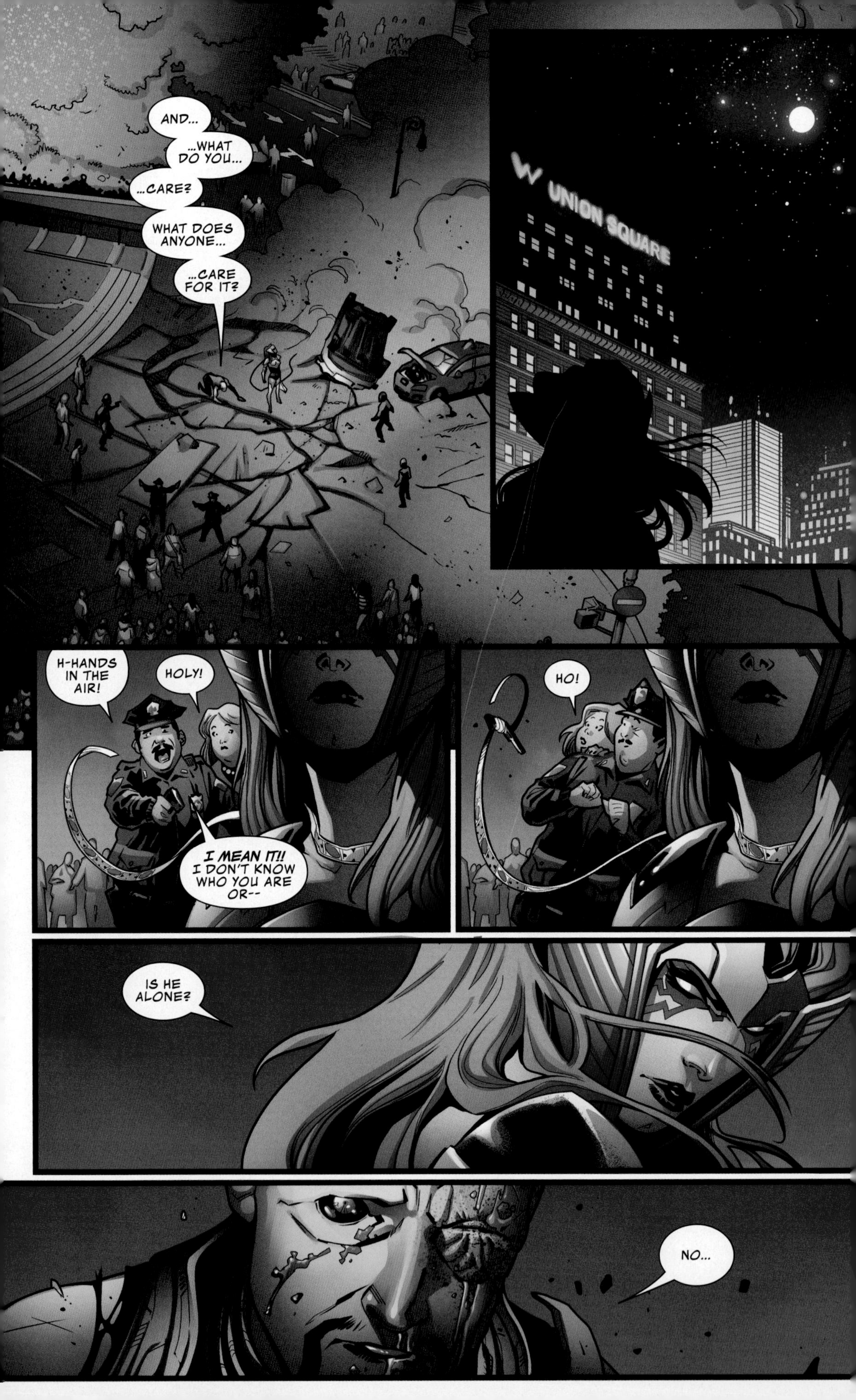
AND...
...WHAT DO YOU...
...CARE?
WHAT DOES ANYONE...
...CARE FOR IT?
UNION SQUARE
H-HANDS IN THE AIR!
HOLY!
I MEAN IT!! I DON'T KNOW WHO YOU ARE OR--
HO!
IS HE ALONE?
NO...

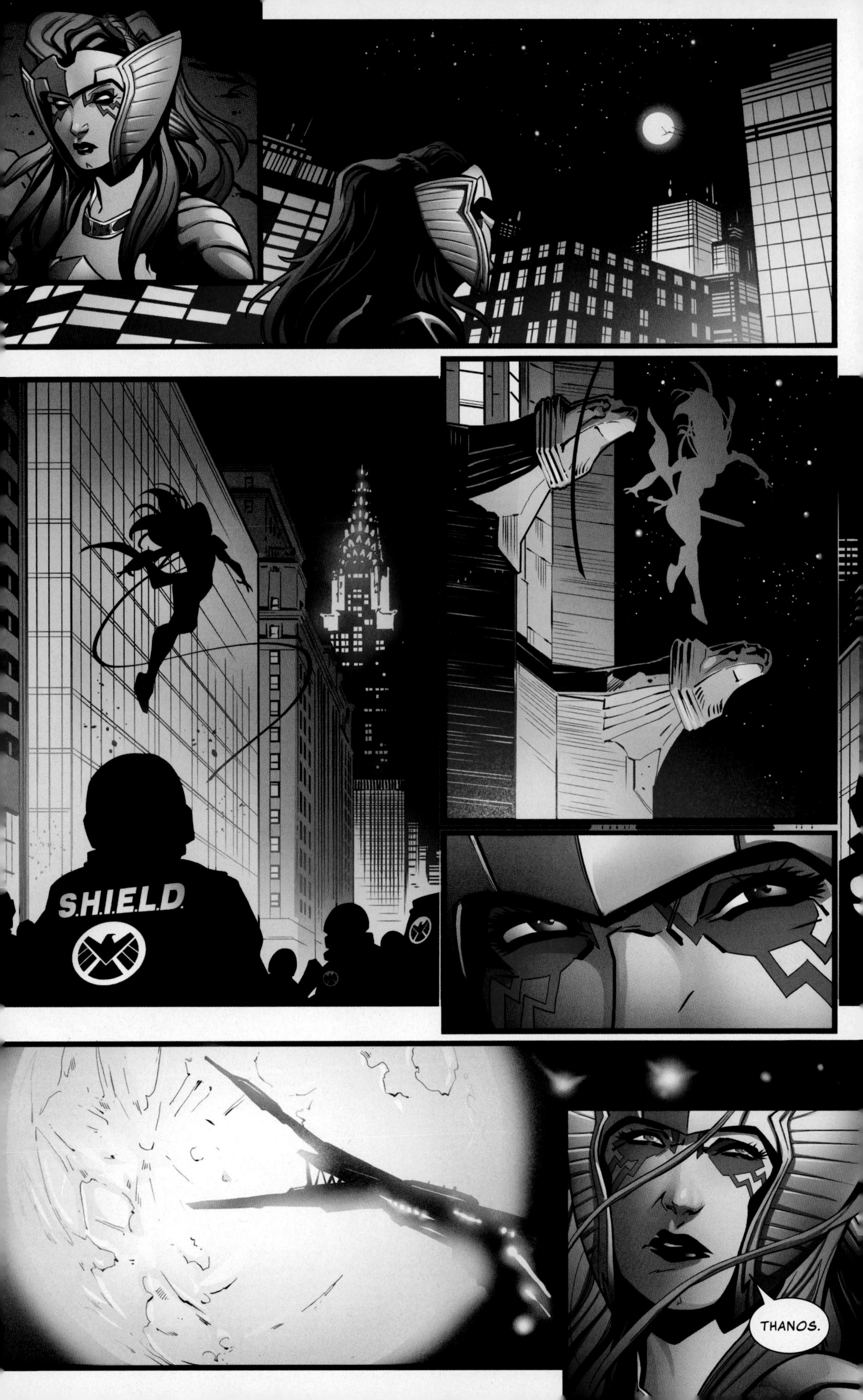
S.H.I.E.L.D.
THANOS.

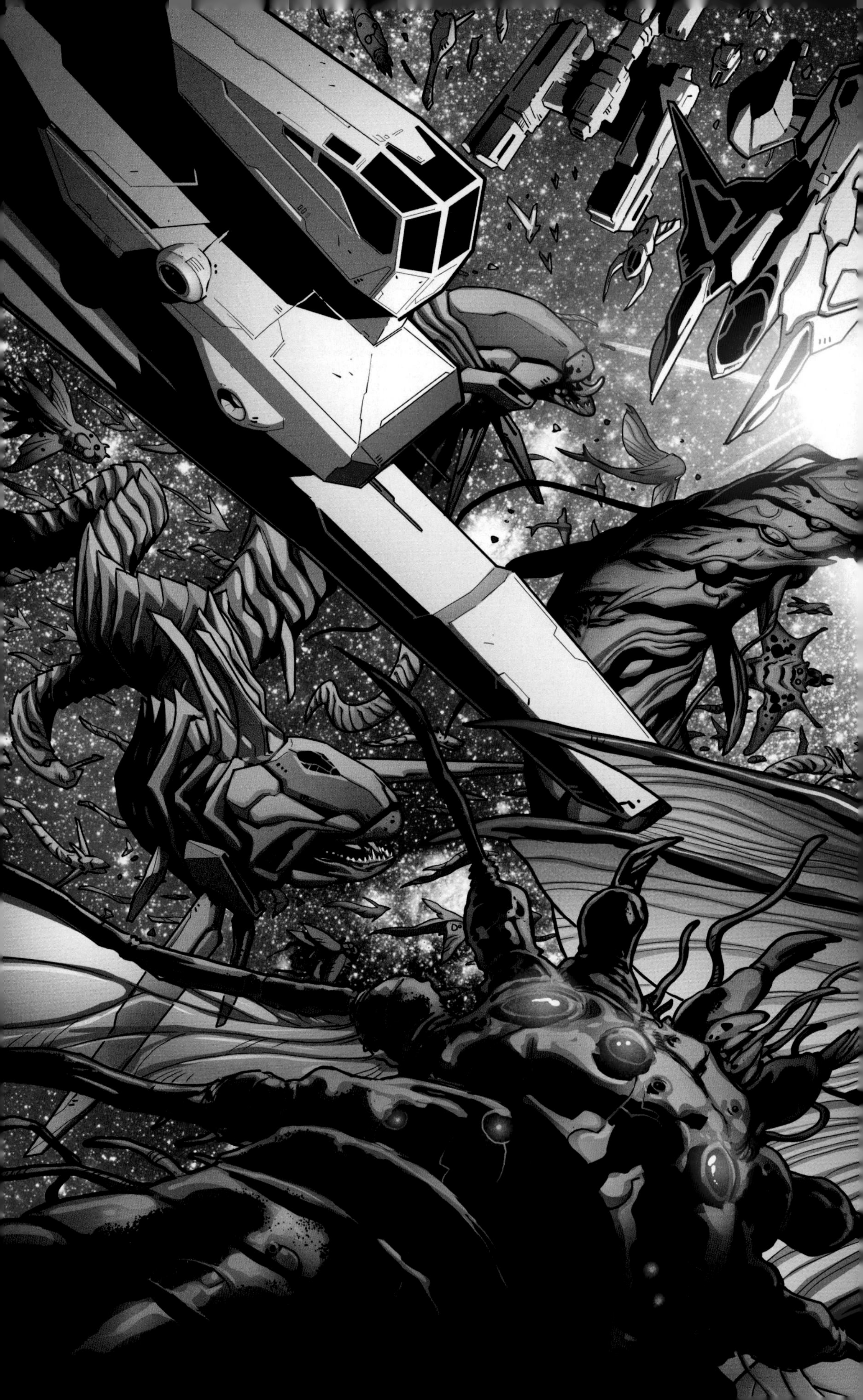

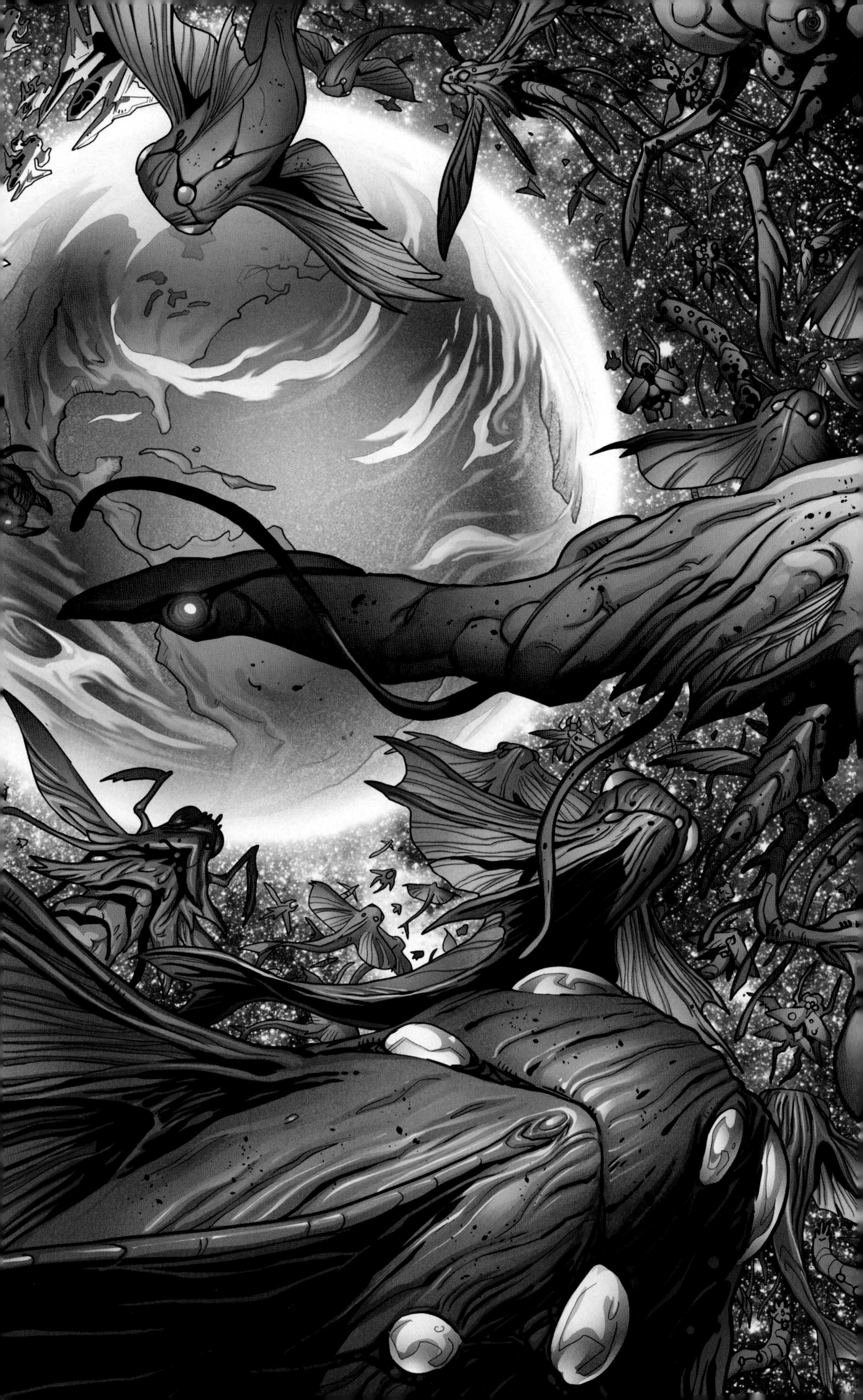

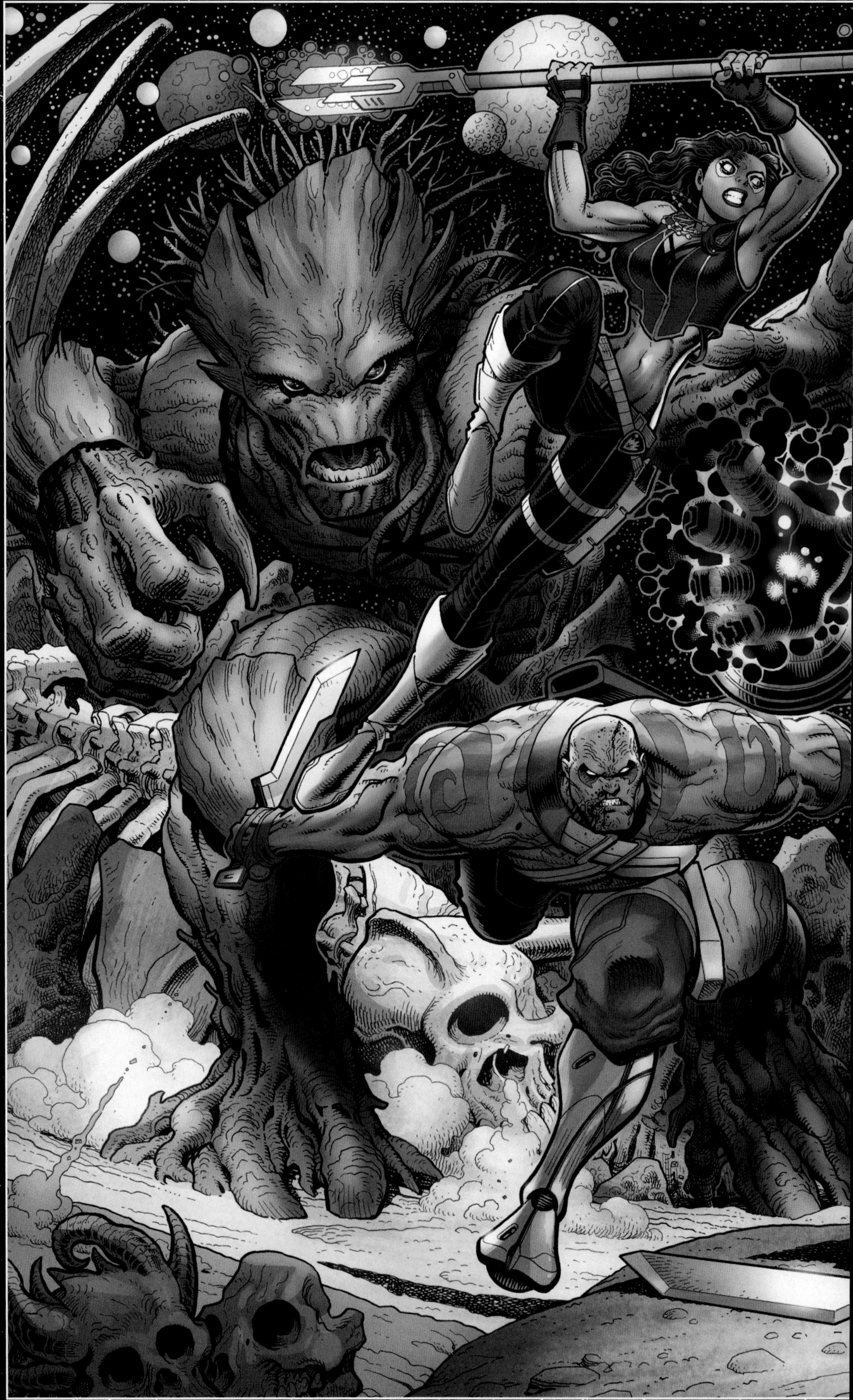

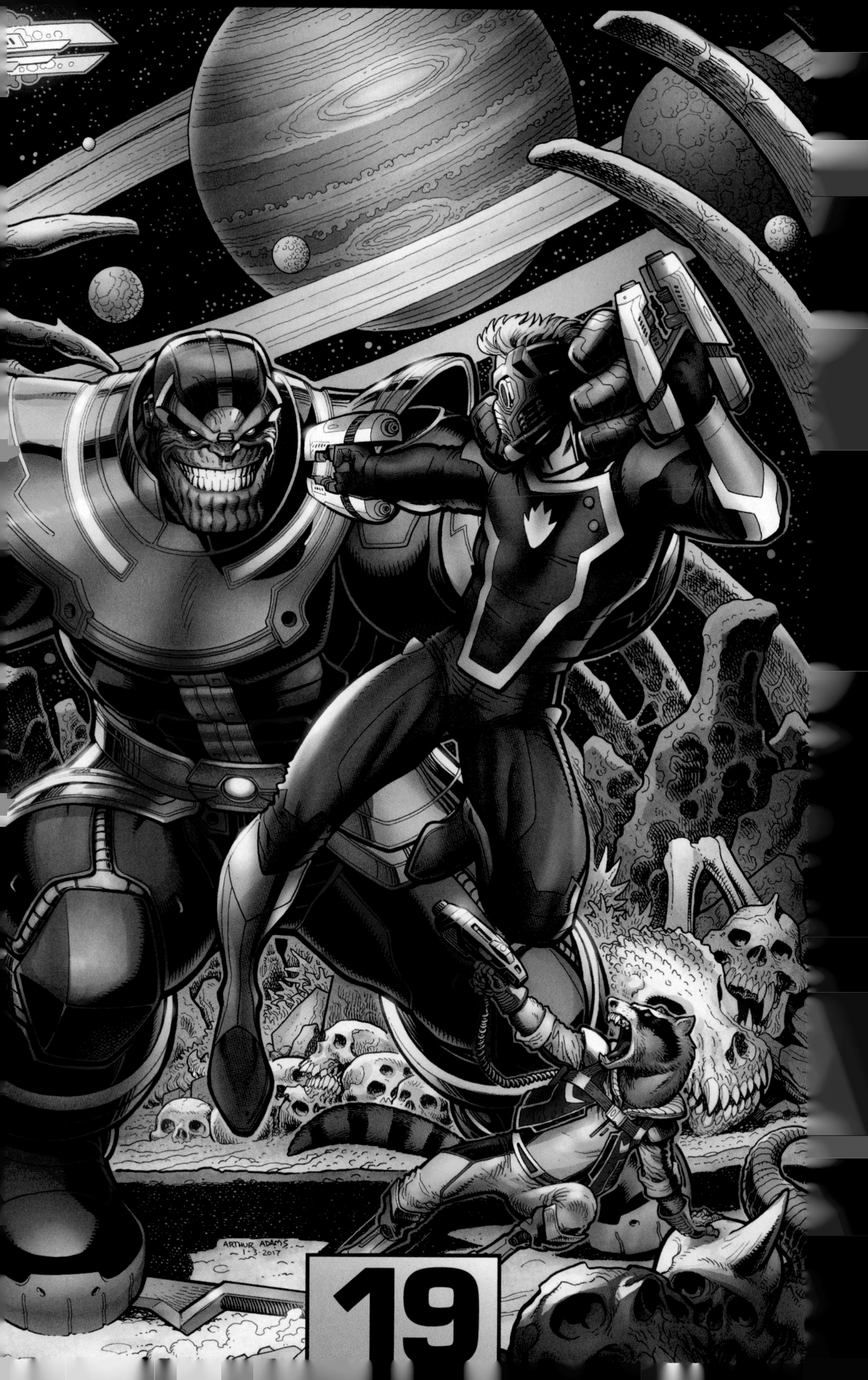
ARTHUR ADAMS
1-3-2017
19

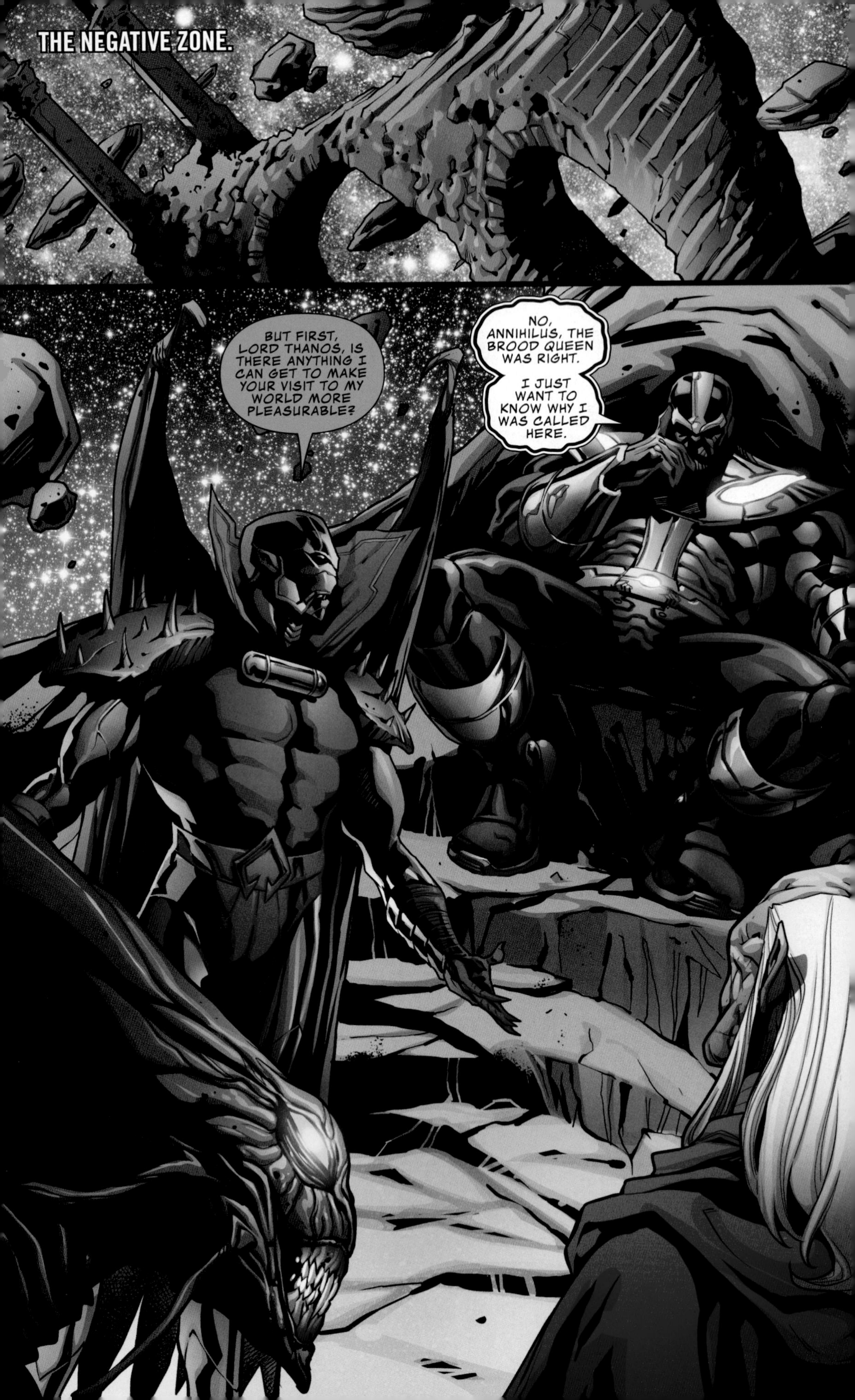
THE NEGATIVE ZONE.
BUT FIRST, LORD THANOS, IS THERE ANYTHING I CAN GET TO MAKE YOUR VISIT TO MY WORLD MORE PLEASURABLE?
NO, ANNIHILUS, THE BROOD QUEEN WAS RIGHT.
I JUST WANT TO KNOW WHY I WAS CALLED HERE.

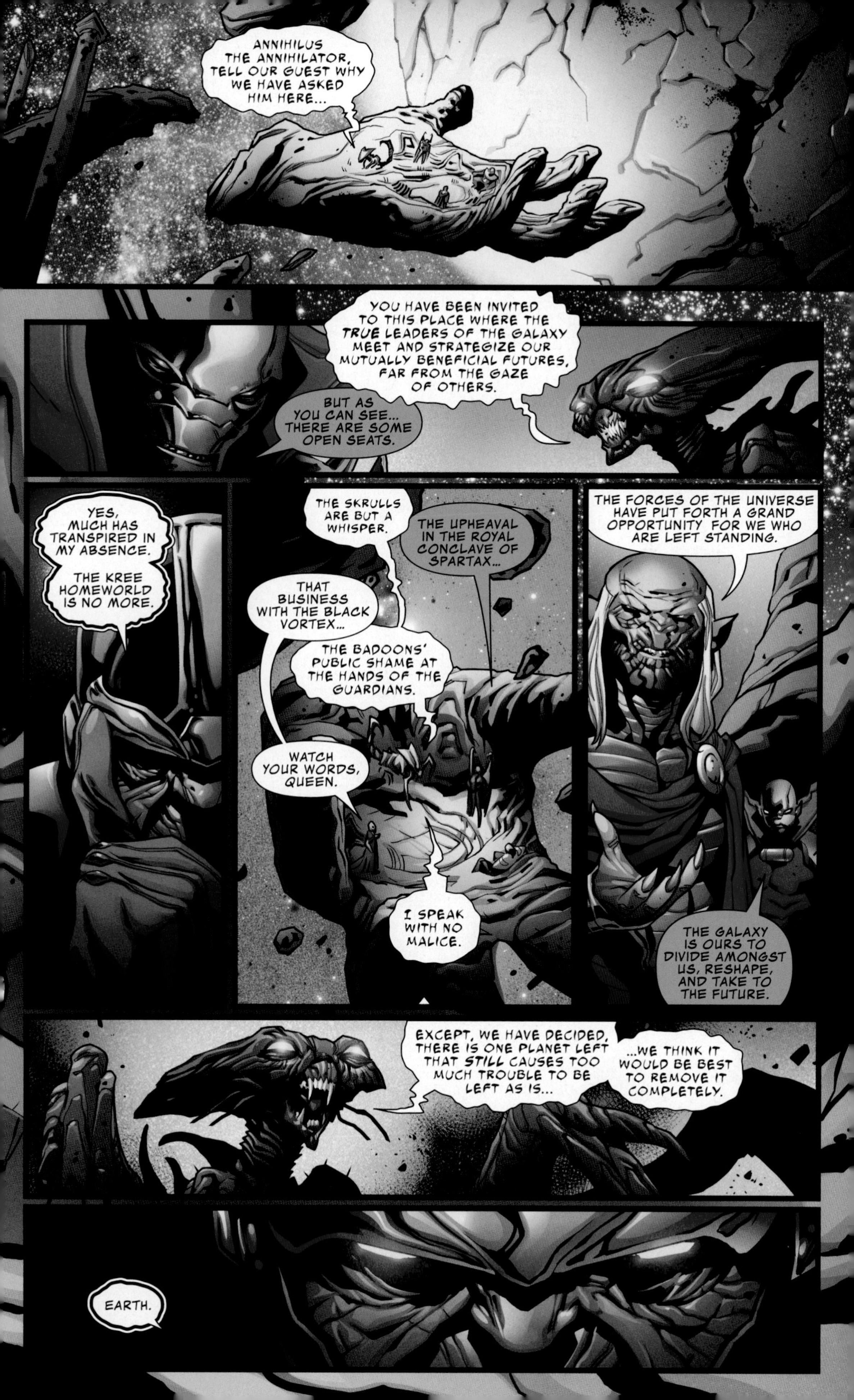
ANNIHILUS THE ANNIHILATOR, TELL OUR GUEST WHY WE HAVE ASKED HIM HERE...
YOU HAVE BEEN INVITED TO THIS PLACE WHERE THE TRUE LEADERS OF THE GALAXY MEET AND STRATEGIZE OUR MUTUALLY BENEFICIAL FUTURES, FAR FROM THE GAZE OF OTHERS.
BUT AS YOU CAN SEE... THERE ARE SOME OPEN SEATS.
YES, MUCH HAS TRANSPIRED IN MY ABSENCE.
THE KREE HOMEWORLD IS NO MORE.
THE SKRULLS ARE BUT A WHISPER.
THE UPHEAVAL IN THE ROYAL CONCLAVE OF SPARTAX...
THAT BUSINESS WITH THE BLACK VORTEX...
THE BADOONS' PUBLIC SHAME AT THE HANDS OF THE GUARDIANS.
WATCH YOUR WORDS, QUEEN.
I SPEAK WITH NO MALICE.
THE FORCES OF THE UNIVERSE HAVE PUT FORTH A GRAND OPPORTUNITY FOR WE WHO ARE LEFT STANDING.
THE GALAXY IS OURS TO DIVIDE AMONGST US, RESHAPE, AND TAKE TO THE FUTURE.
EXCEPT, WE HAVE DECIDED, THERE IS ONE PLANET LEFT THAT STILL CAUSES TOO MUCH TROUBLE TO BE LEFT AS IS...
...WE THINK IT WOULD BE BEST TO REMOVE IT COMPLETELY.
EARTH.

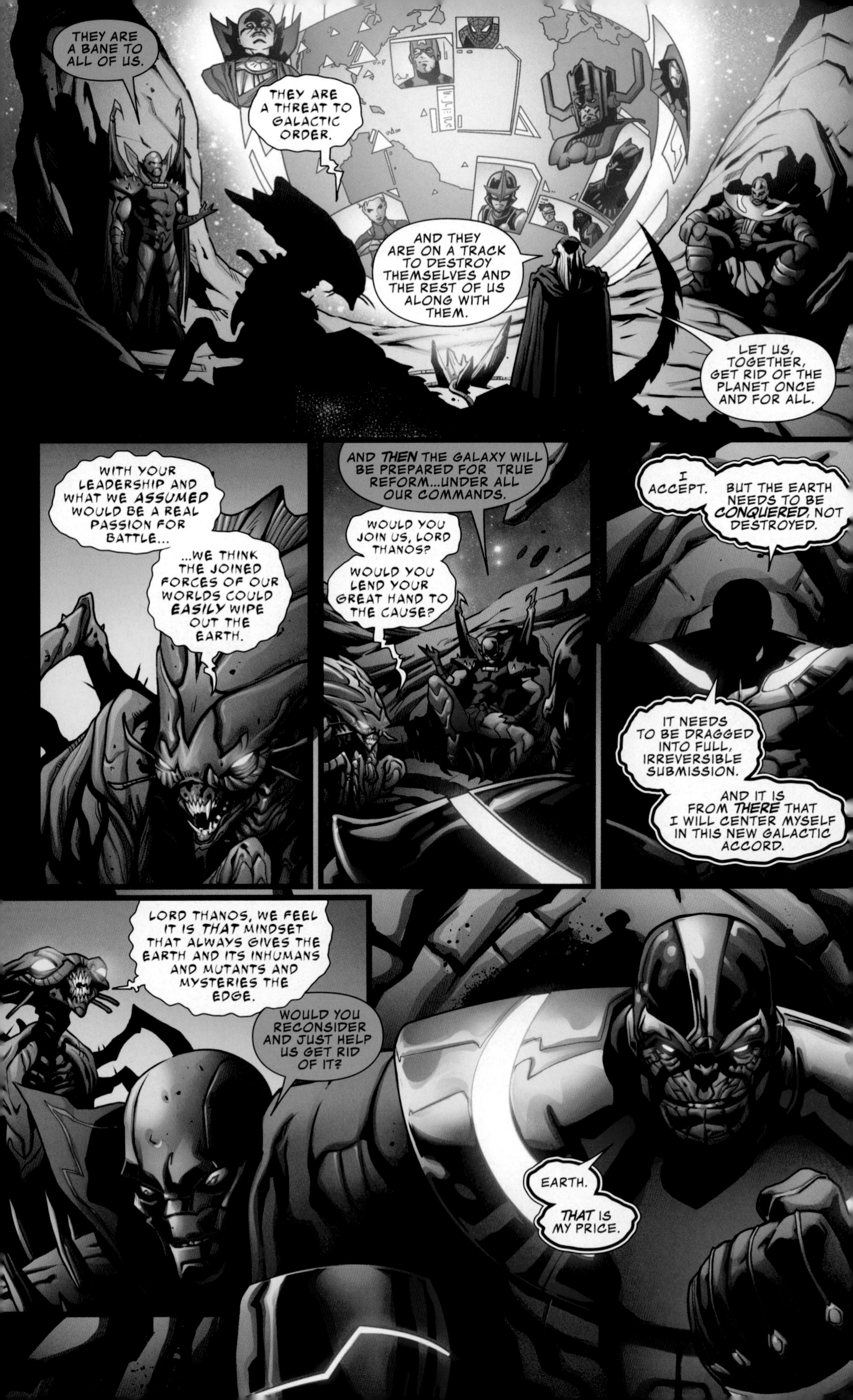
THEY ARE A BANE TO ALL OF US.
THEY ARE A THREAT TO GALACTIC ORDER.
AND THEY ARE ON A TRACK TO DESTROY THEMSELVES AND THE REST OF US ALONG WITH THEM.
LET US, TOGETHER, GET RID OF THE PLANET ONCE AND FOR ALL.
WITH YOUR LEADERSHIP AND WHAT WE ASSUMED WOULD BE A REAL PASSION FOR BATTLE...
...WE THINK THE JOINED FORCES OF OUR WORLDS COULD EASILY WIPE OUT THE EARTH.
AND THEN THE GALAXY WILL BE PREPARED FOR TRUE REFORM...UNDER ALL OUR COMMANDS.
WOULD YOU JOIN US, LORD THANOS?
WOULD YOU LEND YOUR GREAT HAND TO THE CAUSE?
I ACCEPT.
BUT THE EARTH NEEDS TO BE CONQUERED, NOT DESTROYED.
IT NEEDS TO BE DRAGGED INTO FULL, IRREVERSIBLE SUBMISSION.
AND IT IS FROM THERE THAT I WILL CENTER MYSELF IN THIS NEW GALACTIC ACCORD.
LORD THANOS, WE FEEL IT IS THAT MINDSET THAT ALWAYS GIVES THE EARTH AND ITS INHUMANS AND MUTANTS AND MYSTERIES THE EDGE.
WOULD YOU RECONSIDER AND JUST HELP US GET RID OF IT?
EARTH.
THAT IS MY PRICE.

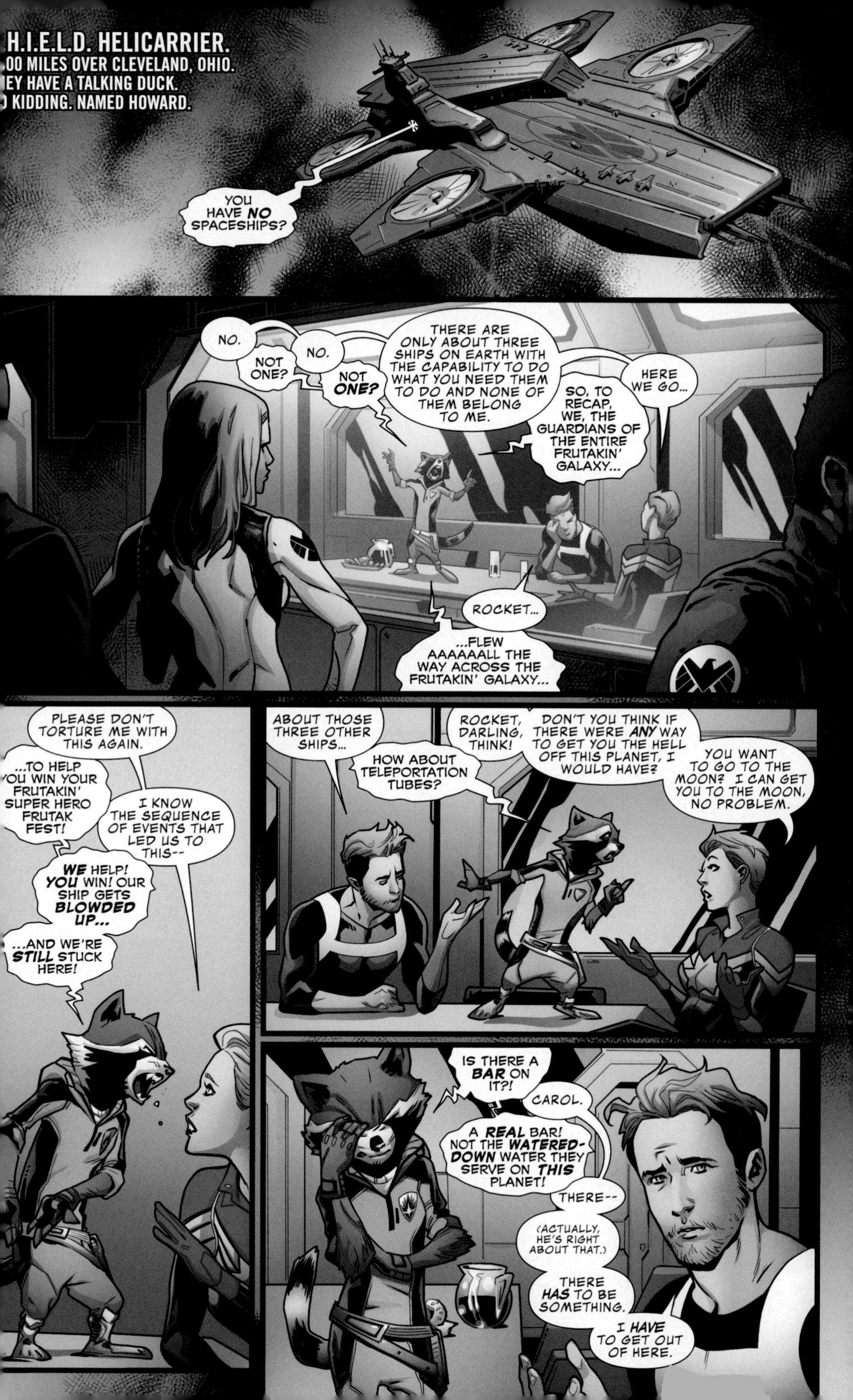

H.I.E.L.D. HELICARRIER.
00 MILES OVER CLEVELAND, OHIO.
EY HAVE A TALKING DUCK.
KIDDING. NAMED HOWARD.
YOU HAVE NO SPACESHIPS?
NO.
NOT ONE?
NO.
NOT ONE?
THERE ARE ONLY ABOUT THREE SHIPS ON EARTH WITH THE CAPABILITY TO DO WHAT YOU NEED THEM TO DO AND NONE OF THEM BELONG TO ME.
HERE WE GO...
SO, TO RECAP, WE, THE GUARDIANS OF THE ENTIRE FRUTAKIN' GALAXY...
ROCKET...
...FLEW AAAAAALL THE WAY ACROSS THE FRUTAKIN' GALAXY...
PLEASE DON'T TORTURE ME WITH THIS AGAIN.
...TO HELP YOU WIN YOUR FRUTAKIN' SUPER HERO FRUTAK FEST!
I KNOW THE SEQUENCE OF EVENTS THAT LED US TO THIS--
WE HELP! YOU WIN! OUR SHIP GETS BLOWDED UP...
...AND WE'RE STILL STUCK HERE!
ABOUT THOSE THREE OTHER SHIPS...
HOW ABOUT TELEPORTATION TUBES?
ROCKET, DARLING, THINK!
DON'T YOU THINK IF THERE WERE ANY WAY TO GET YOU THE HELL OFF THIS PLANET, I WOULD HAVE?
YOU WANT TO GO TO THE MOON? I CAN GET YOU TO THE MOON, NO PROBLEM.
IS THERE A BAR ON IT?!
CAROL.
A REAL BAR! NOT THE WATERED-DOWN WATER THEY SERVE ON THIS PLANET!
THERE--
(ACTUALLY, HE'S RIGHT ABOUT THAT.)
THERE HAS TO BE SOMETHING.
I HAVE TO GET OUT OF HERE.

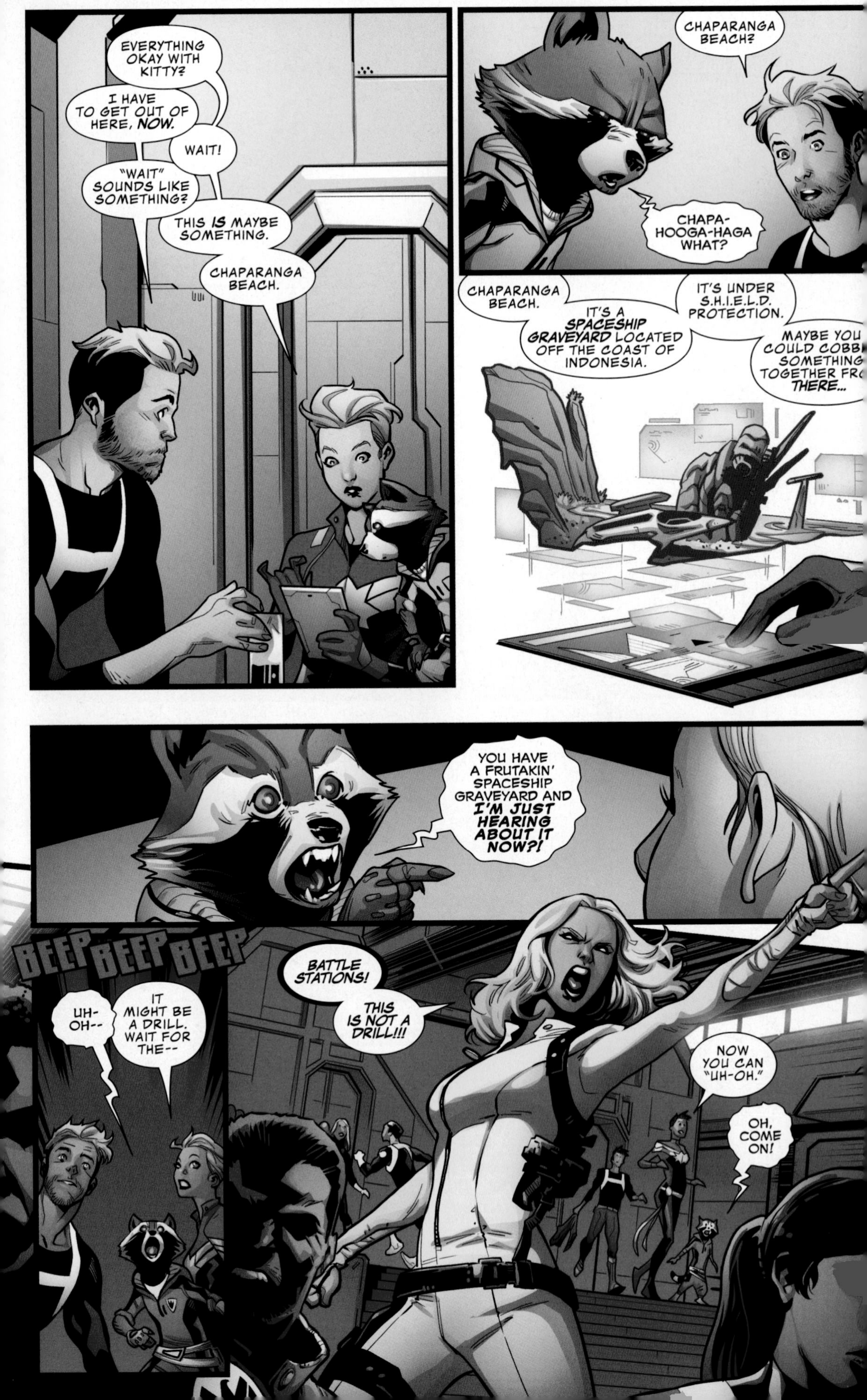
EVERYTHING OKAY WITH KITTY?
I HAVE TO GET OUT OF HERE, NOW.
WAIT!
"WAIT" SOUNDS LIKE SOMETHING?
THIS IS MAYBE SOMETHING.
CHAPARANGA BEACH.
CHAPARANGA BEACH?
CHAPA-HOOGA-HAGA WHAT?
CHAPARANGA BEACH.
IT'S A SPACESHIP GRAVEYARD LOCATED OFF THE COAST OF INDONESIA.
IT'S UNDER S.H.I.E.L.D. PROTECTION.
MAYBE YOU COULD COBB SOMETHING TOGETHER FR THERE...
YOU HAVE A FRUTAKIN' SPACESHIP GRAVEYARD AND I'M JUST HEARING ABOUT IT NOW?!
BEEP BEEP BEEP
UH-OH--
IT MIGHT BE A DRILL. WAIT FOR THE--
BATTLE STATIONS!
THIS IS NOT A DRILL!!!
NOW YOU CAN "UH-OH."
OH, COME ON!

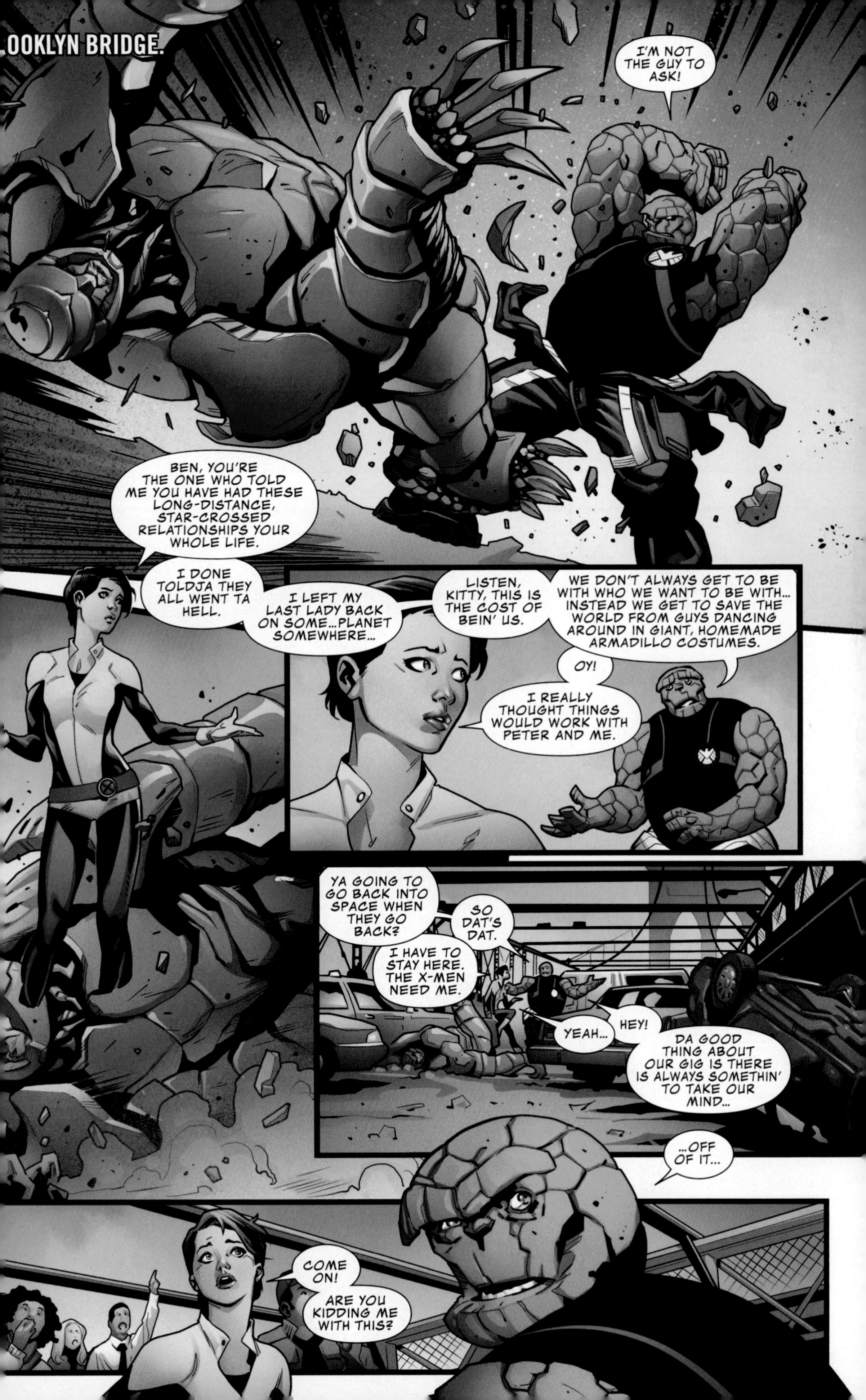
OOKLYN BRIDGE.
I'M NOT THE GUY TO ASK!
BEN, YOU'RE THE ONE WHO TOLD ME YOU HAVE HAD THESE LONG-DISTANCE, STAR-CROSSED RELATIONSHIPS YOUR WHOLE LIFE.
I DONE TOLDJA THEY ALL WENT TA HELL.
I LEFT MY LAST LADY BACK ON SOME...PLANET SOMEWHERE...
LISTEN, KITTY, THIS IS THE COST OF BEIN' US.
WE DON'T ALWAYS GET TO BE WITH WHO WE WANT TO BE WITH... INSTEAD WE GET TO SAVE THE WORLD FROM GUYS DANCING AROUND IN GIANT, HOMEMADE ARMADILLO COSTUMES.
OY!
I REALLY THOUGHT THINGS WOULD WORK WITH PETER AND ME.
YA GOING TO GO BACK INTO SPACE WHEN THEY GO BACK?
SO DAT'S DAT.
I HAVE TO STAY HERE. THE X-MEN NEED ME.
YEAH...
HEY!
DA GOOD THING ABOUT OUR GIG IS THERE IS ALWAYS SOMETHIN' TO TAKE OUR MIND...
...OFF OF IT...
COME ON!
ARE YOU KIDDING ME WITH THIS?

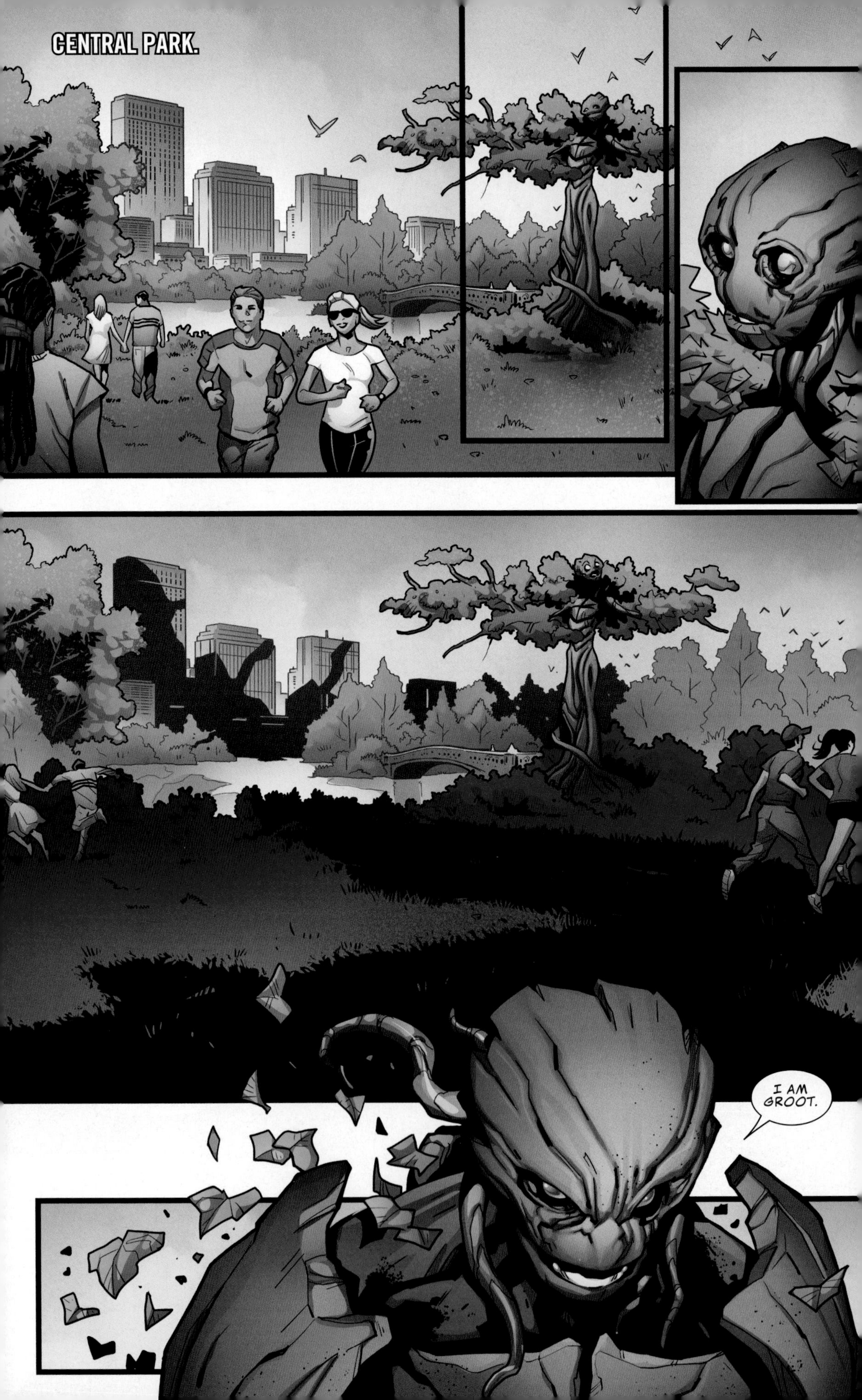
CENTRAL PARK.
I AM GROOT.

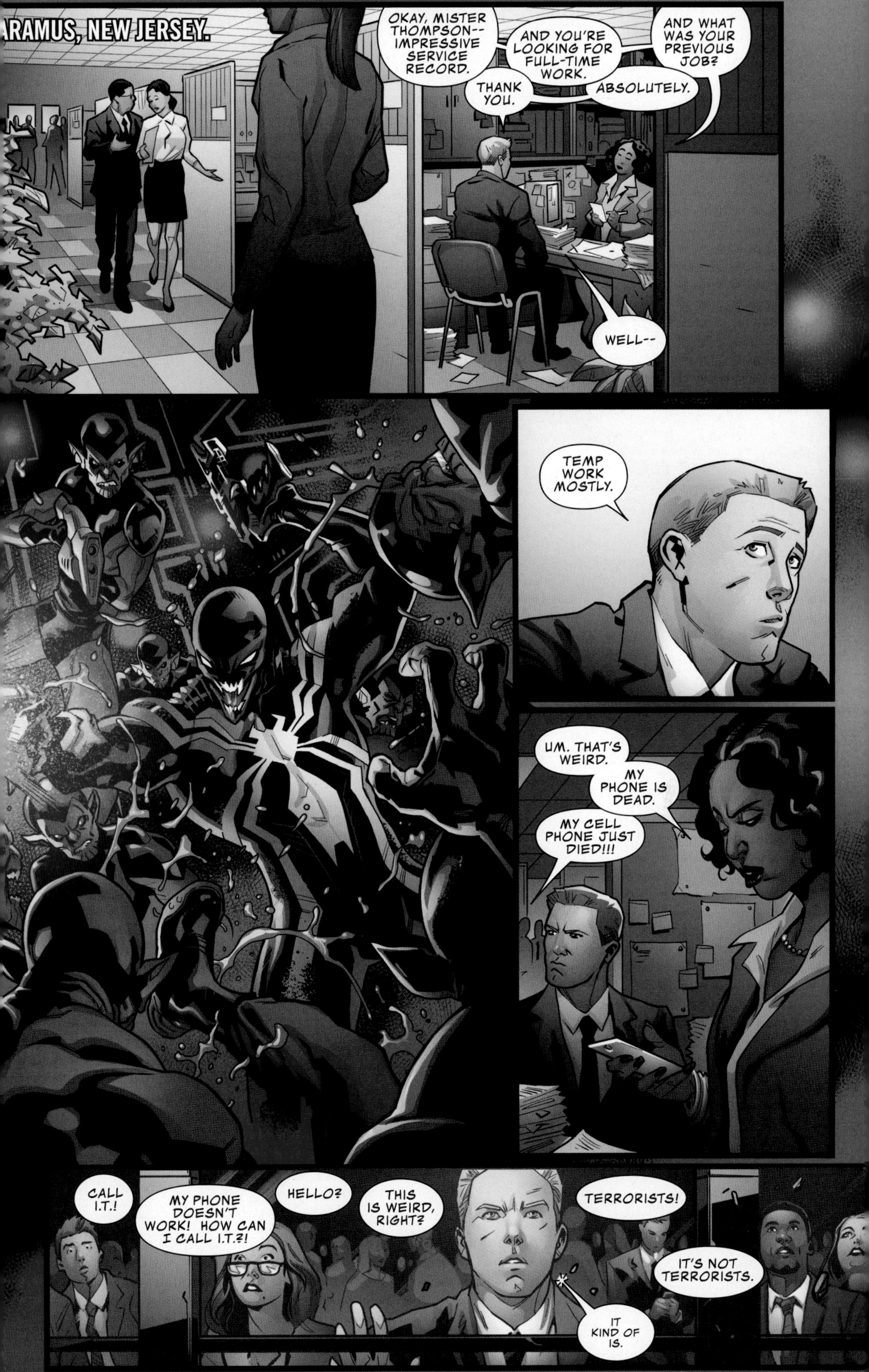
ARAMUS, NEW JERSEY.
OKAY, MISTER THOMPSON-- IMPRESSIVE SERVICE RECORD.
THANK YOU.
AND YOU'RE LOOKING FOR FULL-TIME WORK.
ABSOLUTELY.
AND WHAT WAS YOUR PREVIOUS JOB?
WELL--
TEMP WORK MOSTLY.
UM. THAT'S WEIRD.
MY PHONE IS DEAD.
MY CELL PHONE JUST DIED!!!
CALL I.T.!
MY PHONE DOESN'T WORK! HOW CAN I CALL I.T.?!
HELLO?
THIS IS WEIRD, RIGHT?
TERRORISTS!
IT'S NOT TERRORISTS.
IT KIND OF IS.

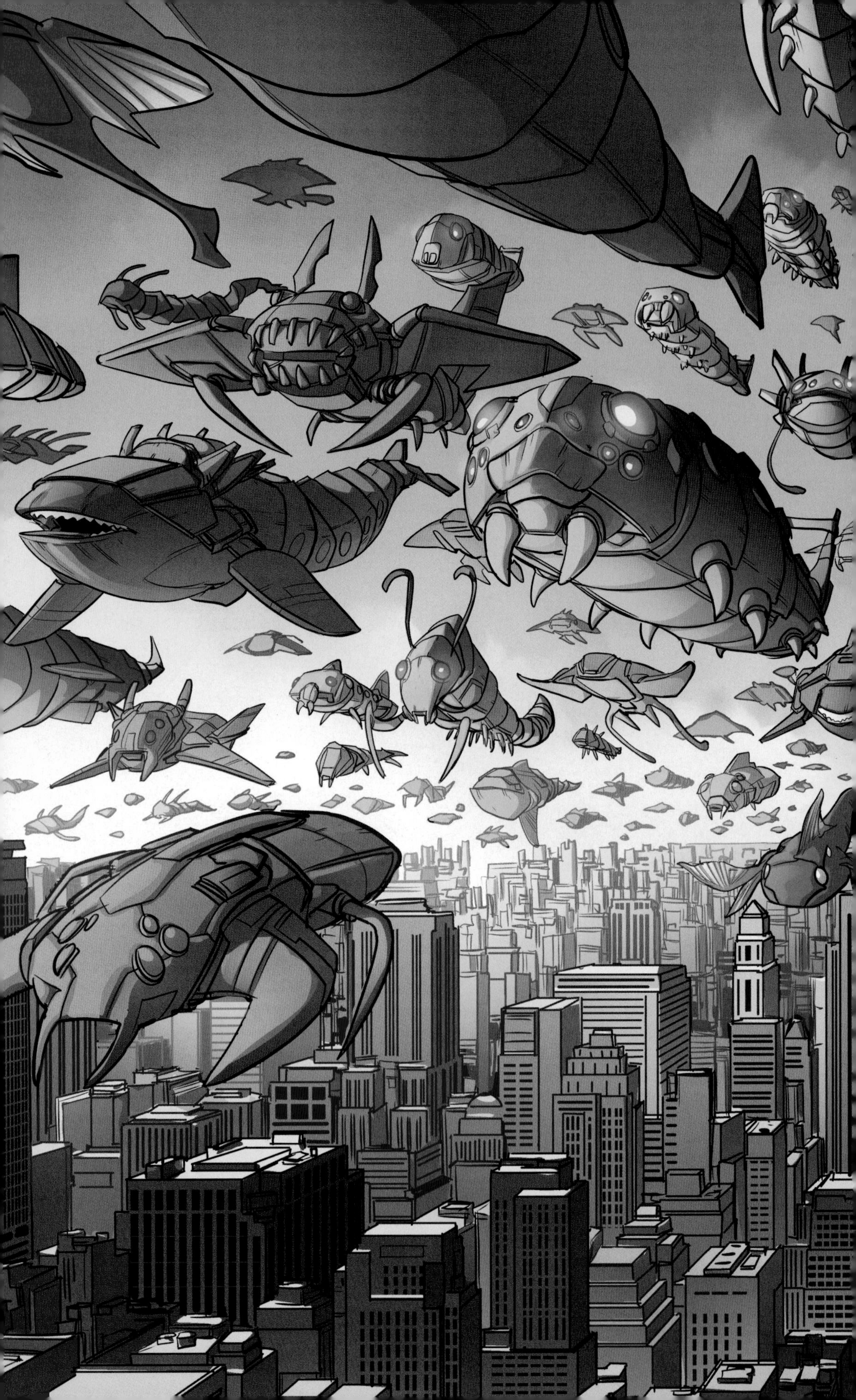

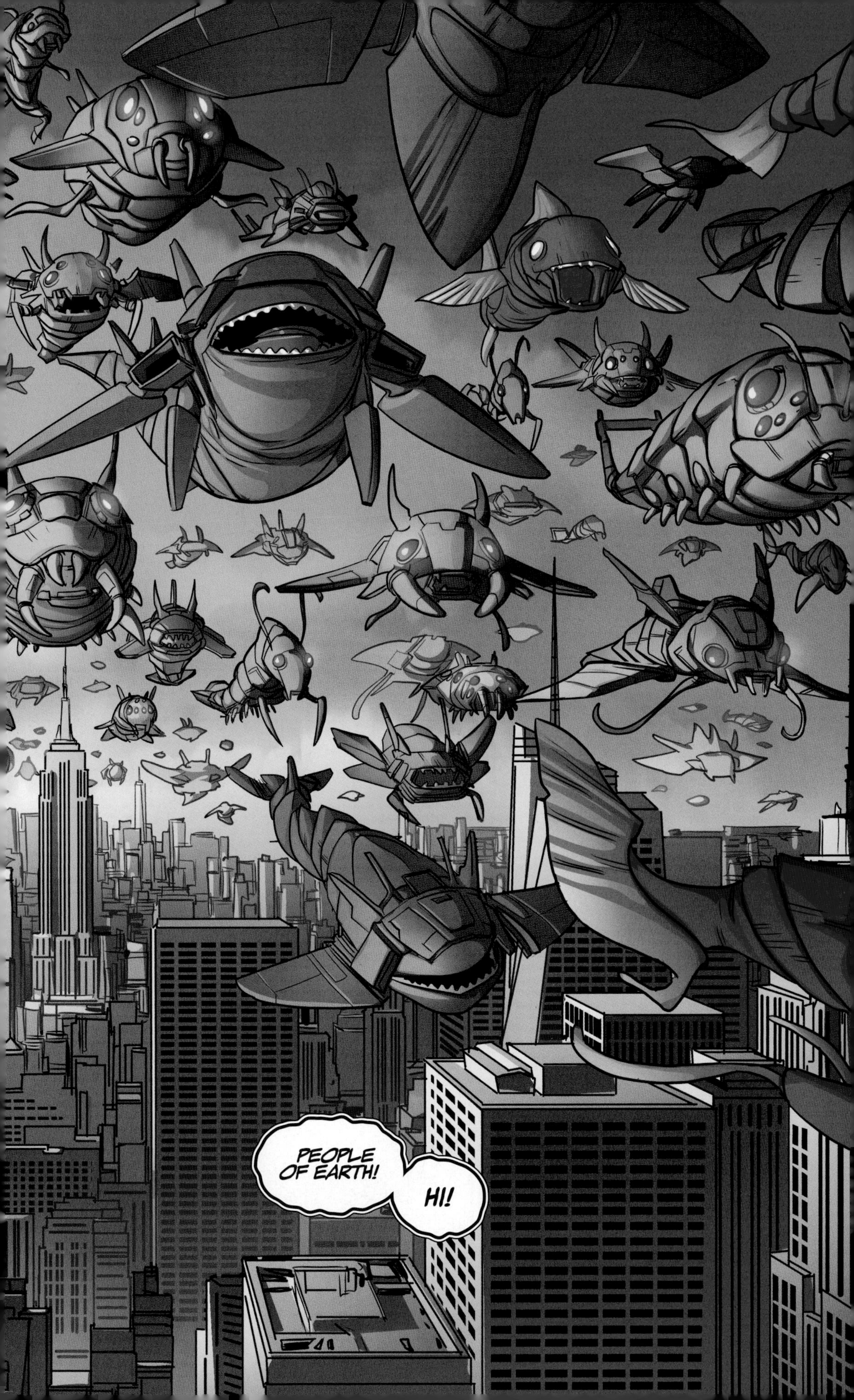
PEOPLE OF EARTH!
HI!

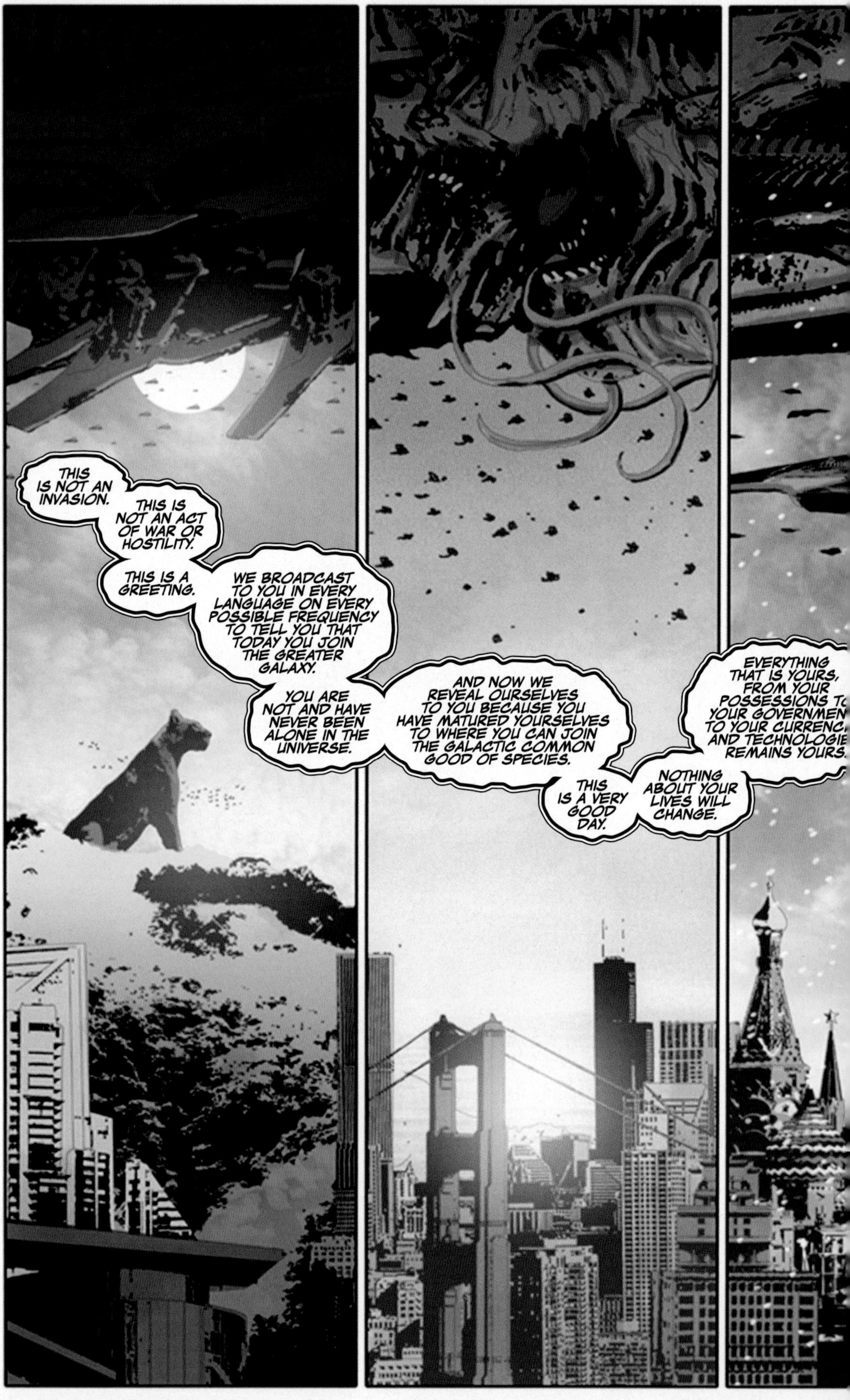
THIS IS NOT AN INVASION.
THIS IS NOT AN ACT OF WAR OR HOSTILITY.
THIS IS A GREETING.
WE BROADCAST TO YOU IN EVERY LANGUAGE ON EVERY POSSIBLE FREQUENCY TO TELL YOU THAT TODAY YOU JOIN THE GREATER GALAXY.
YOU ARE NOT AND HAVE NEVER BEEN ALONE IN THE UNIVERSE.
AND NOW WE REVEAL OURSELVES TO YOU BECAUSE YOU HAVE MATURED YOURSELVES TO WHERE YOU CAN JOIN THE GALACTIC COMMON GOOD OF SPECIES.
THIS IS A VERY GOOD DAY.
NOTHING ABOUT YOUR LIVES WILL CHANGE.
EVERYTHING THAT IS YOURS, FROM YOUR POSSESSIONS TO YOUR GOVERNMEN TO YOUR CURRENC AND TECHNOLOGIE REMAINS YOURS.

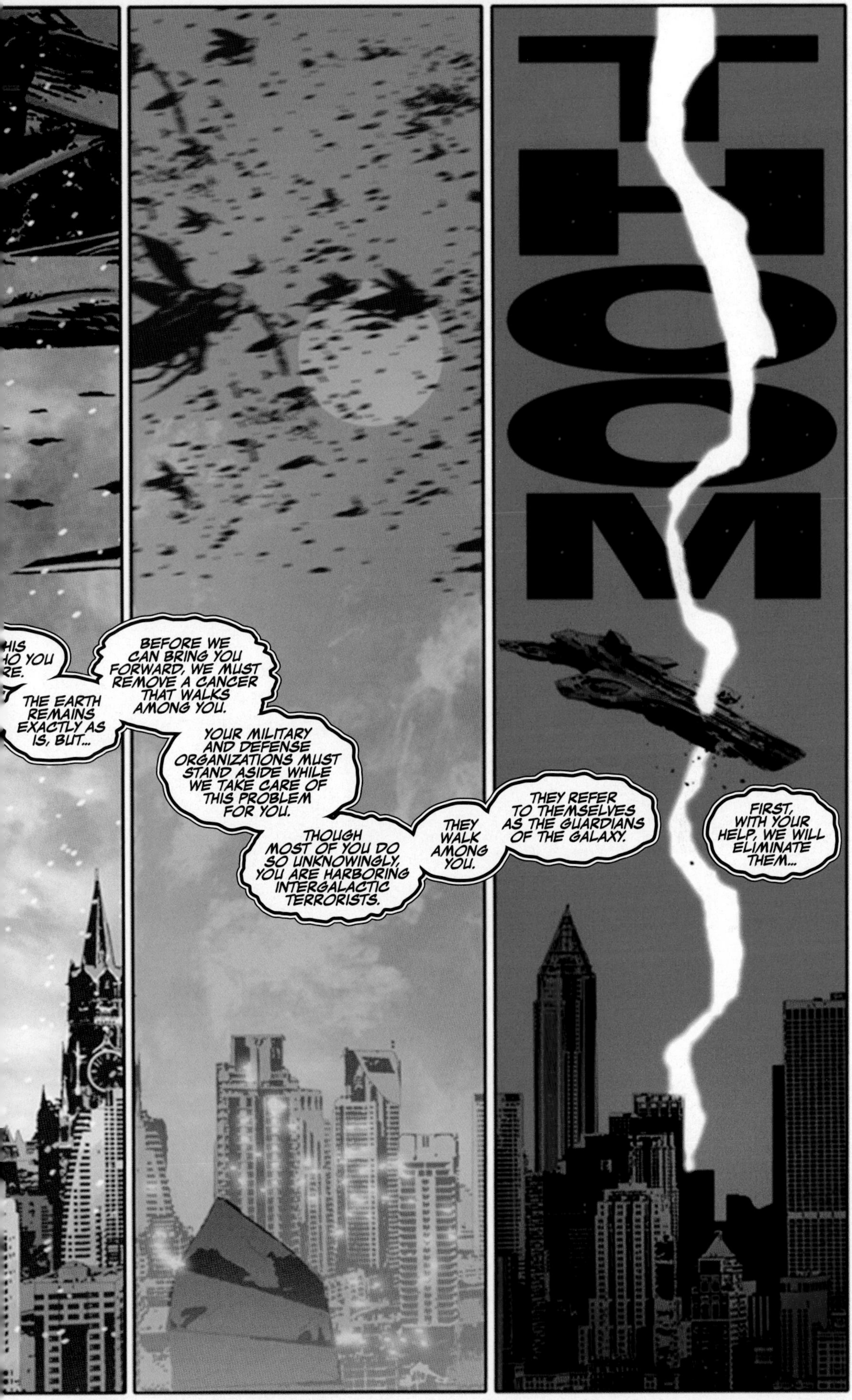
THE EARTH REMAINS EXACTLY AS IS, BUT...
BEFORE WE CAN BRING YOU FORWARD, WE MUST REMOVE A CANCER THAT WALKS AMONG YOU.
YOUR MILITARY AND DEFENSE ORGANIZATIONS MUST STAND ASIDE WHILE WE TAKE CARE OF THIS PROBLEM FOR YOU.
THOUGH MOST OF YOU DO SO UNKNOWINGLY, YOU ARE HARBORING INTERGALACTIC TERRORISTS.
THEY WALK AMONG YOU.
THEY REFER TO THEMSELVES AS THE GUARDIANS OF THE GALAXY.
THOOM
FIRST, WITH YOUR HELP, WE WILL ELIMINATE THEM...

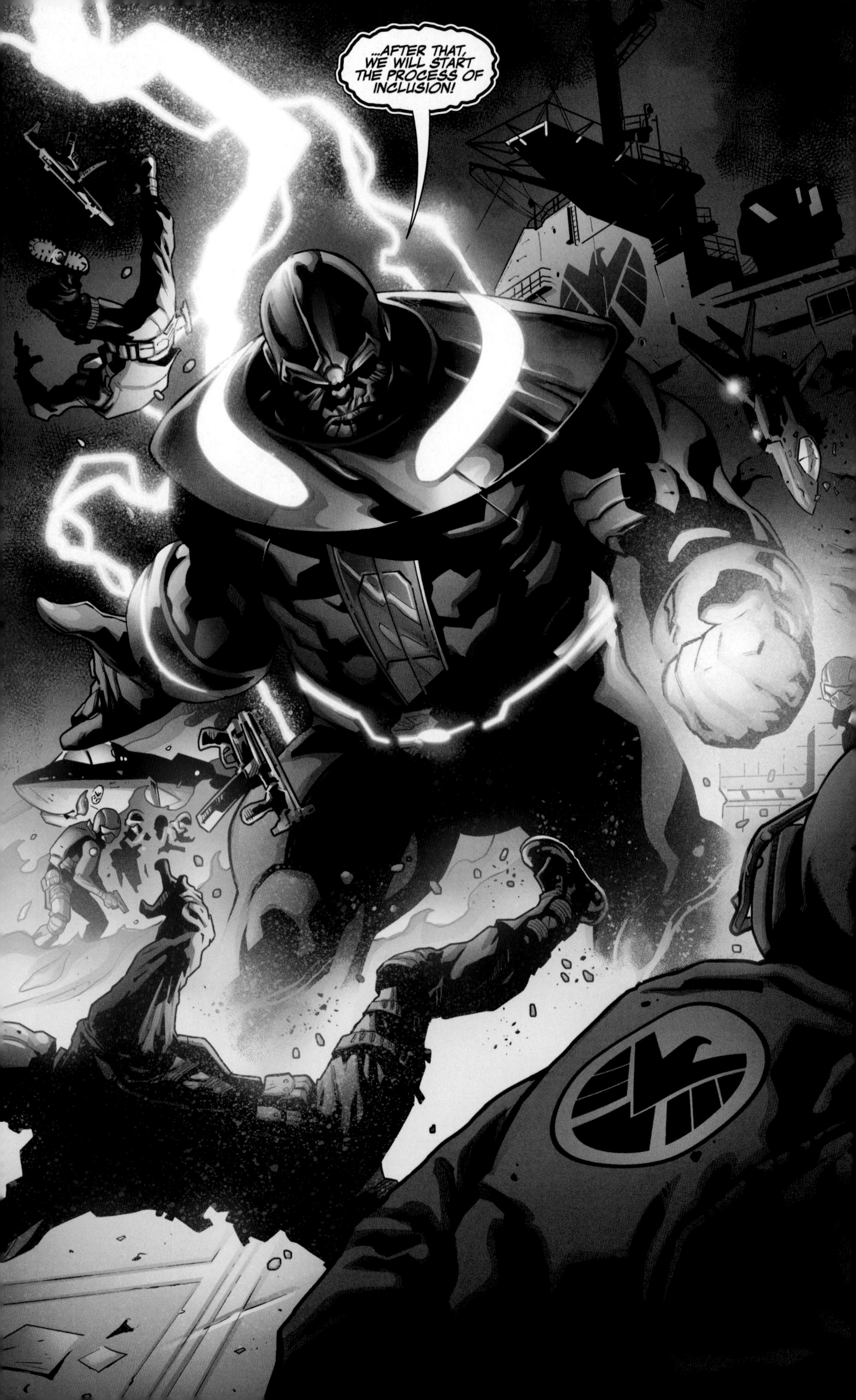
...AFTER THAT, WE WILL START THE PROCESS OF INCLUSION!

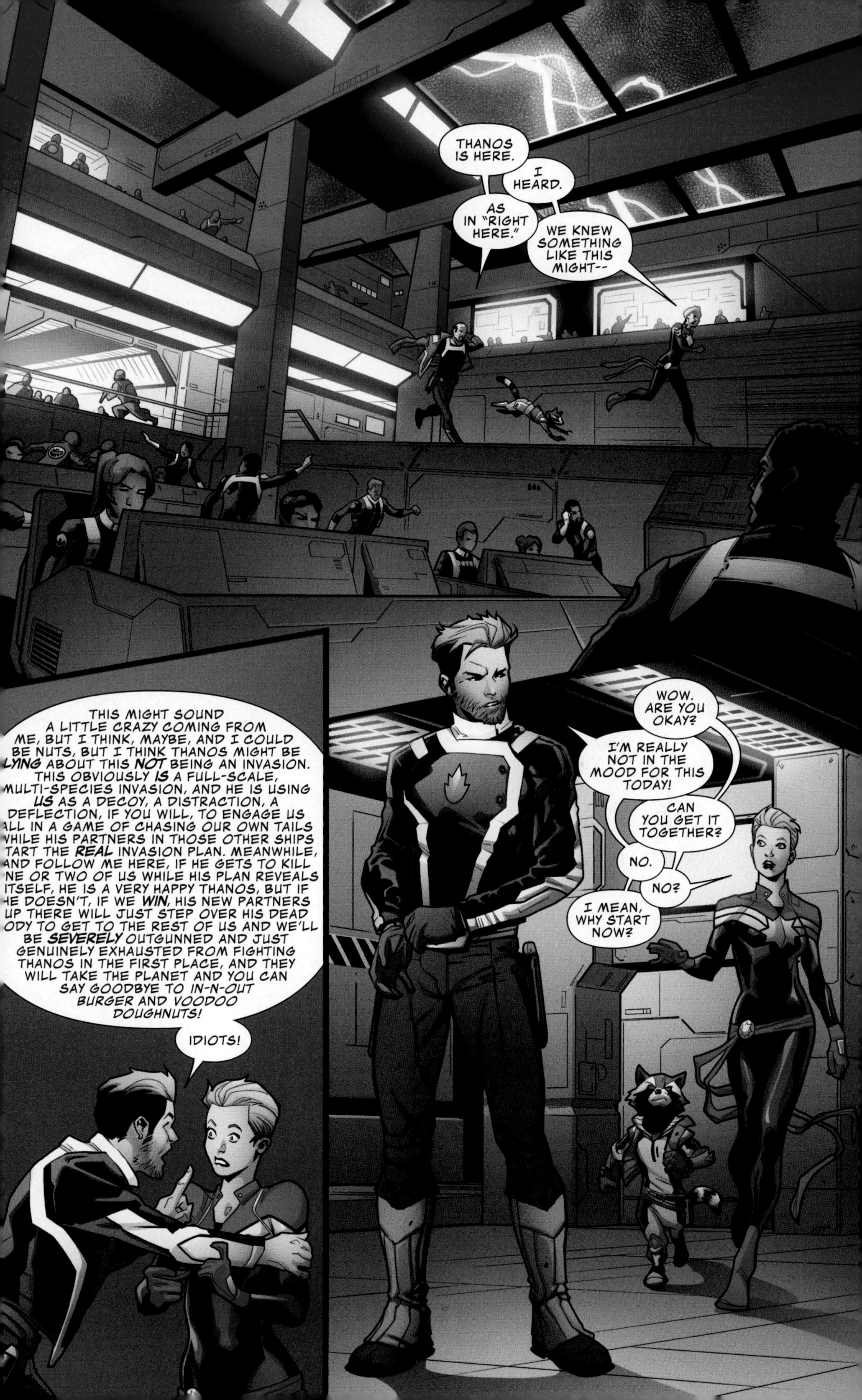
THANOS IS HERE.
I HEARD.
AS IN "RIGHT HERE."
WE KNEW SOMETHING LIKE THIS MIGHT--
THIS MIGHT SOUND A LITTLE CRAZY COMING FROM ME, BUT I THINK, MAYBE, AND I COULD BE NUTS, BUT I THINK THANOS MIGHT BE LYING ABOUT THIS NOT BEING AN INVASION. THIS OBVIOUSLY IS A FULL-SCALE, MULTI-SPECIES INVASION, AND HE IS USING US AS A DECOY, A DISTRACTION, A DEFLECTION, IF YOU WILL, TO ENGAGE US LL IN A GAME OF CHASING OUR OWN TAILS HILE HIS PARTNERS IN THOSE OTHER SHIPS TART THE REAL INVASION PLAN. MEANWHILE, AND FOLLOW ME HERE, IF HE GETS TO KILL NE OR TWO OF US WHILE HIS PLAN REVEALS ITSELF, HE IS A VERY HAPPY THANOS, BUT IF HE DOESN'T, IF WE WIN, HIS NEW PARTNERS UP THERE WILL JUST STEP OVER HIS DEAD ODY TO GET TO THE REST OF US AND WE'LL BE SEVERELY OUTGUNNED AND JUST GENUINELY EXHAUSTED FROM FIGHTING THANOS IN THE FIRST PLACE, AND THEY WILL TAKE THE PLANET AND YOU CAN SAY GOODBYE TO IN-N-OUT BURGER AND VOODOO DOUGHNUTS!
IDIOTS!
WOW. ARE YOU OKAY?
I'M REALLY NOT IN THE MOOD FOR THIS TODAY!
CAN YOU GET IT TOGETHER?
NO.
NO?
I MEAN, WHY START NOW?

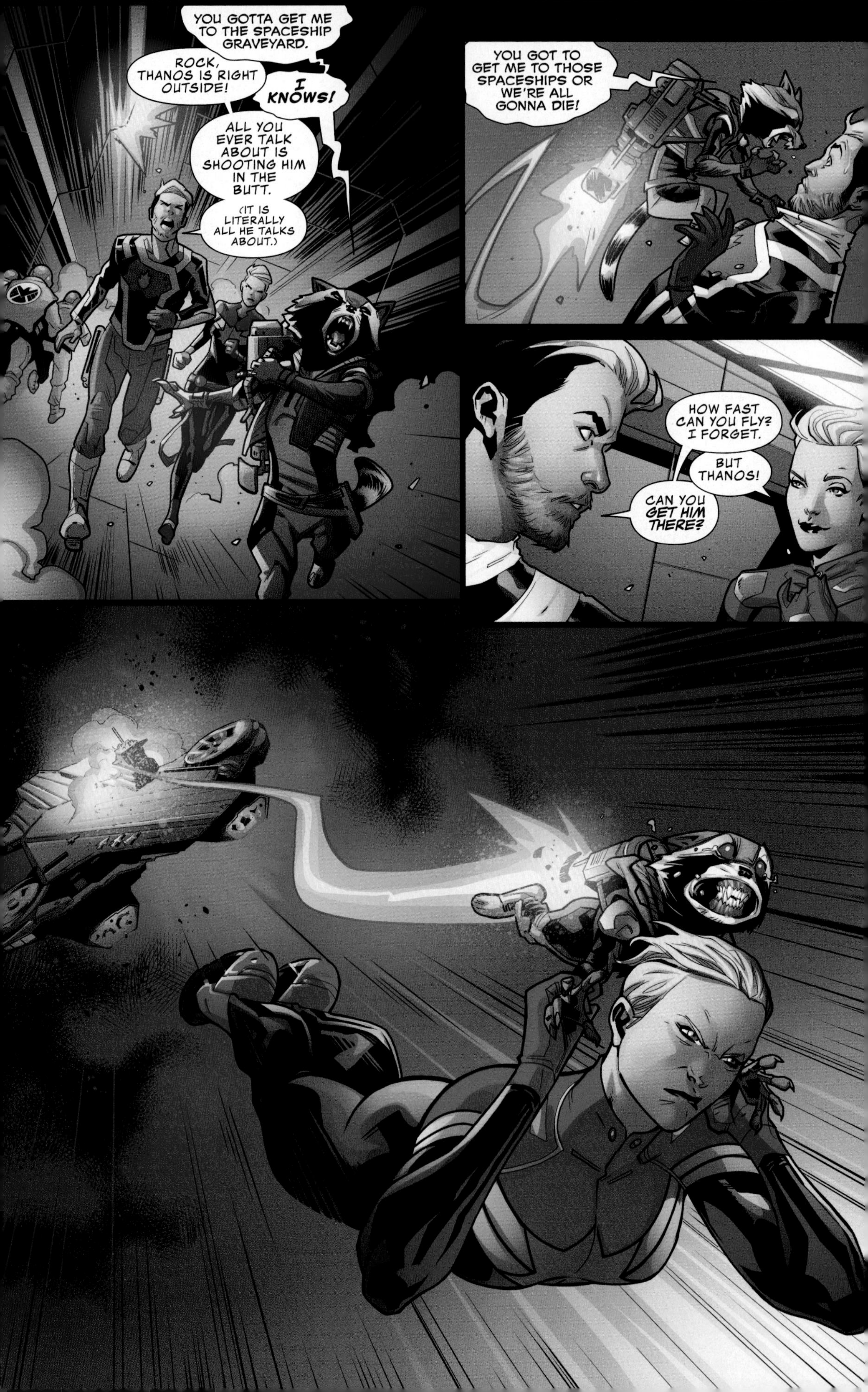
YOU GOTTA GET ME TO THE SPACESHIP GRAVEYARD.
ROCK, THANOS IS RIGHT OUTSIDE!
I KNOWS!
ALL YOU EVER TALK ABOUT IS SHOOTING HIM IN THE BUTT.
(IT IS LITERALLY ALL HE TALKS ABOUT.)
YOU GOT TO GET ME TO THOSE SPACESHIPS OR WE'RE ALL GONNA DIE!
HOW FAST CAN YOU FLY? I FORGET.
BUT THANOS!
CAN YOU GET HIM THERE?

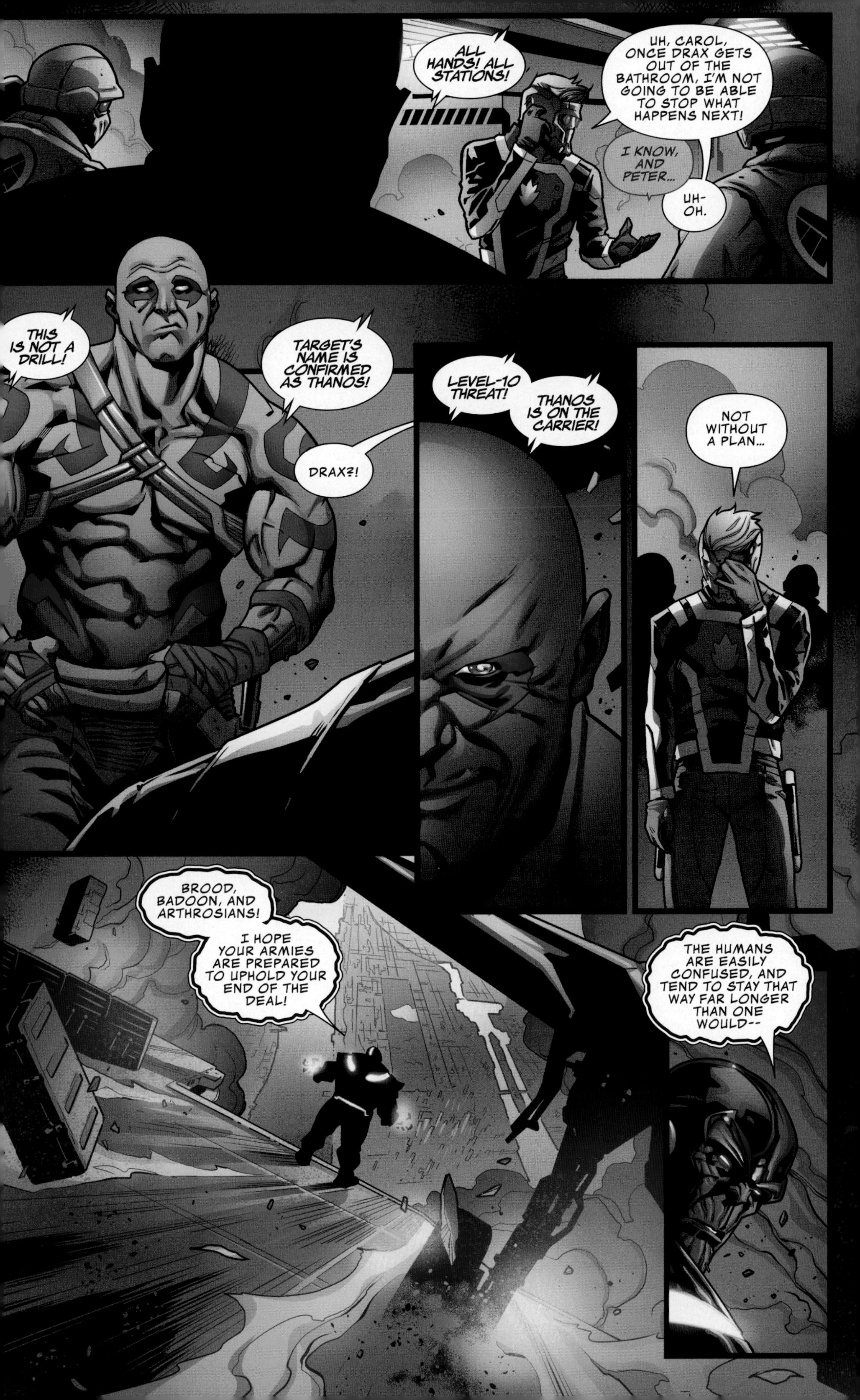
ALL HANDS! ALL STATIONS!
UH, CAROL, ONCE DRAX GETS OUT OF THE BATHROOM, I'M NOT GOING TO BE ABLE TO STOP WHAT HAPPENS NEXT!
I KNOW, AND PETER...
UH-OH.
THIS IS NOT A DRILL!
TARGET'S NAME IS CONFIRMED AS THANOS!
DRAX?!
LEVEL-10 THREAT!
THANOS IS ON THE CARRIER!
NOT WITHOUT A PLAN...
BROOD, BADOON, AND ARTHROSIANS!
I HOPE YOUR ARMIES ARE PREPARED TO UPHOLD YOUR END OF THE DEAL!
THE HUMANS ARE EASILY CONFUSED, AND TEND TO STAY THAT WAY FAR LONGER THAN ONE WOULD--

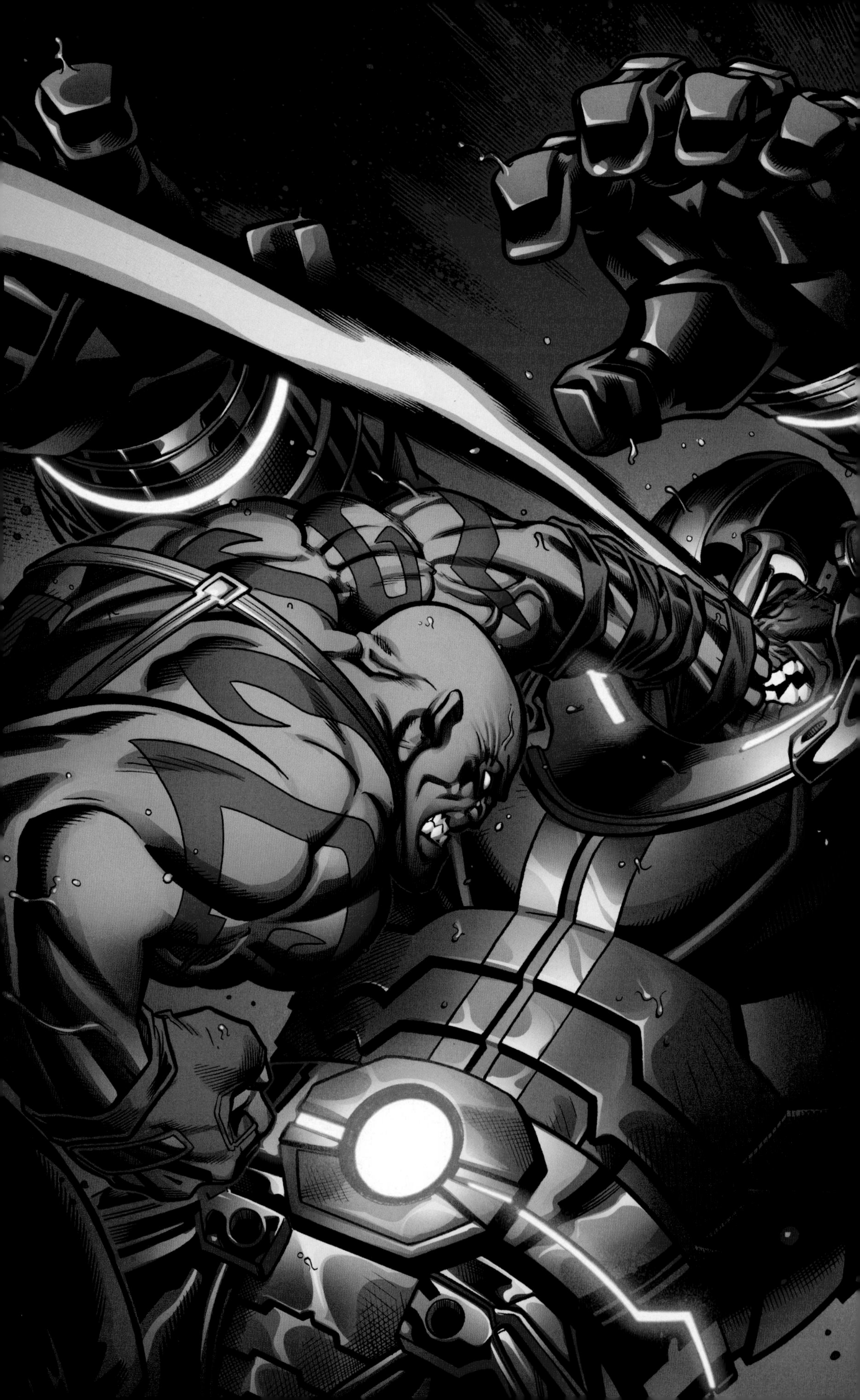

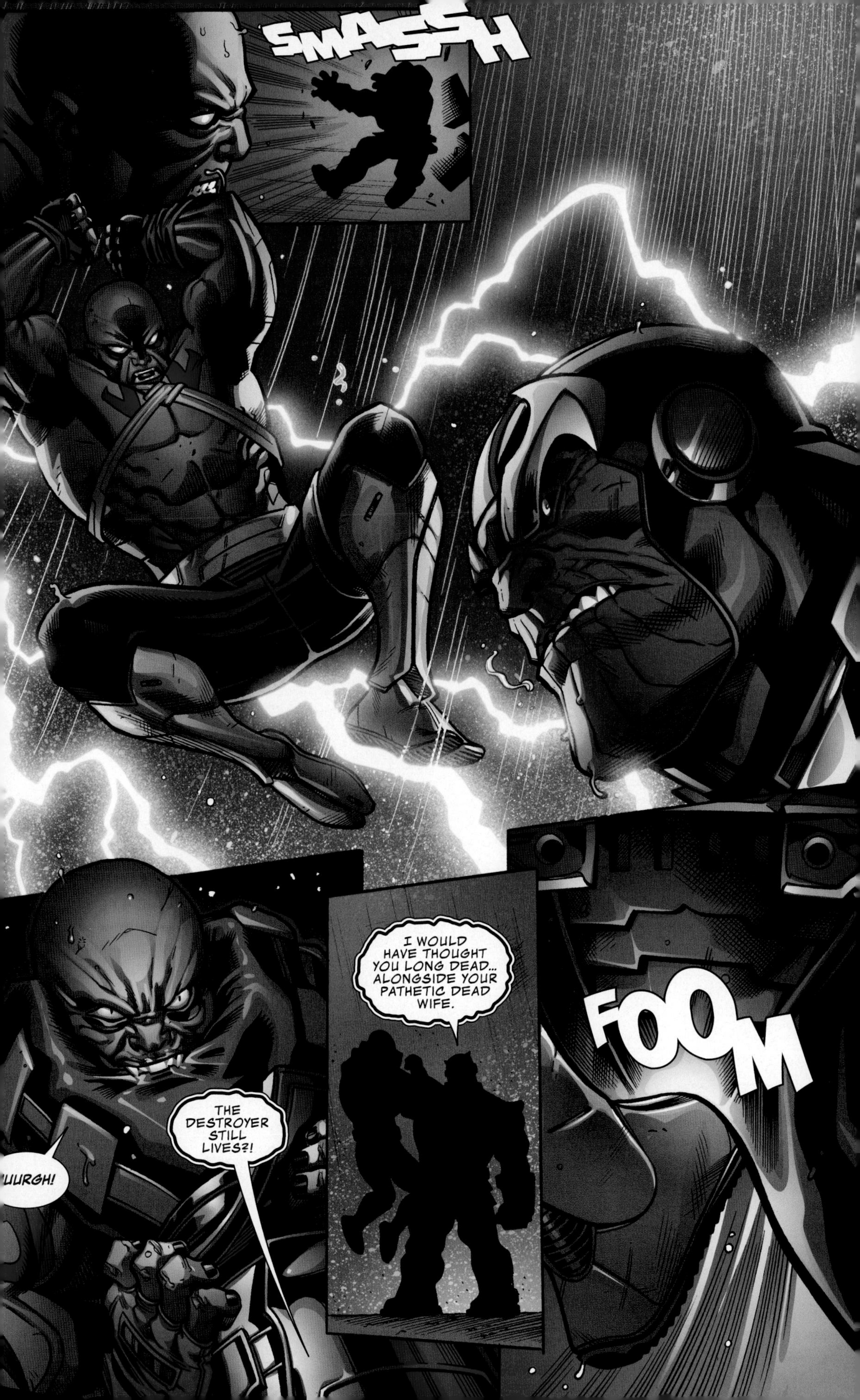
SMASSH
THE DESTROYER STILL LIVES?!
UURGH!
I WOULD HAVE THOUGHT YOU LONG DEAD... ALONGSIDE YOUR PATHETIC DEAD WIFE.
FOOM

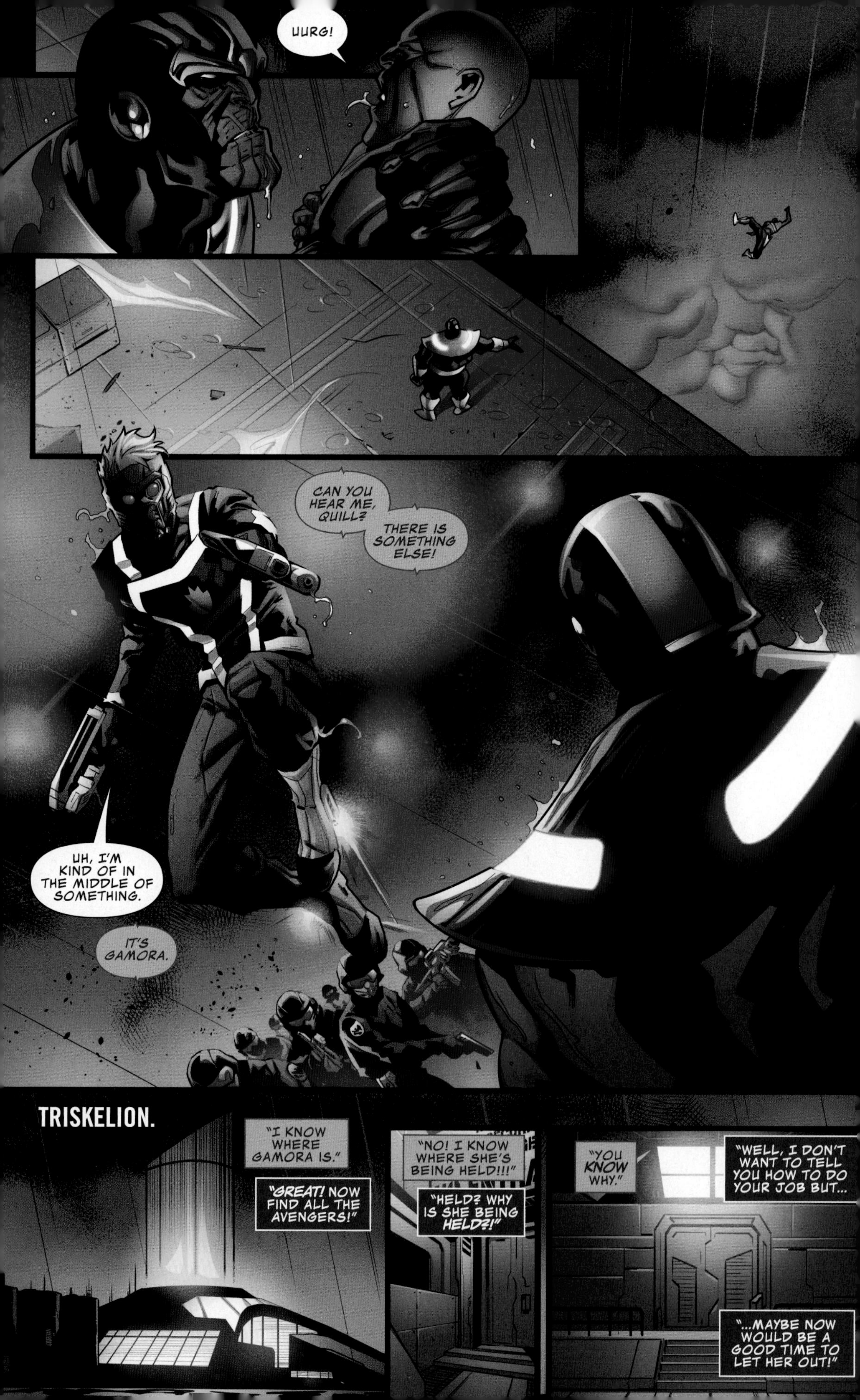
UURG!
CAN YOU HEAR ME, QUILL?
THERE IS SOMETHING ELSE!
UH, I'M KIND OF IN THE MIDDLE OF SOMETHING.
IT'S GAMORA.
TRISKELION.
"I KNOW WHERE GAMORA IS."
"GREAT! NOW FIND ALL THE AVENGERS!"
"NO! I KNOW WHERE SHE'S BEING HELD!!!"
"HELD? WHY IS SHE BEING HELD?!"
"YOU KNOW WHY."
"WELL, I DON'T WANT TO TELL YOU HOW TO DO YOUR JOB BUT...
"...MAYBE NOW WOULD BE A GOOD TIME TO LET HER OUT!"

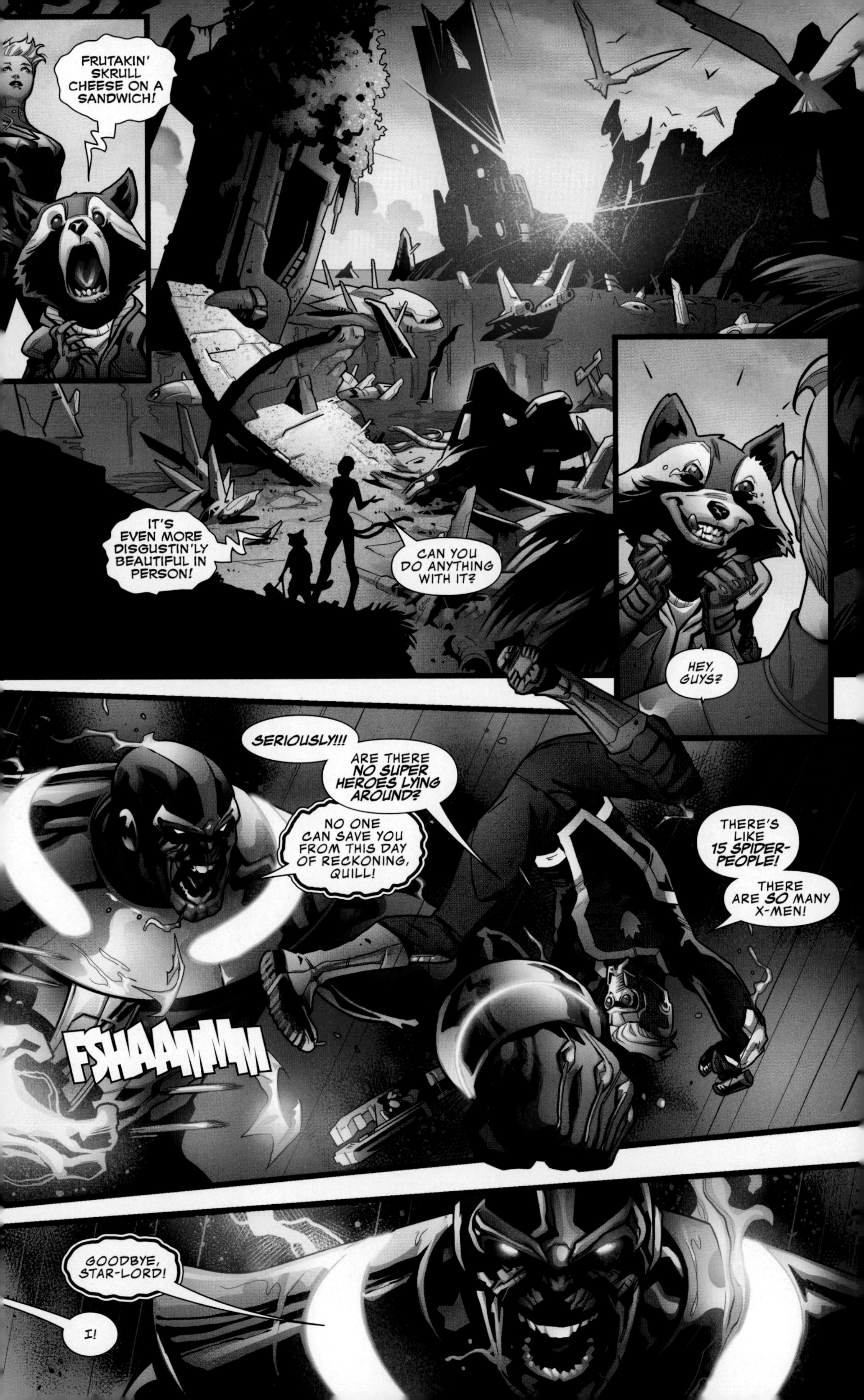
FRUTAKIN' SKRULL CHEESE ON A SANDWICH!
IT'S EVEN MORE DISGUSTIN'LY BEAUTIFUL IN PERSON!
CAN YOU DO ANYTHING WITH IT?
HEY, GUYS?
SERIOUSLY!!!
ARE THERE NO SUPER HEROES LYING AROUND?
NO ONE CAN SAVE YOU FROM THIS DAY OF RECKONING, QUILL!
THERE'S LIKE 15 SPIDER-PEOPLE!
THERE ARE SO MANY X-MEN!
FSHAAMMM
GOODBYE, STAR-LORD!
I!

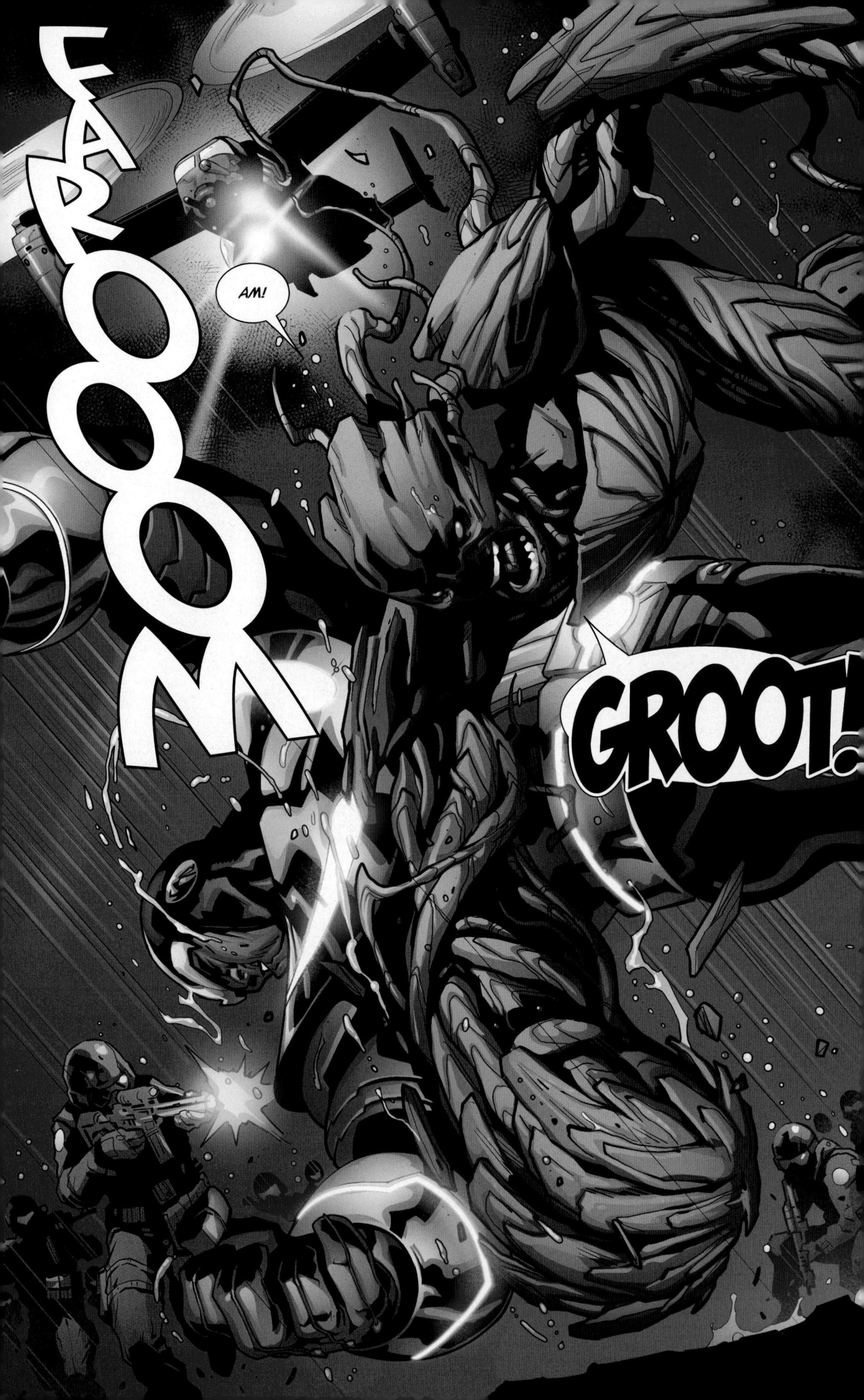
CAROOOM
AM!
GROOT!

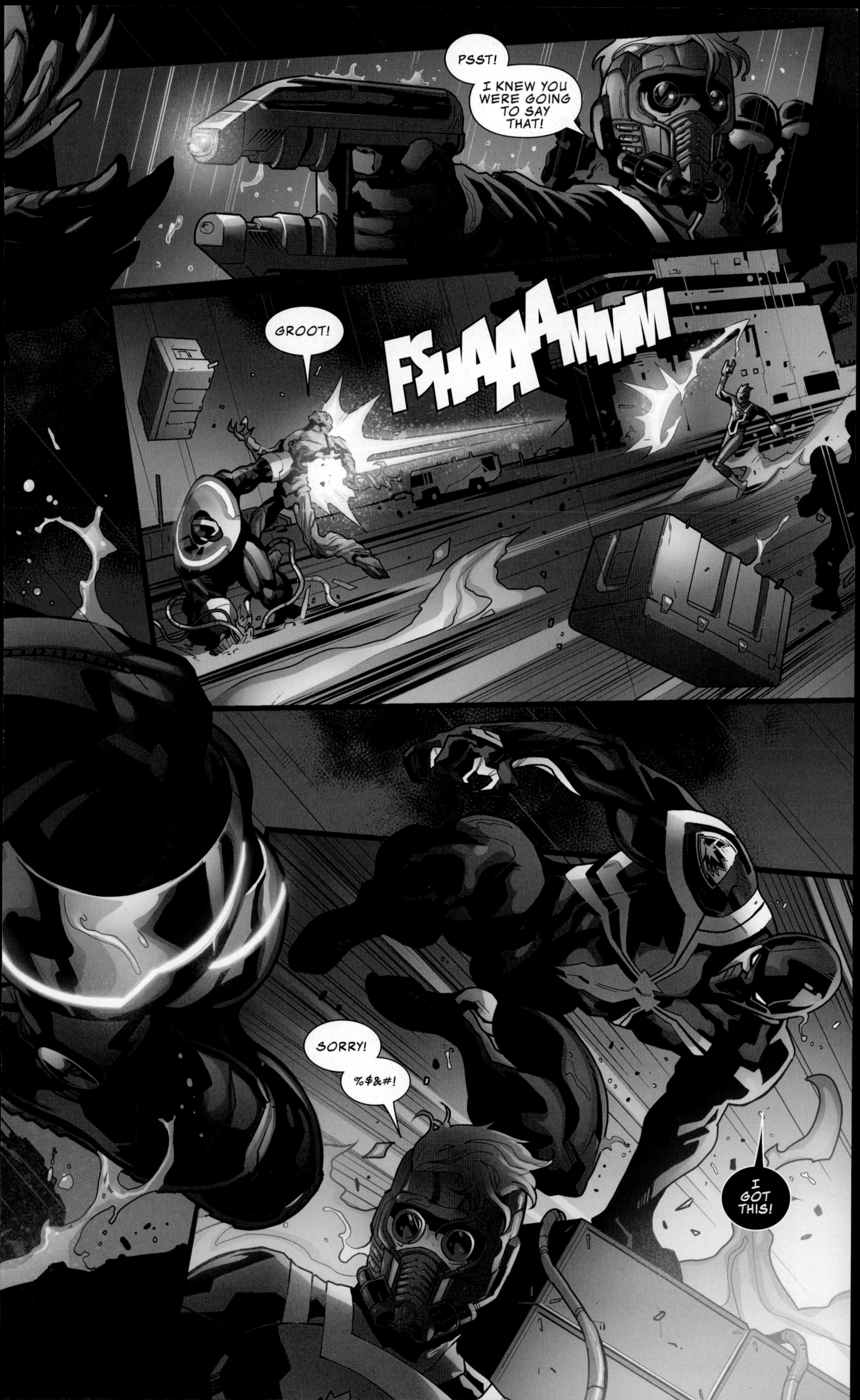
PSST!
I KNEW YOU WERE GOING TO SAY THAT!
GROOT!
FSHAAAMMMM
SORRY!
%$&#!
I GOT THIS!

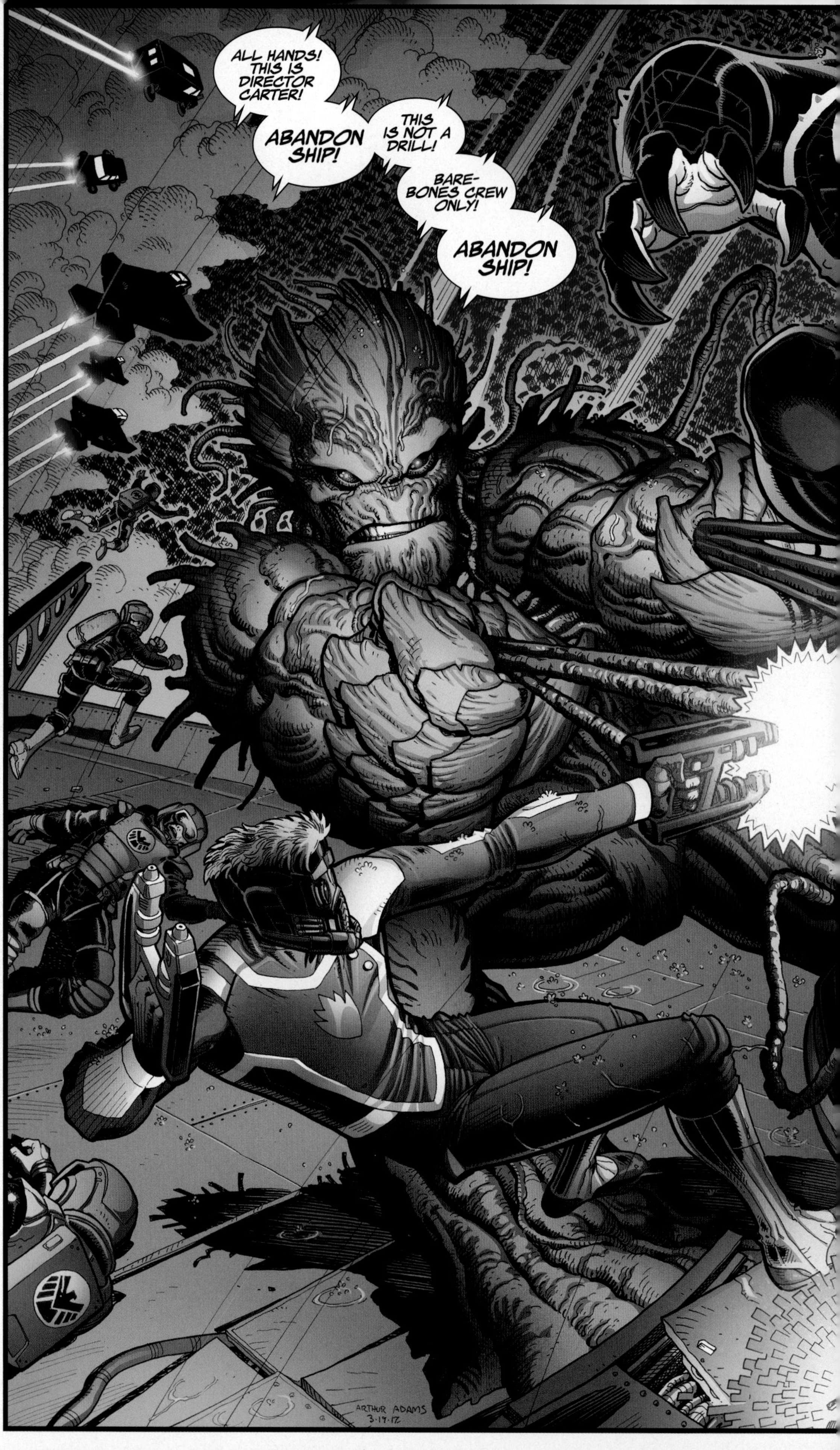
ALL HANDS! THIS IS DIRECTOR CARTER!
ABANDON SHIP!
THIS IS NOT A DRILL!
BARE-BONES CREW ONLY!
ABANDON SHIP!
ARTHUR ADAMS 3-19-17

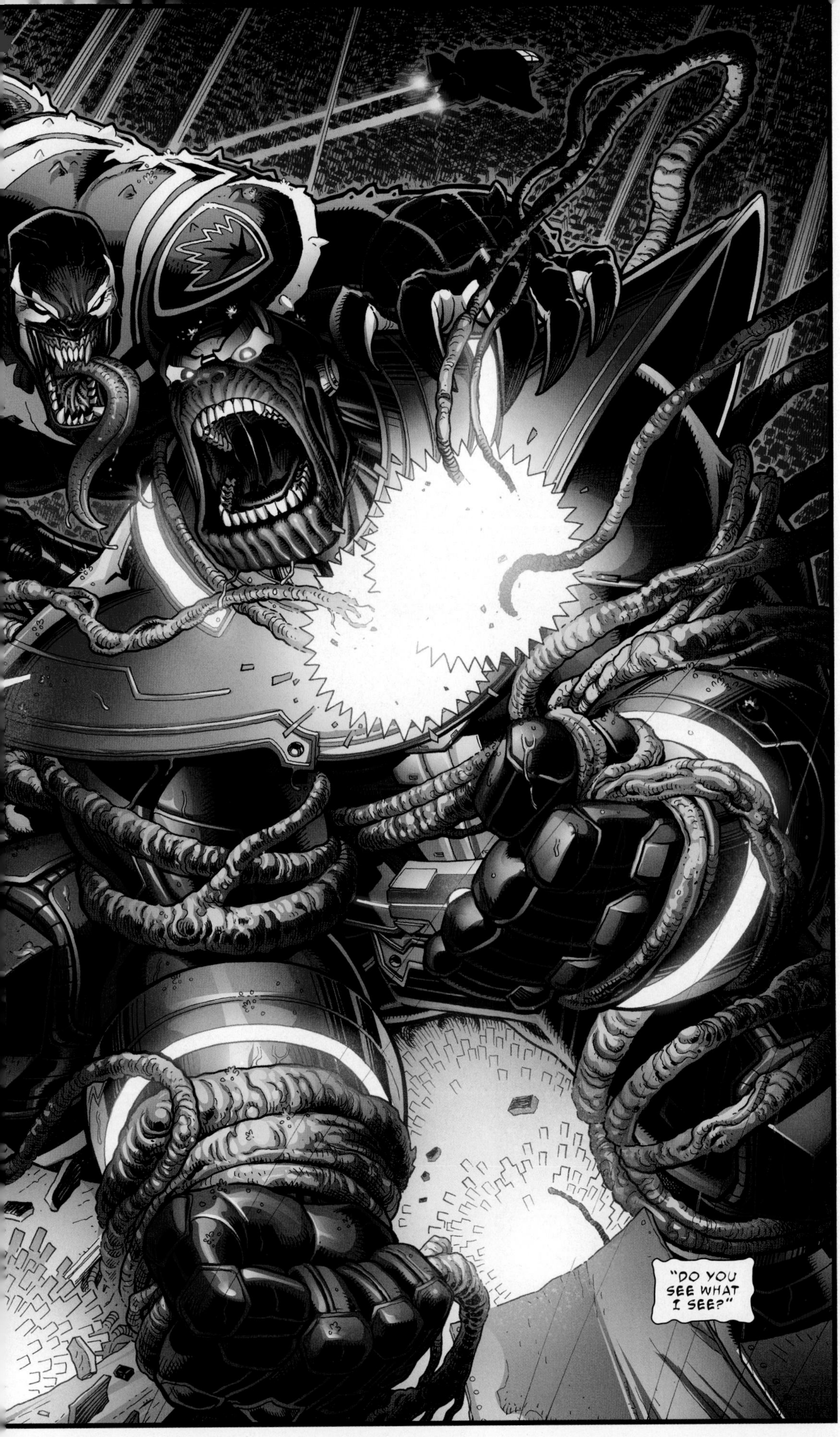
"DO YOU SEE WHAT I SEE?"

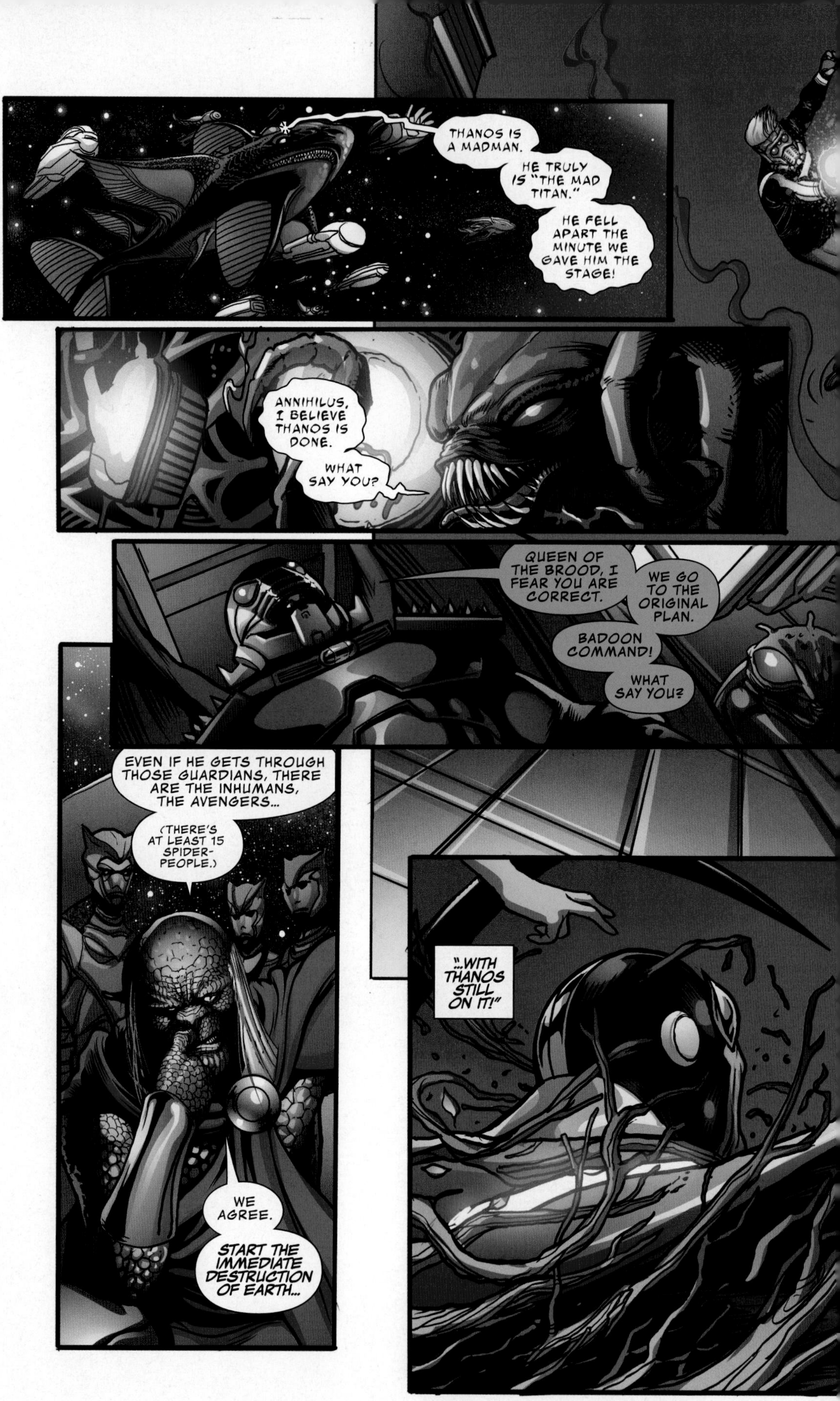
THANOS IS A MADMAN.
HE TRULY IS "THE MAD TITAN."
HE FELL APART THE MINUTE WE GAVE HIM THE STAGE!
ANNIHILUS, I BELIEVE THANOS IS DONE.
WHAT SAY YOU?
QUEEN OF THE BROOD, I FEAR YOU ARE CORRECT.
WE GO TO THE ORIGINAL PLAN.
BADOON COMMAND!
WHAT SAY YOU?
EVEN IF HE GETS THROUGH THOSE GUARDIANS, THERE ARE THE INHUMANS, THE AVENGERS...
(THERE'S AT LEAST 15 SPIDER-PEOPLE.)
WE AGREE.
START THE IMMEDIATE DESTRUCTION OF EARTH...
"...WITH THANOS STILL ON IT!"

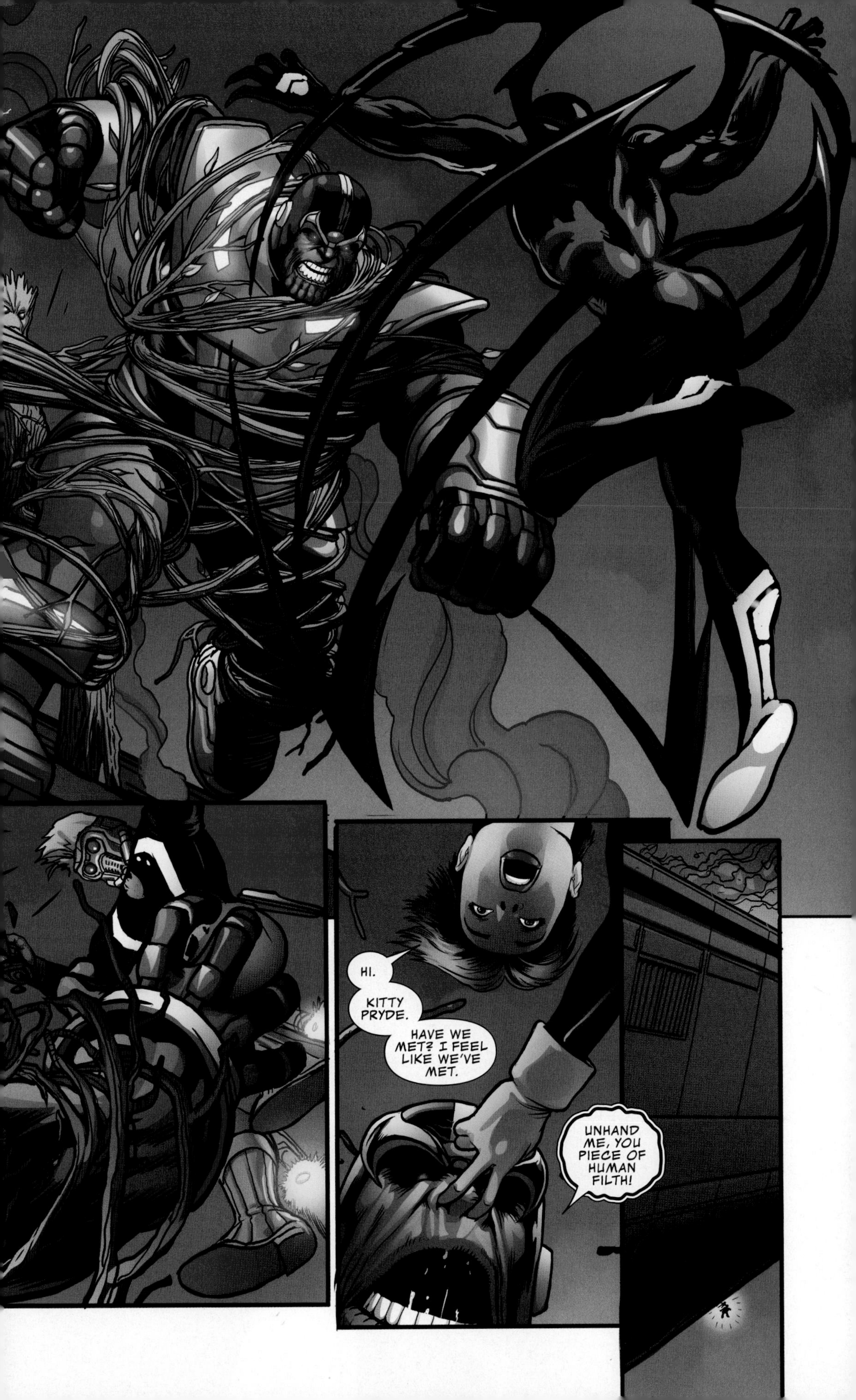
HI.
KITTY PRYDE.
HAVE WE MET? I FEEL LIKE WE'VE MET.
UNHAND ME, YOU PIECE OF HUMAN FILTH!

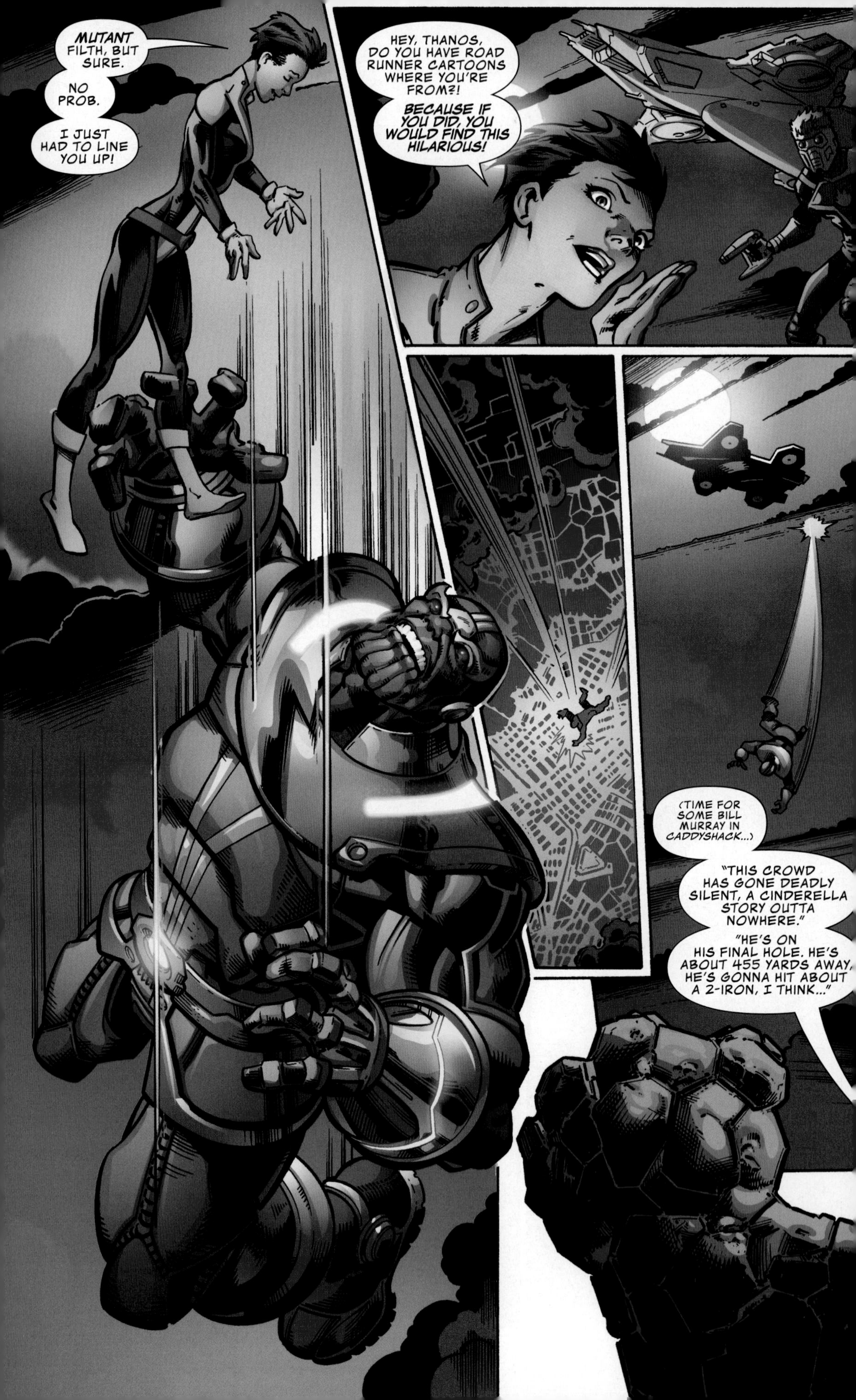
MUTANT FILTH, BUT SURE.
NO PROB.
I JUST HAD TO LINE YOU UP!
HEY, THANOS, DO YOU HAVE ROAD RUNNER CARTOONS WHERE YOU'RE FROM?!
BECAUSE IF YOU DID, YOU WOULD FIND THIS HILARIOUS!
(TIME FOR SOME BILL MURRAY IN CADDYSHACK...)
"THIS CROWD HAS GONE DEADLY SILENT, A CINDERELLA STORY OUTTA NOWHERE."
"HE'S ON HIS FINAL HOLE. HE'S ABOUT 455 YARDS AWAY, HE'S GONNA HIT ABOUT A 2-IRON, I THINK..."

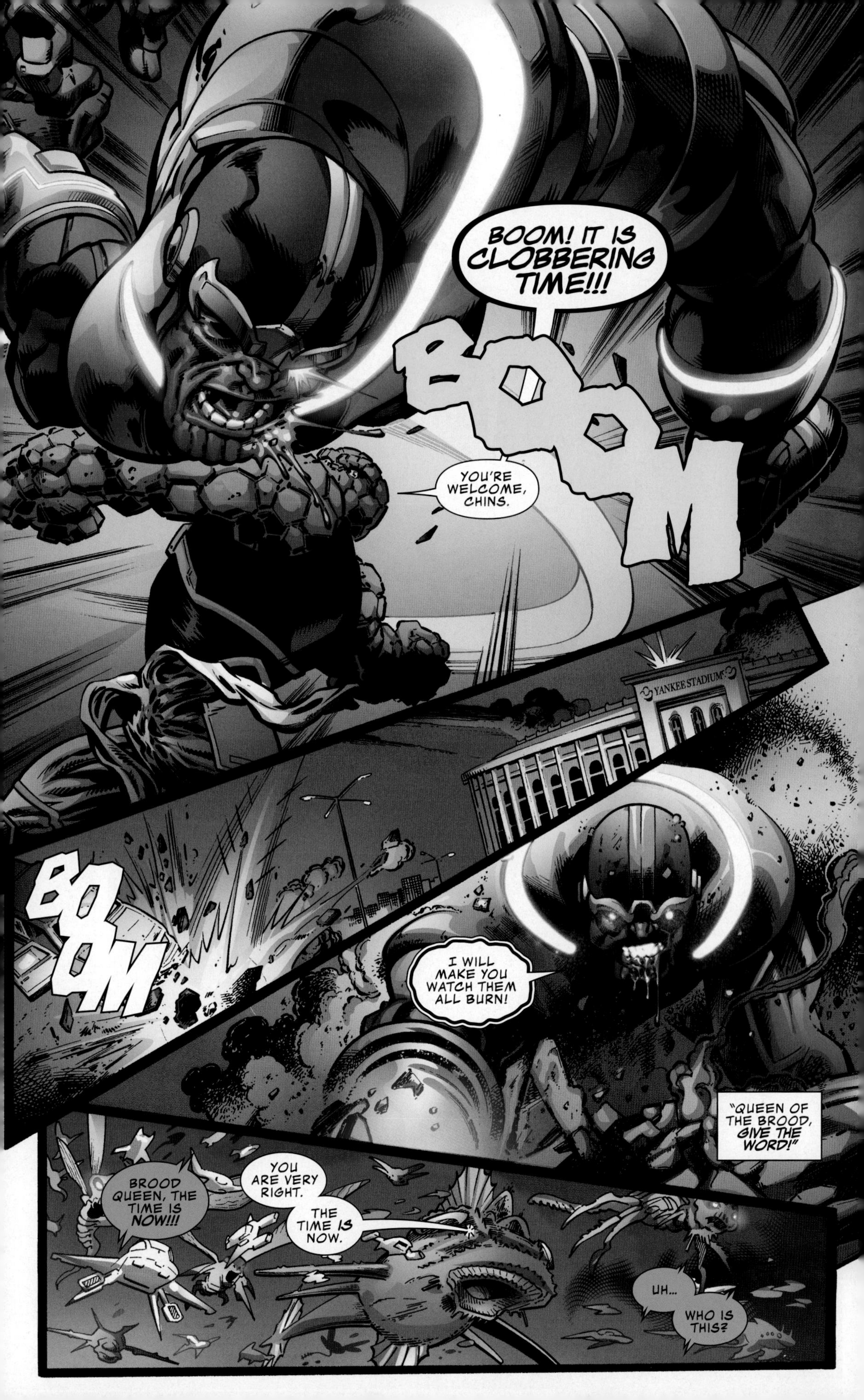
BOOM! IT IS CLOBBERING TIME!!!
BOOM
YOU'RE WELCOME, CHINS.
YANKEE STADIUM
BOOM
I WILL MAKE YOU WATCH THEM ALL BURN!
"QUEEN OF THE BROOD, GIVE THE WORD!"
BROOD QUEEN, THE TIME IS NOW!!!
YOU ARE VERY RIGHT.
THE TIME IS NOW.
UH...
WHO IS THIS?

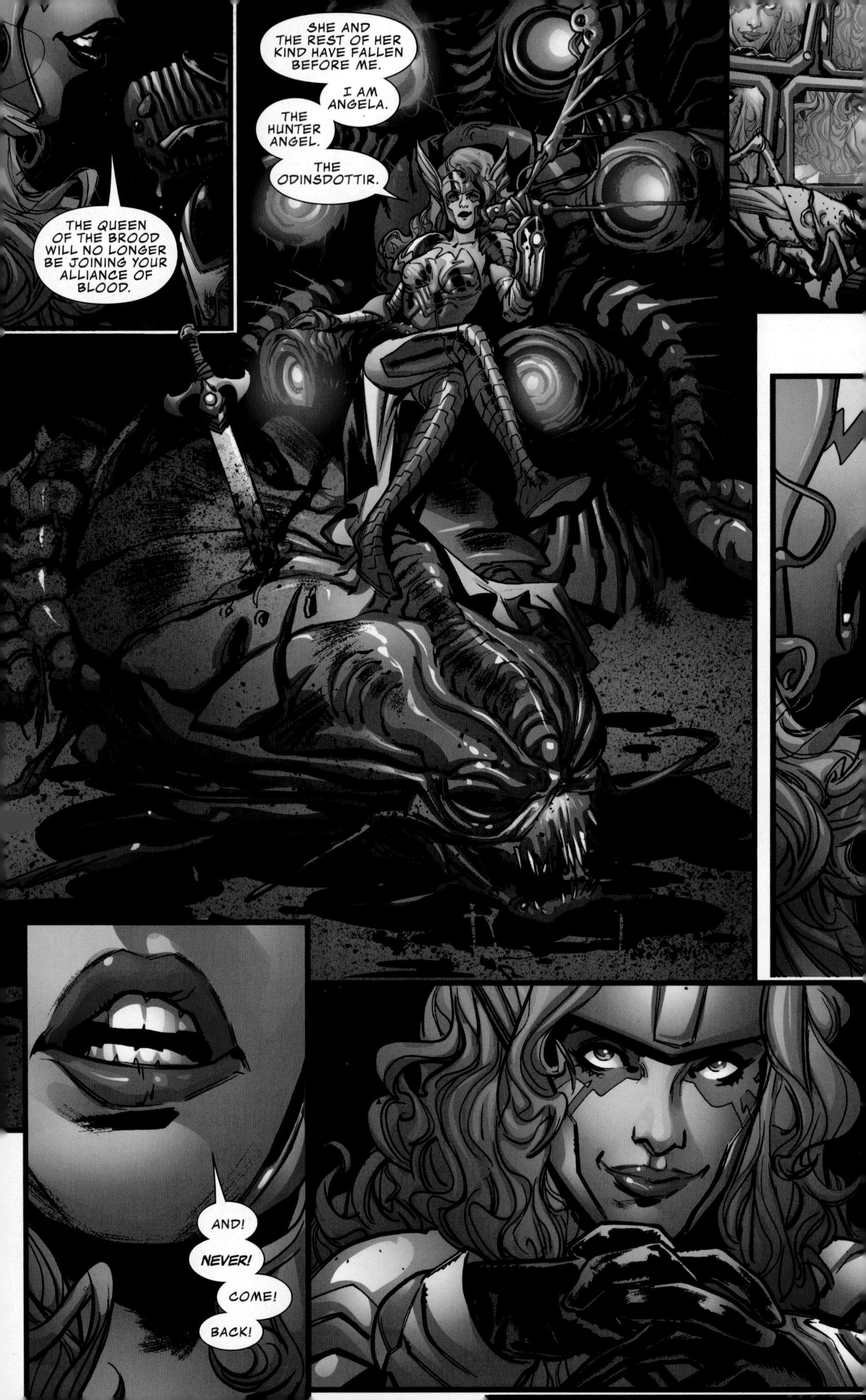
THE QUEEN OF THE BROOD WILL NO LONGER BE JOINING YOUR ALLIANCE OF BLOOD.
SHE AND THE REST OF HER KIND HAVE FALLEN BEFORE ME.
I AM ANGELA.
THE HUNTER ANGEL.
THE ODINSDOTTIR.
AND!
NEVER!
COME!
BACK!

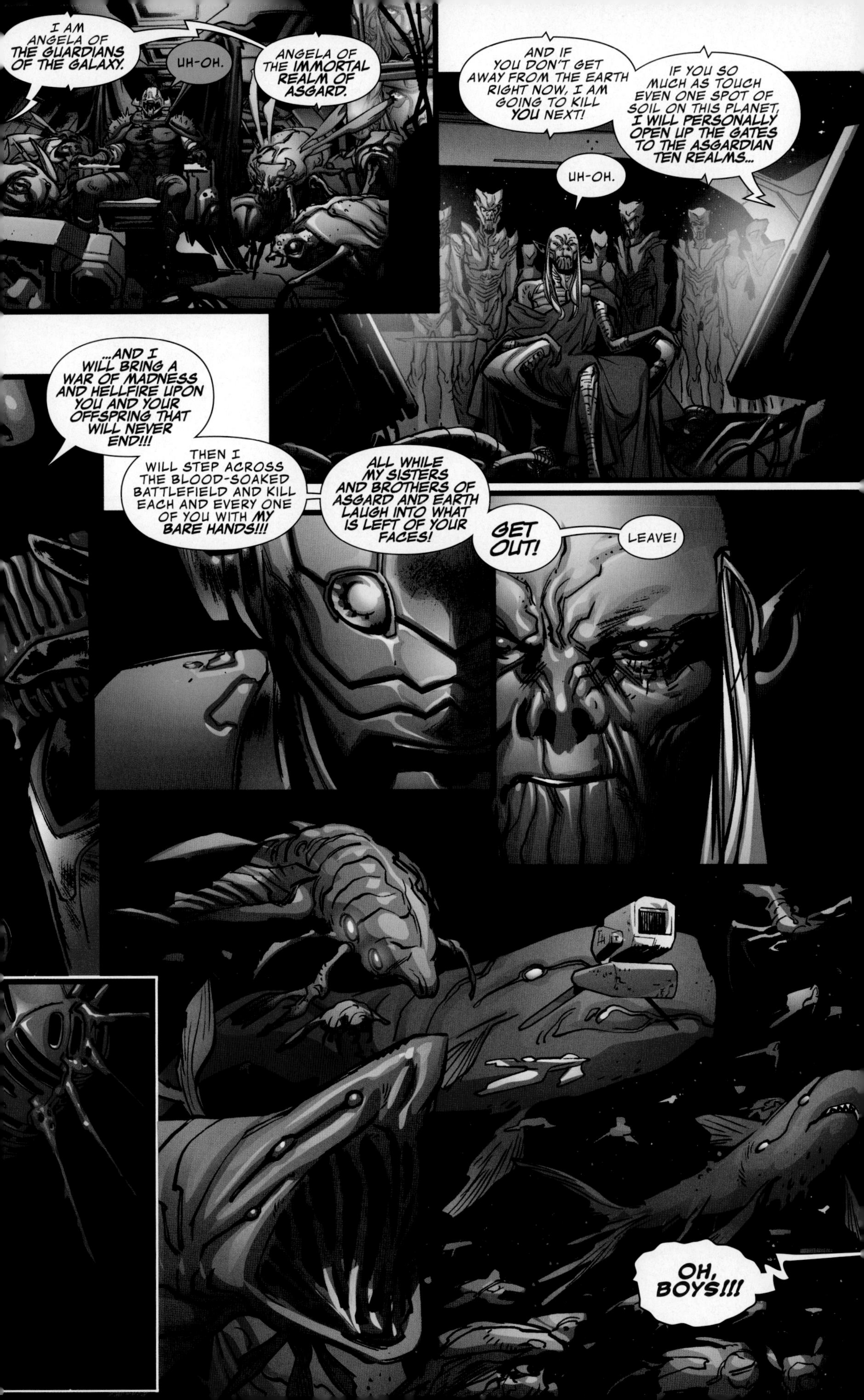
I AM ANGELA OF THE GUARDIANS OF THE GALAXY.
UH-OH.
ANGELA OF THE IMMORTAL REALM OF ASGARD.
AND IF YOU DON'T GET AWAY FROM THE EARTH RIGHT NOW, I AM GOING TO KILL YOU NEXT!
IF YOU SO MUCH AS TOUCH EVEN ONE SPOT OF SOIL ON THIS PLANET, I WILL PERSONALLY OPEN UP THE GATES TO THE ASGARDIAN TEN REALMS...
UH-OH.
...AND I WILL BRING A WAR OF MADNESS AND HELLFIRE UPON YOU AND YOUR OFFSPRING THAT WILL NEVER END!!!
THEN I WILL STEP ACROSS THE BLOOD-SOAKED BATTLEFIELD AND KILL EACH AND EVERY ONE OF YOU WITH MY BARE HANDS!!!
ALL WHILE MY SISTERS AND BROTHERS OF ASGARD AND EARTH LAUGH INTO WHAT IS LEFT OF YOUR FACES!
GET OUT!
LEAVE!
OH, BOYS!!!

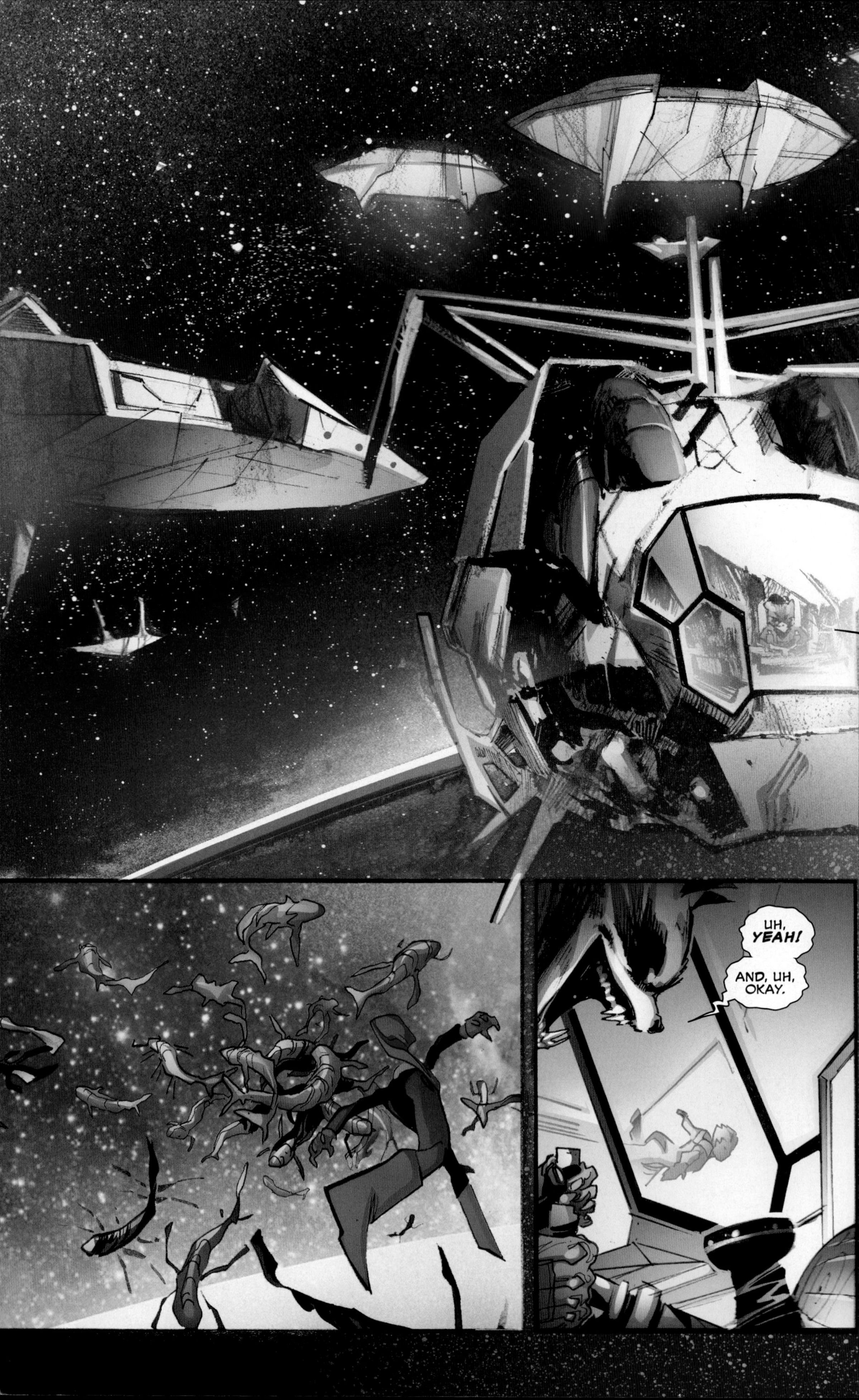
UH, YEAH!
AND, UH, OKAY.

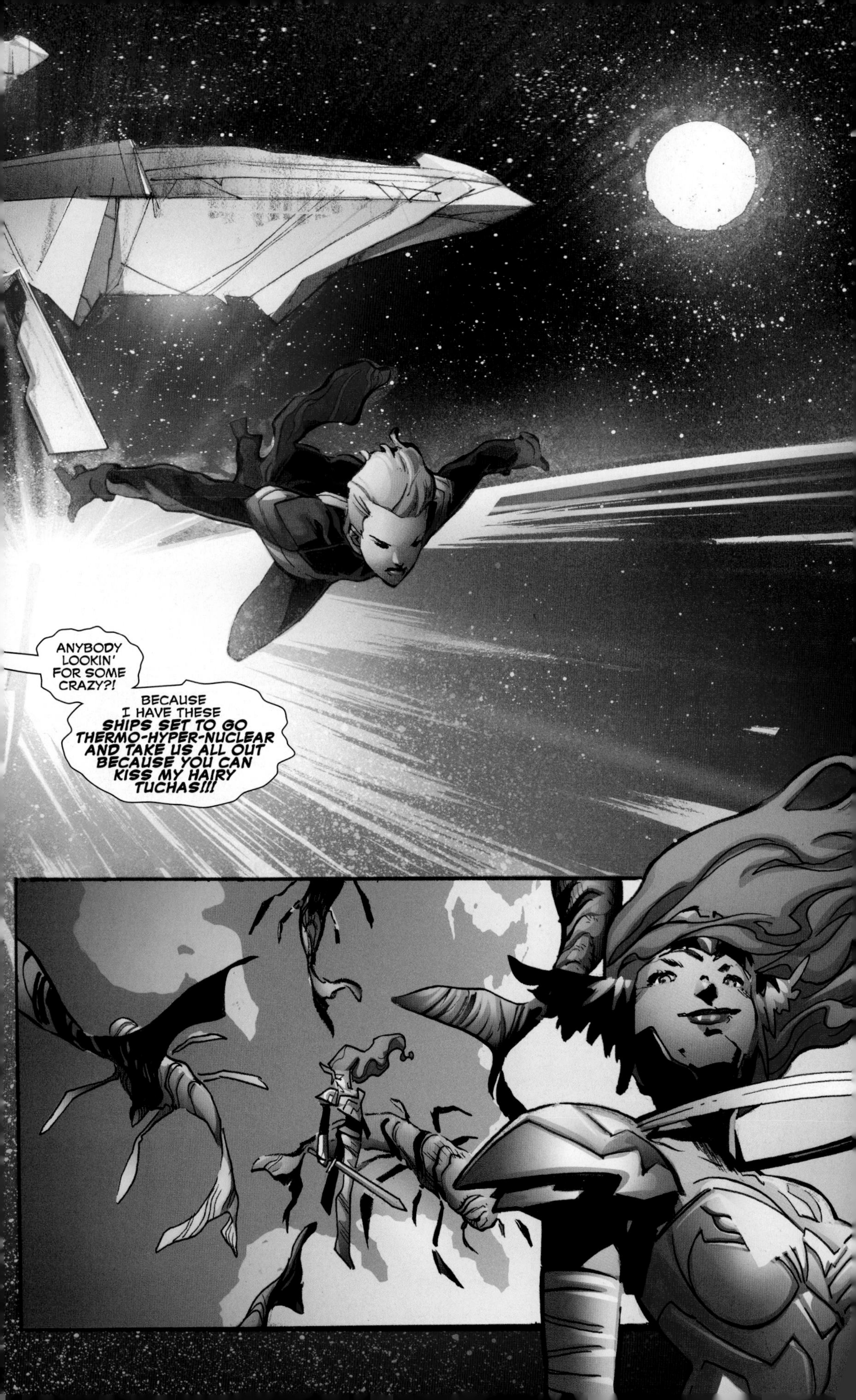
ANYBODY LOOKIN' FOR SOME CRAZY?!
BECAUSE I HAVE THESE SHIPS SET TO GO THERMO-HYPER-NUCLEAR AND TAKE US ALL OUT BECAUSE YOU CAN KISS MY HAIRY TUCHAS!!!

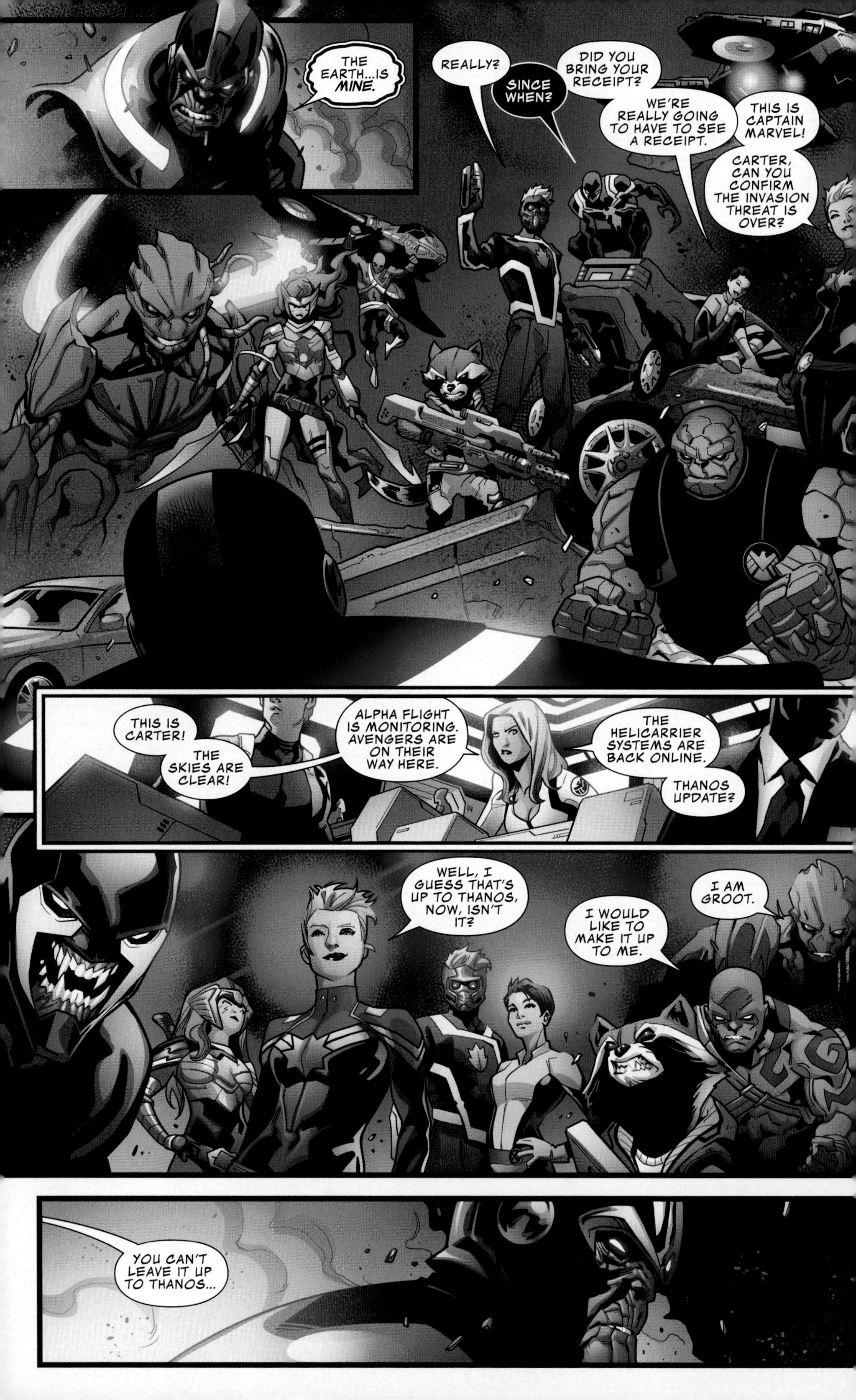
THE EARTH...IS MINE.
REALLY?
SINCE WHEN?
DID YOU BRING YOUR RECEIPT?
WE'RE REALLY GOING TO HAVE TO SEE A RECEIPT.
THIS IS CAPTAIN MARVEL!
CARTER, CAN YOU CONFIRM THE INVASION THREAT IS OVER?
THIS IS CARTER!
THE SKIES ARE CLEAR!
ALPHA FLIGHT IS MONITORING. AVENGERS ARE ON THEIR WAY HERE.
THE HELICARRIER SYSTEMS ARE BACK ONLINE.
THANOS UPDATE?
WELL, I GUESS THAT'S UP TO THANOS, NOW, ISN'T IT?
I WOULD LIKE TO MAKE IT UP TO ME.
I AM GROOT.
YOU CAN'T LEAVE IT UP TO THANOS...

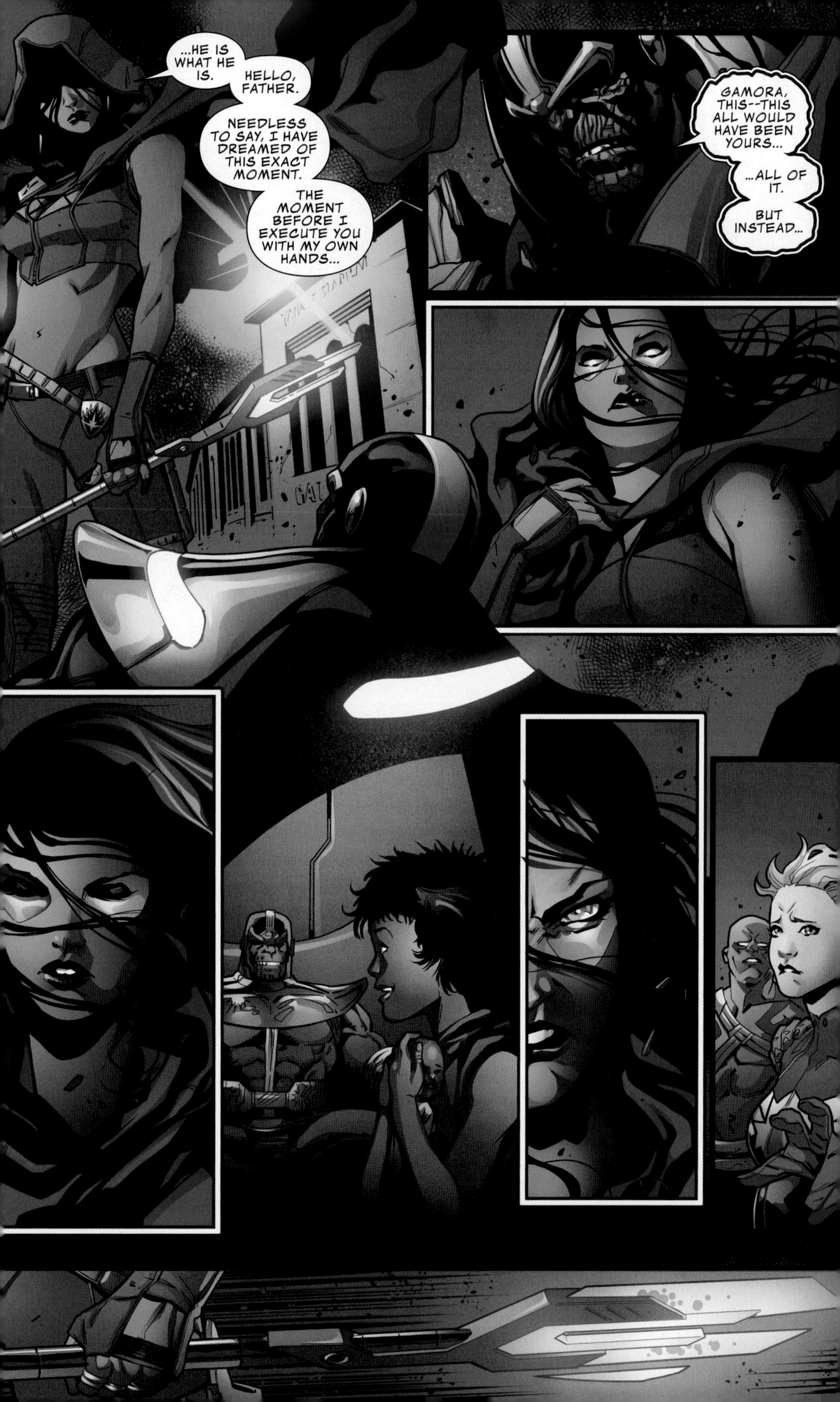
...HE IS WHAT HE IS.
HELLO, FATHER.
NEEDLESS TO SAY, I HAVE DREAMED OF THIS EXACT MOMENT.
THE MOMENT BEFORE I EXECUTE YOU WITH MY OWN HANDS...
GAMORA, THIS--THIS ALL WOULD HAVE BEEN YOURS...
...ALL OF IT.
BUT INSTEAD...

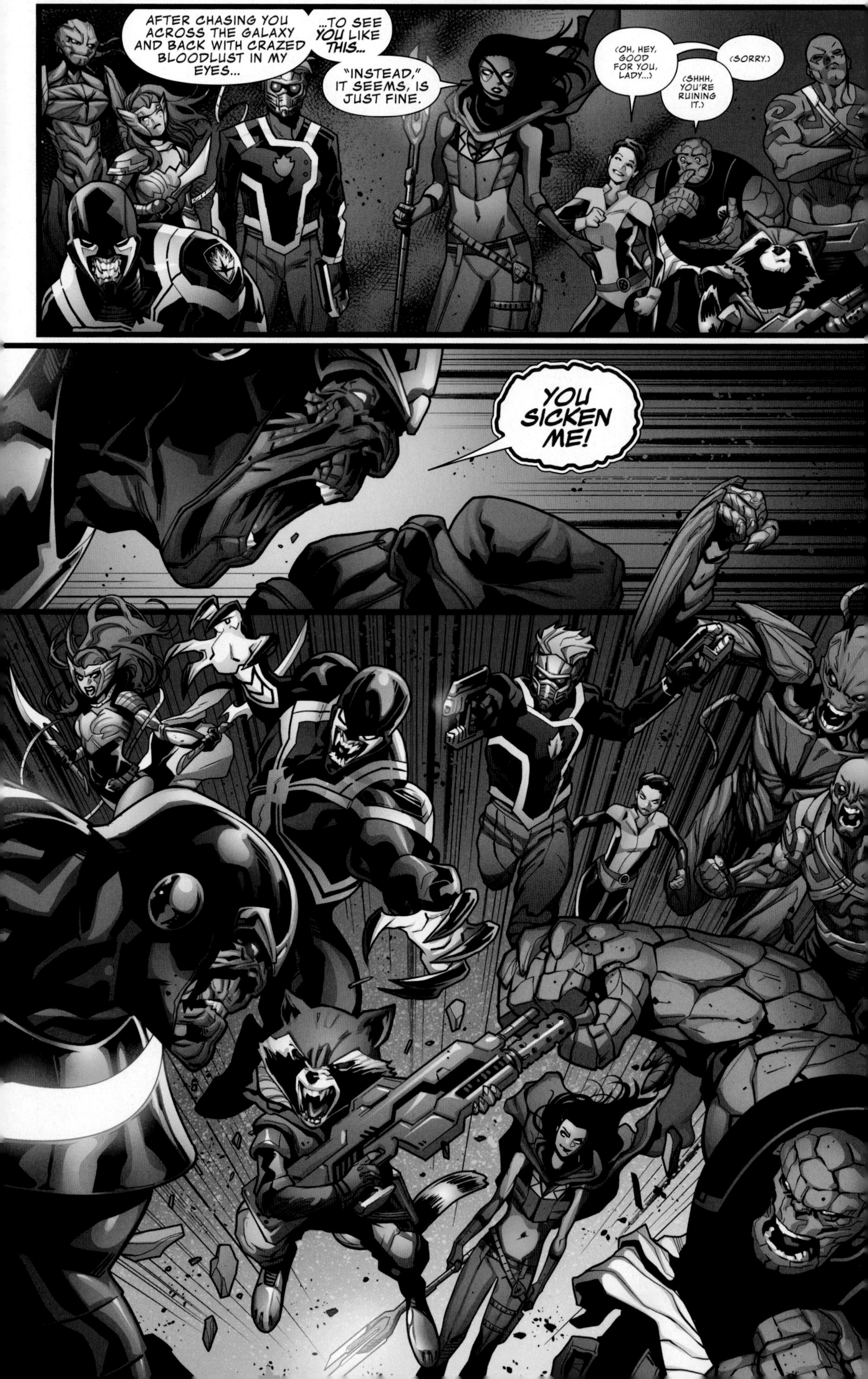
AFTER CHASING YOU ACROSS THE GALAXY AND BACK WITH CRAZED BLOODLUST IN MY EYES...
...TO SEE YOU LIKE THIS...
"INSTEAD," IT SEEMS, IS JUST FINE.
(OH, HEY, GOOD FOR YOU, LADY...)
(SORRY.)
(SHHH, YOU'RE RUINING IT.)
YOU SICKEN ME!

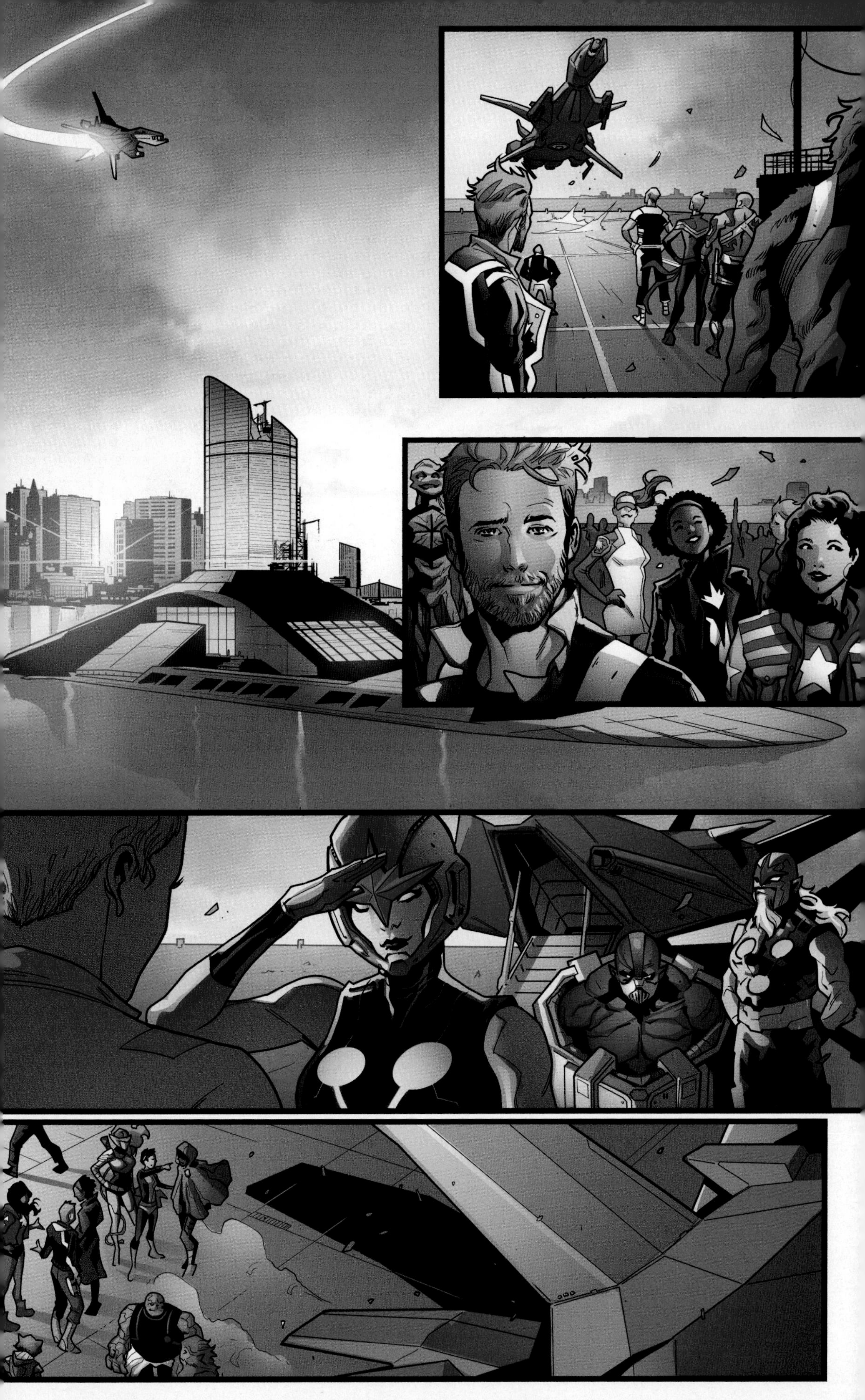

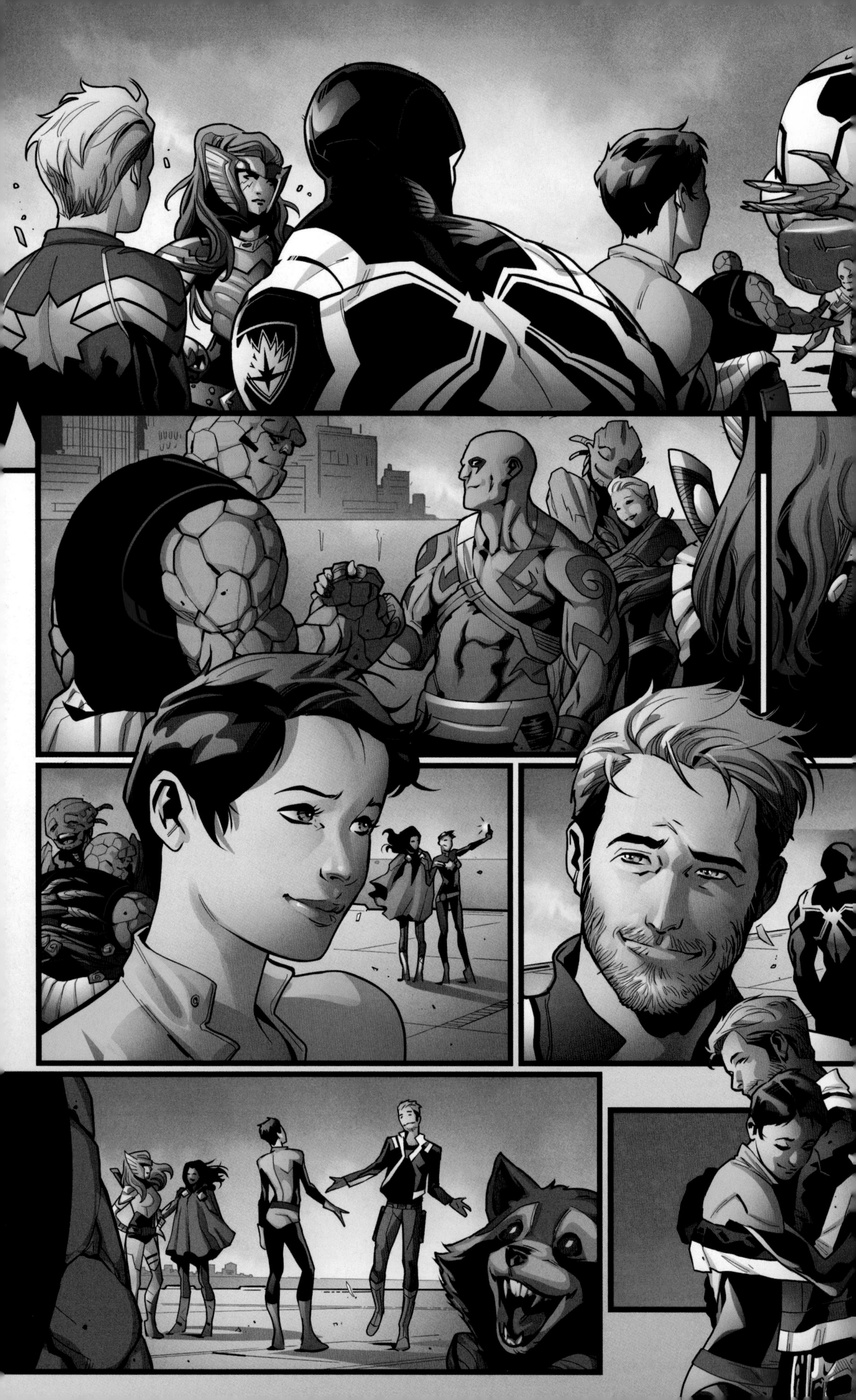

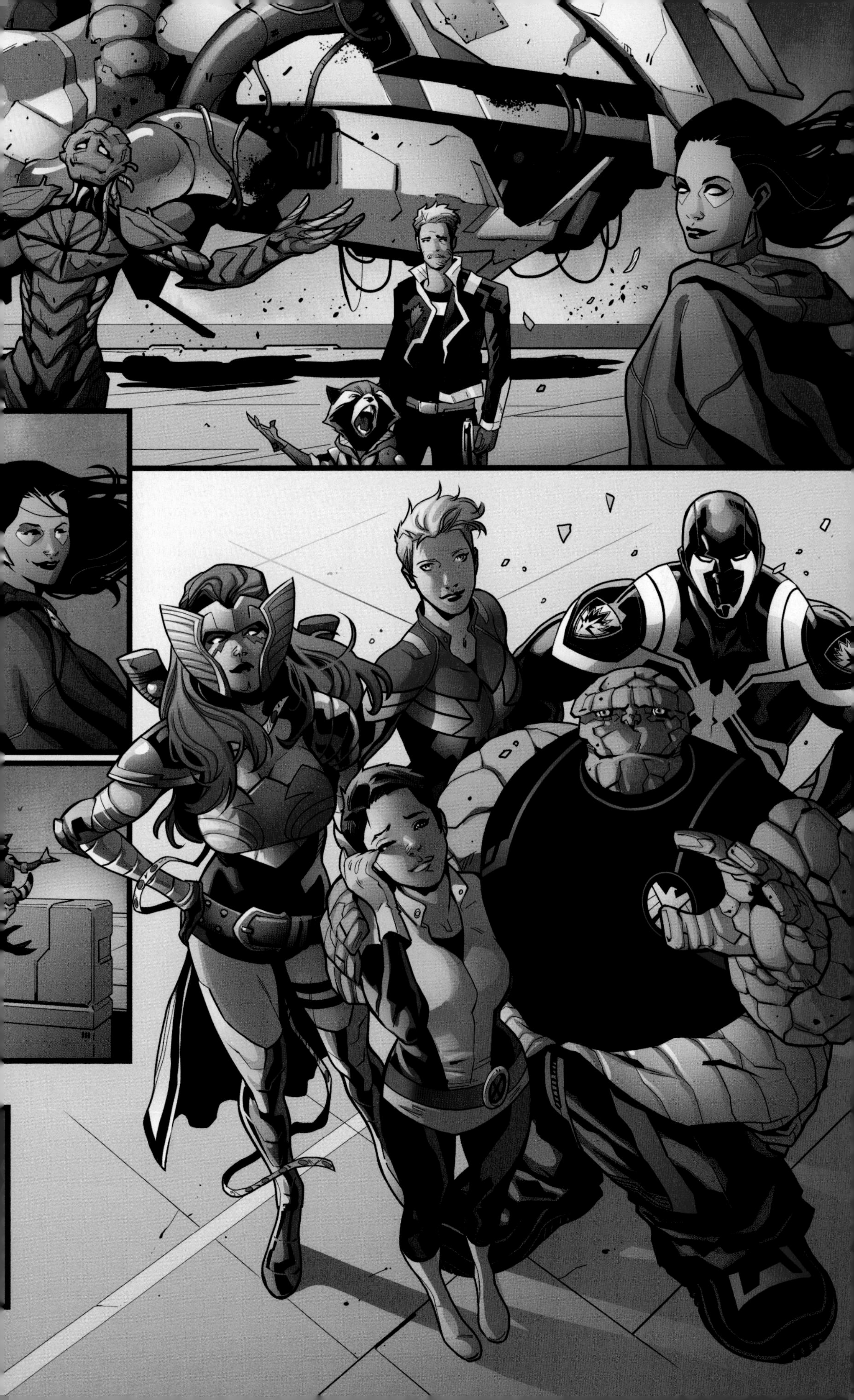

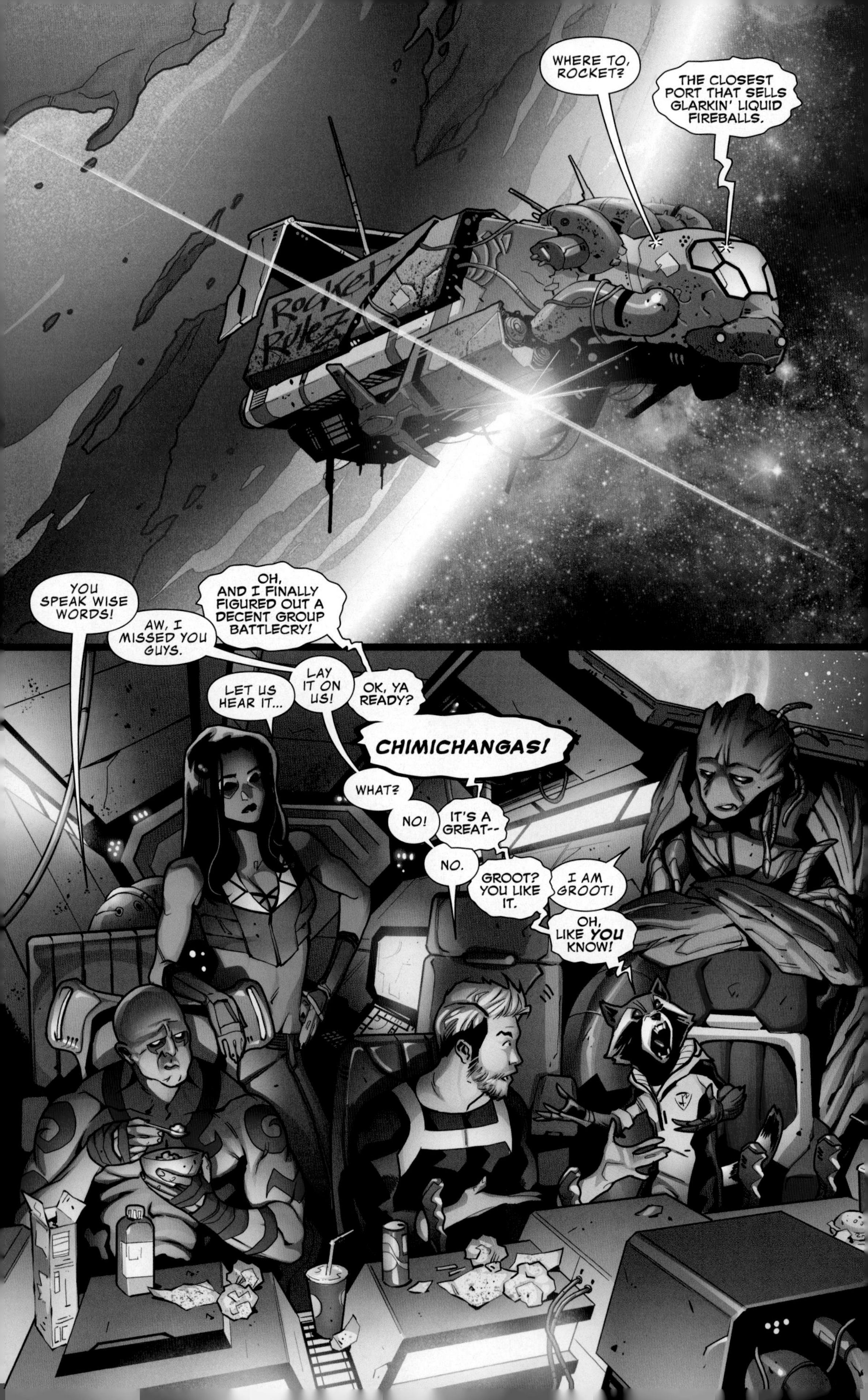
Rocket Rulez
WHERE TO, ROCKET?
THE CLOSEST PORT THAT SELLS GLARKIN' LIQUID FIREBALLS.
YOU SPEAK WISE WORDS!
AW, I MISSED YOU GUYS.
OH, AND I FINALLY FIGURED OUT A DECENT GROUP BATTLECRY!
LET US HEAR IT...
LAY IT ON US!
OK, YA READY?
CHIMICHANGAS!
WHAT?
NO!
IT'S A GREAT--
NO.
GROOT? YOU LIKE IT.
I AM GROOT!
OH, LIKE YOU KNOW!

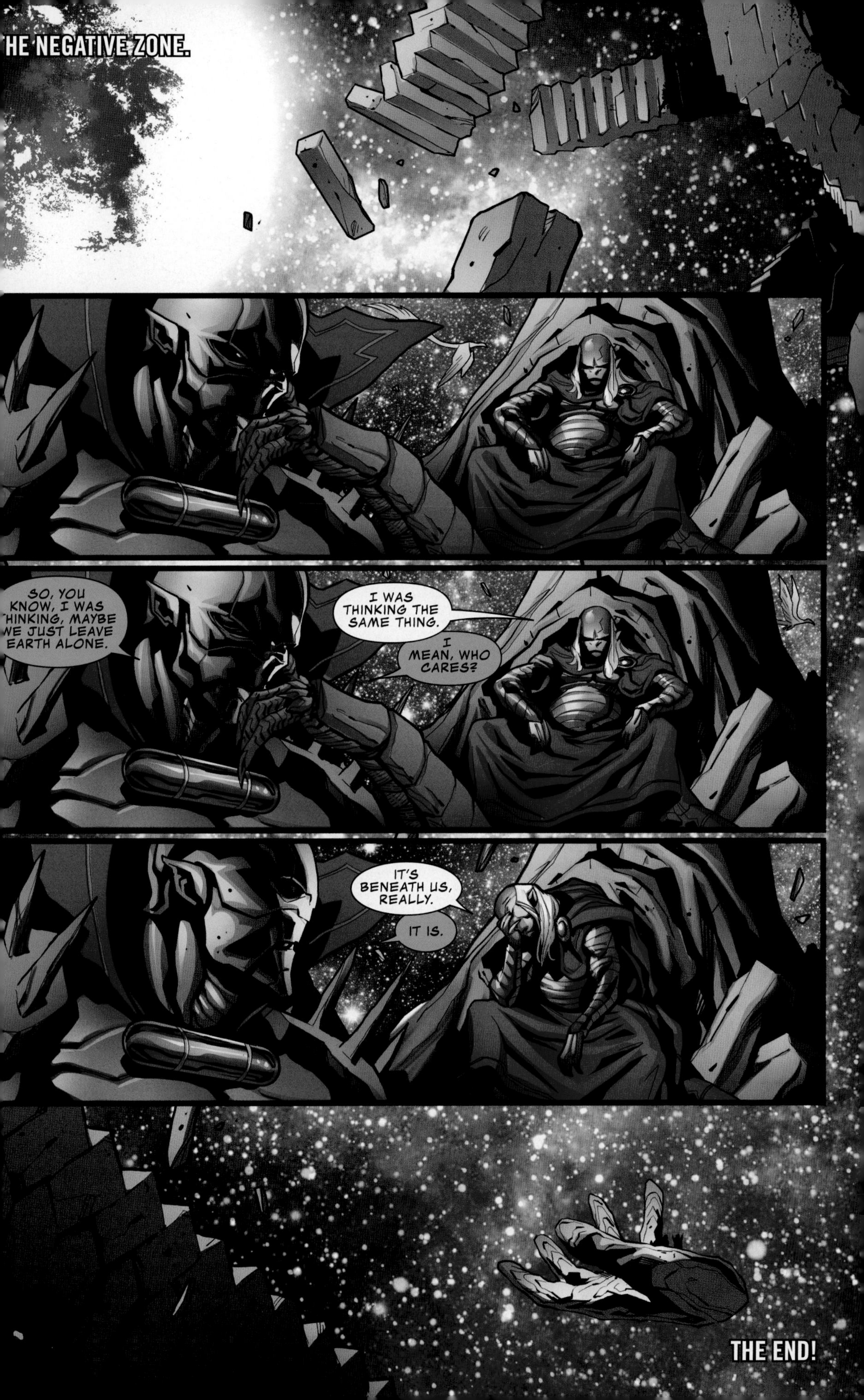
HE NEGATIVE ZONE.
SO, YOU KNOW, I WAS THINKING, MAYBE WE JUST LEAVE EARTH ALONE.
I WAS THINKING THE SAME THING.
I MEAN, WHO CARES?
IT'S BENEATH US, REALLY.
IT IS.
THE END!

# GUARDIANS OF THE GALAXY

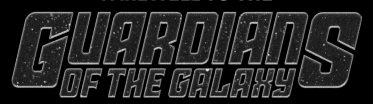

## ...FOR NOW

By the time you read this I will have already written my final issue months ago. I have some perspective and, goo
Lord, I do miss GUARDIANS.

It was never a book I ever thought I would write. First of all, I broke into comics as a crime fiction writer and artist. I got whatever success I have off of creations like Jessica Jones. I wasn't the "space" guy. And I certainly wasn't th "talking-raccoon-alien space" guy, I was the "face down in the gutter" guy.

I got the job in an unusual way. Years ago, for quite a few years, the only people who had ever heard of the Guardian of the Galaxy was us deep-level, hard-core, not-messin'-around, always-ahead-of-the-pop-culture-curve-and-neve never-getting-any-credit-for-it Marvel zombies. We Marvel zombies know what's coming before everyone else.

Abnett and Lanning knew.

Everybody else was stuck watching the trailer for the remake of *The Day the Earth Stood Still.* (It starts off well...)

It was around this time that I was part of Marvel's Cinematic Universe Creative Committee—a group of executive and creators brought together to consult on the bigger choices being made in what is now the most successful film studio in history. Once the hits really started rolling, Kevin Feige and the group started taking a hard look at what th next wave of movies could and should be. They even had writers working on drafts to see what would come out—t see what would rise up.

Because of this I read the early draft of Nicole Perlman's "Guardians of the Galaxy" script. It was she—and sh doesn't get enough credit for this, in my opinion—who, with her writing, proved to the studio that the Abnett an Lanning GUARDIANS was a franchise of *Star Wars* potential. It was reading those outlines and drafts that sent m back to the earlier classic source material. I had read almost all of it as a fan but never as someone considering th true potential of these characters on a worldwide basis.

Going back and rereading the '70s origin of Peter Quill and all of the early Starlin material put me in a bit of a creativ craze. I said it when we were first promoting this series and I'll say it now: Quill's original origin is as strong as Spide Man's or Superman's. It's just not as well known.

I was so over-the-top excited about the potential of the Guardians, I guess I never shut up about it. And I guess som of my co-workers were so surprised to see me so passionate about a genre I had shown so little interest in creativel that when Marvel decided to bring back the comic book, Marvel President Dan Buckley recommended me.

The crime fiction guy accidentally talked his way into a book about talking raccoons and ray guns. (I know that's no what it's really about, shh!)

I actually wasn't sure how long I would write the book for. A year? I had so many projects I wanted to do. And then, a often happens to me, once I start writing I can't stop. The characters start pitching stories themselves. They interac with each other without consulting me as I'm writing them. The entire Marvel galaxy started to take shape in my heac All these ideas. New characters. And, oh my God! I'm also the writer of X-MEN! I love when the X-Men go into oute space. The X-Men have to go to outer space and team up with the Guardians. Like that cool Alpha Flight/X-Men serie from years ago that—oh no! Kitty and Peter just fell in love! Neil Gaiman (What? Yes!) just gave Angela to Marvel! Sar Humphries just told me about his idea for "Black Vortex." Oh good, the movie was a hit and now everybody knows wh

...nd all this time the book was so much fun to make. The best artists in comics love to draw the Guardians.

And as if I weren't having a creatively awesome time, as if I weren't working with great artists, there's the fact that every single child that I, as a father of four, come in contact with stares at me as if I'm David Bowie when they hear I work on the GUARDIANS OF THE GALAXY.

I have worked on so many major franchises, braggy time, that have been turned into movies, including co-creating JESSICA JONES with Michael Gaydos, but the most awestruck looks I've ever gotten from strangers and friends are when they hear I work on GUARDIANS OF THE GALAXY!

Just today, I'm waiting outside for my son and daughters to get off the school bus and my 4-year-old son is carrying the brand-new GUARDIANS Treasury Edition that Marvel put out. And from the look of it he's been dragging it around all day, and it's about the same size as him. I asked him why he took it to school. He said, "I can't wait to learn to read because I've been staring at this all day thinking reading it would be a lot of fun. Which words did you write, Dad?"

So, writing GUARDIANS has been creatively rewarding and fun (and comics should be fun once in a while), and I am honored to have worked with every single artist, colorist, letterer, editor, intern, production assistant, proofreader, and designer who worked on this book.

The artist names you know. I can tell you that every single one of them, from the ship-launching Steve McNiven to Valerio Schiti, in whose magnificent hands the book finally settled, there hasn't been one bad-looking page on this book since we began. Every single page was world-class, top-to-bottom gorgeous. Everyone was a pleasure to work with.

Take this issue as an example of everything I love about working with Marvel Comics. Jordan, who leads the outstanding editing team of Kathleen and Darren for all these galactic books and *Star Wars* and all kinds of other projects, really went out of his way to make sure that my last issue had the pages and the talent for a special send-off. He lined up some of my all-time favorite artists for the big jam fight. (And if you think coordinating that is easy, nuh-uh.)

It all just shows the kind of love and dedication that goes on behind the scenes. Jordan leads a team of editors and craftsmen who work tirelessly and, on Fridays, sometimes until the wee hours of the morning...making sure that your books go to press on time and that the stories are well told.

It's a thankless job. Except right here. If you enjoyed anything that has gone on in this book over the years, take a look at the names of the editors and thank them for the job well done.

To all the original creators of the original incarnations of the characters, to the creators on the DnA books that came before us, to the filmmakers and animators who helped craft everyone's shared love of these characters on a global scale, thank you for allowing me to be part of the team.

I'm not leaving the book because I'm sick of it. I'm leaving it because it's time and I've been DYING to do this DEFENDERS book for years! I'm telling you this because for what comics cost I would think you'd like to know that every single issue of this book was made with love and passion.

What will I miss most of all? Making up alien swear words and getting away with it.

If you're looking for me, I'll be over at IRON MAN, SPIDER-MAN, and THE DEFENDERS (please buy it, it's so gorgeous) and I always have a couple of surprises coming.

As for readers of this book, stay right where you are because I know what Gerry and the gang have planned. I will be reading right along with you. Well, not right along next to you but, you know, spiritually.

But for now, may the Force be—no, that's not right. What was the thing for this one? There was nothing for this one right? Oh, it's classic rock. We can't do ... ack in the letter column!! Flarknard!!

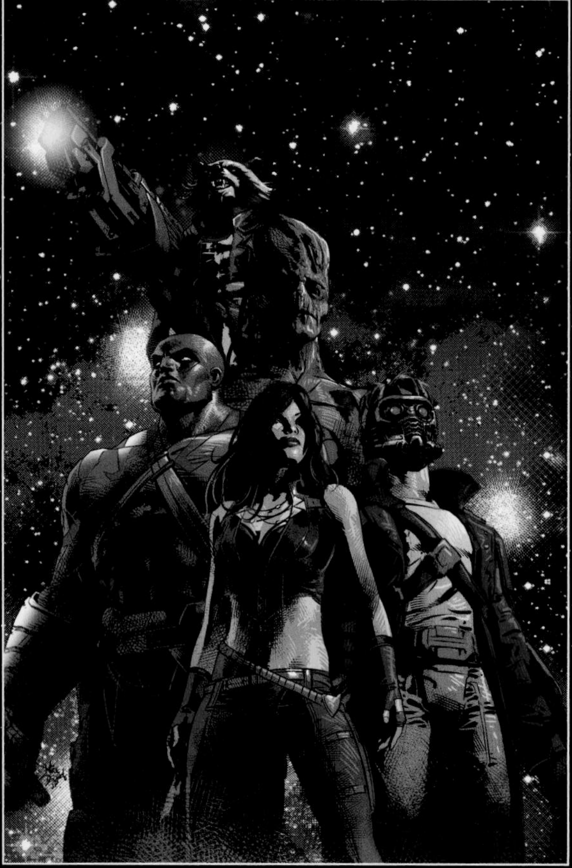

#19 VARIANT BY
MIKE DEODATO JR. & RAIN BEREDO

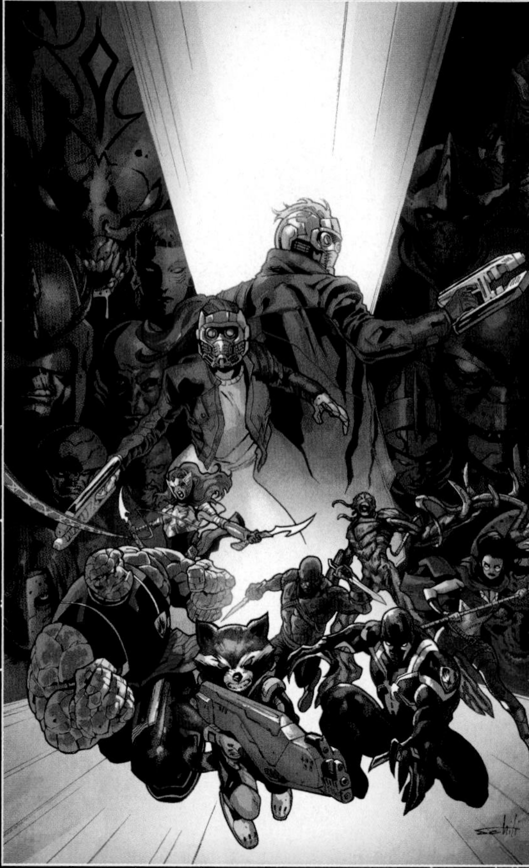

#19 VARIANT BY
VALERO SCHITI & RAIN BEREDO

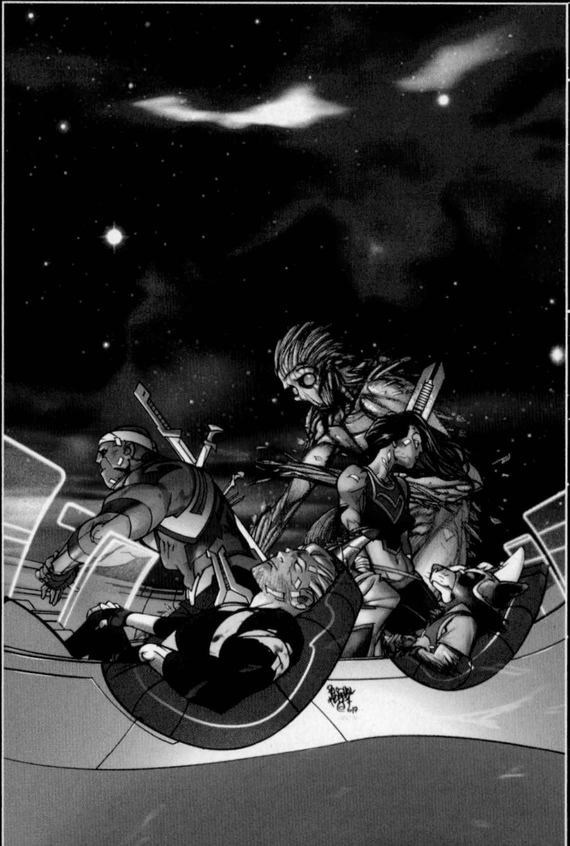

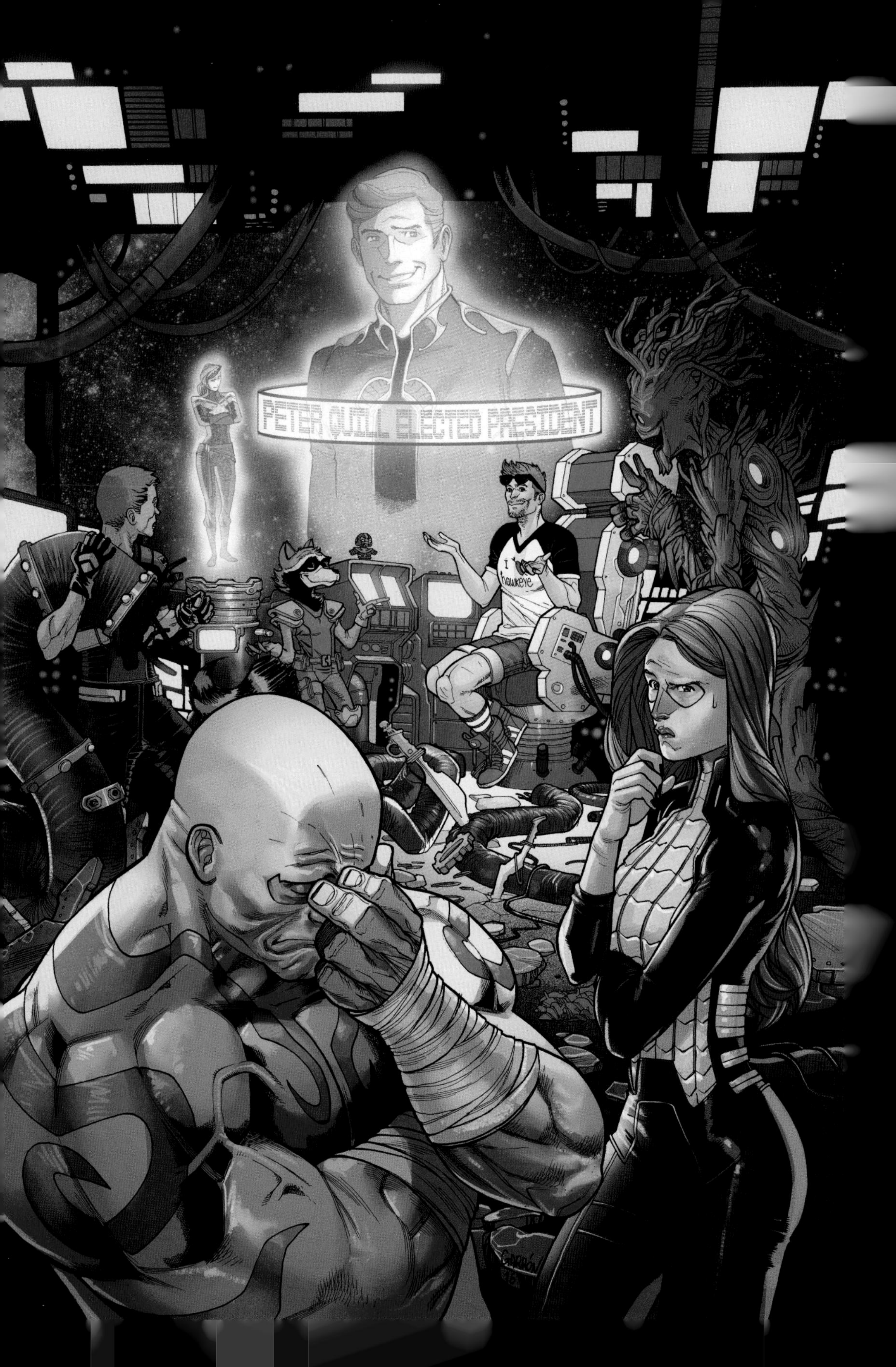
PETER QUILL ELECTED PRESIDENT

#16 BEST OF BENDIS VARIANT BY
**MARCO CHECCHETTO**

#17 BEST OF BENDIS VARIANT BY
**FRANCESCO FRANCAVILLA**

#18 BEST OF BENDIS VARIANT BY
**PASQUAL FERRY & CHRIS SOTOMAYOR**

#19 BEST OF BENDIS VARIANT BY
**JACEN BURROWS & ANDY TROY**